PENGUIN CLASSICS

LIVES OF THE LATER CAESARS

FOUNDER EDITOR (1944–64): E. V. RIEU

Editor: Betty Radice

The Augustan History is a mysterious work ostensibly composed by six biographers writing in the late third and early fourth centuries A.D., under the emperors Diocletian and Constantine, and covering the *Lives* of emperors and usurpers from A.D. 117–284 (with a gap from 244–53). Most modern scholars now believe that a single author was responsible, writing in the late fourth century, and, for obscure reasons, concealing his identity. Fiction predominates in the *Lives* of the usurpers and other minor figures, and in the whole of the second half of the work. The present translation is of the first half only, from Hadrian to Heliogabalus (A.D. 117–222), but the translator has prefaced it with newly compiled *Lives* of Nerva and Trajan to fill the gap (A.D. 96–117) between the *Augustan History* and its prototype, the *Twelve Caesars* of Suetonius.

Anthony Birley was born at Chesterholm, Northumberland, in 1937 and was educated at Clifton College and Magdalen College, Oxford. He is married with two children. After posts at Birmingham and Leeds he is now Professor of Ancient History at Manchester University. His previous publications include *Life in Roman Britain* (1964), *Marcus Aurelius* (1966) and *Septimius Severus the African Emperor* (1971).

LIVES
OF THE
LATER CAESARS

The first part of the Augustan History,
with newly compiled Lives of Nerva and Trajan

TRANSLATED AND INTRODUCED BY
ANTHONY BIRLEY

Penguin Books

Penguin Books Ltd, Harmondsworth, Middlesex, England
Penguin Books Inc., 7110 Ambassador Road, Baltimore, Maryland 21207, U.S.A.
Penguin Books Australia Ltd, Ringwood, Victoria, Australia
Penguin Books Canada Ltd, 41 Steelcase Road West, Markham, Ontario, Canada
Penguin Books (N.Z.) Ltd, 182–190 Wairau Road, Auckland 10, New Zealand

—

This translation first published 1976

—

—

Made and printed in Great Britain by
Cox and Wyman Ltd, London, Reading and Fakenham
Set in Monotype Bembo

CONTENTS

CONTENTS

INTRODUCTION

'**D**ILIGENCE and accuracy are the only merits which an historical writer may ascribe to himself,' wrote Gibbon in the preface[1] to *The History of the Decline and Fall of the Roman Empire*. He went on to make a tentative promise (never fulfilled) to provide 'a critical account of the authors consulted' at the end of the work, when it was completed. 'At present,' he added,

I shall content myself with a single observation. The biographers, who, under the reigns of Diocletian and Constantine, composed, or rather compiled, the lives of the emperors, from Hadrian to the sons of Carus, are usually mentioned under the names of Aelius Spartianus, Julius Capitolinus, Aelius Lampridius, Vulcatius Gallicanus, Trebellius Pollio, and Flavius Vobiscus [*sic*]. But there is so much perplexity in the titles of the MSS., and so many disputes have arisen among the critics . . . concerning their number, their names, and their respective property, that for the most part I have quoted them without distinction, under the general and well-known title of the *Augustan History*.[2]

The problem that Gibbon describes may now be regarded as one of the least vexing that afflict students of this strange work. Most are now agreed on 'number, names and respective property'. In 1889 Hermann Dessau produced the remarkable hypothesis[3] that the *Augustan History* was the work of one man, not six, writing at the end of the fourth century, nearly a hundred years after the ostensible period of composition or compilation. His identity and exact motives for this curious piece of deceit must remain unknown; but there is now a fairly

1. Volume I of the octavo edition, 1783.
2. The name originally given it by the early seventeenth-century editor Isaac Casaubon: see Hohl, p. vii, n. 1.
3. *Hermes*, 1889, pp. 337ff.

wide consensus[4] that Dessau's basic contention is correct. In the meantime, eighty-five years of vigorous research and scholarly controversy[5] have succeeded in solving at least some of the difficulties associated with the work. But more remains to be done. The second and third centuries A.D. are among the worst provided in the history of Rome, as far as literary authorities are concerned. For the period up till the year 229 the major source is the *Roman History* of Cassius Dio, a Bithynian Greek who held his second consulship in that year. But Dio's account of the reign of Antoninus Pius, A.D. 138–61, is missing and had already been lost in the time of his Byzantine epitomator John Xiphilinus. Most of what remains is not Dio's complete text, only a brief epitome.[6] For the years 180–238 there is also Herodian's *History of the Empire from the Time of Marcus*, but this is a feeble product, heavily indebted to Dio. Weak on chronology, names and facts, Herodian has been justifiably described as 'a Greek rhetorician passing himself off as a writer of history'.[7] Hence, use of the *Augustan History* cannot be avoided.

The present translation is of the first half of the *Augustan History* only, the biographies from Hadrian to Elagabalus. I should have liked to tackle the whole, but the first half alone already makes a substantial enough volume. Besides, it is in the first half that one finds a reasonable basis of fact, and the student of Roman imperial history can use the earlier *Lives* with some profit, if due precautions are taken. The same cannot be said for the second half, where fiction predominates – not without considerable charm, to be sure, but dangerously beguiling stuff for the historian. *The Twelve Caesars* of Suetonius ends with the

4. A few sceptics remain, see p. 13, n. 21 below.

5. For an introduction, see A. Chastagnol, *HAC*, 1963, pp. 43ff.; A. Birley, *Latin Biography* (ed. T. A. Dorey), Routledge, 1967, pp. 113ff.; Syme, *AHA* and *EB*, *passim*.

6. See F. Millar, *A Study of Cassius Dio*, Oxford U.P., 1964.

7. Syme, *EB*, p. 235.

Life of Domitian, and the *Augustan History* begins with Hadrian;
and there are no extant ancient biographies of Nerva (reigned
A.D. 96–8) and Trajan (reigned A.D. 98–117). After some hesi-
tation I have attempted to make good this deficiency by
cobbling together extracts from such sources as Cassius Dio,
Aurelius Victor and the *Epitome de Caesaribus*, to produce brief
Lives of Nerva and Trajan in the manner of Suetonius or the
Augustan History. I have been careful to supply references for
every statement and can only hope that the result will be of
some interest and utility, and that it will not mislead the unwary.

The *Augustan History* itself may have originally commenced
with biographies of Nerva and Trajan. As it is, the work
launches off into the *Life of Hadrian* with no word of introduction or explanation, and it is not unreasonable to postulate
that some pages may have been lost from the beginning of the
original manuscript. Certainly, there is apparent evidence of
damage to the manuscript later in the work; after the biographies of the emperors of the year 238 there follows what is
evidently the concluding portion of a *Life of Valerian*, dealing
with the aftermath of his capture by the Persians in the year
260. Thus the *Lives* of the emperors between Gordian III
(reigned A.D. 238–44) and Valerian (A.D. 253–60) are evidently
missing. It may be that an opening section covering the years
98–117 has also been lost.[8]

Although there is no preface to the work as it stands, before
long the author, ostensibly addressing his remarks to the
emperor Diocletian, purports to make his intentions and
methods explicit: 'To Diocletian Augustus, his Aelius Spartianus, greeting. I have it in mind, Diocletian Augustus, to bring
to the cognizance of Your Divinity, not only those who have
held the place of *princeps* in that position which you maintain,
as I have done as far as the Deified Hadrian, but also those who

8. However, I have suggested elsewhere that the 'lacuna' may be
bogus, like so much else in the *Augustan History*; see *Latin Biography*,
pp. 125f., and *HAC*, 1972.

have either been called by the name of Caesar but have not
been *principes* or Augusti; or who in any other fashion whatsoever have come either to the fame or the hope of the imperial
power.'[9] And at frequent intervals throughout the rest of the
work there are comments of a similar kind, addressed either to
Diocletian or Constantine, or to a friend of the author.[10]
Allegedly the work is by the six biographers that Gibbon
named. The last of the six, 'Flavius Vopiscus of Syracuse',
responsible for the *Lives* from Aurelian to Carinus (in the
second half of the *Augustan History*), refers both to his immediate predecessor 'Trebellius Pollio'[11] and to two of the other
four *scriptores*, 'Julius Capitolinus' and 'Aelius Lampridius'.[12]
But none of the other five show any awareness of the existence
of any of their 'colleagues'. 'Vopiscus' himself supplies copious
evidence for the time when he is writing, particularly in the
justly celebrated opening of the *Aurelian*, where he relates a
discussion between the prefect of Rome, Junius Tiberianus, and
himself.[13] Two persons of that name are recorded as prefect, in
the years 291–2 and 303–4, while the description of Constantius
Chlorus as 'now emperor' and Diocletian as 'now a private
citizen' later in the *Aurelian* would appear to place the composition of this biography precisely in the years 305–6, after
Diocletian's abdication and before the death of Constantius.[14]
This ostensible date also accords with the references 'Vopiscus'
makes to his father's and grandfather's reminiscences of
Diocletian's activities before his accession and of other late
third-century figures.[15] A difficulty at once arises, however,

9. *Aelius*, 1.1, p. 88 below.
10. cf. for example *Marcus*, 19.12; *Verus*, 11.4; *Avidius*, 3.3; *Severus*,
20.4; etc. (pp. 127f., 148, 151, 220, below).
11. *Aurelian*, 2.1; *Quadrigae tyrannorum*, 1.3.
12. *Probus*, 2.7.
13. *Aurelian*, 1–2.
14. See *Latin Biography*, pp. 120f.
15. e.g. *Aurelian*, 43.2ff.; *Quadrigae tyrannorum*, 9.4, 15.4, 14.1ff.

for both 'Capitolinus' and 'Lampridius', whom 'Vopiscus' – writing in A.D. 305–6 – knows of as biographers, themselves address Constantine. 'Capitolinus', in the main, addresses himself to Diocletian, but in the *Albinus*, *Maximini* and *Gordiani* he refers to Constantine in a way which places the composition not earlier than the year 306. As for 'Lampridius', the tone of his references to Constantine's rival Licinius makes it certain that his work must fall after the latter's defeat in A.D. 324.[16] Hence, without some very elaborate theory about his literary activity, 'Lampridius' can hardly be described as a biographer (as he is by 'Vopiscus') eighteen or more years before he began writing. 'Vulcacius Gallicanus', in the one biography ascribed to him, addresses Diocletian only, but 'Aelius Spartianus', after addressing Diocletian on three occasions, suddenly invokes Constantine in the *Geta*.

Clearly then, even on a cursory inspection, there is something amiss, as Gibbon and his predecessors were well aware. In fact, the biographies are in the wrong order in the manuscripts, with *Didius Julianus* (emperor in A.D. 193, after Pertinax) preceding *Commodus* (emperor A.D. 180–92); and three other *Lives* are also misplaced. Hence it might seem possible to imagine that some of the first four authors' names might have been wrongly attributed to particular biographies in the manuscripts. But no rearrangement would result in chronological consistency.

Three of the first four *scriptores* explicitly state, and the fourth implies, that they are writing considerably more than the biographies extant under their names in the *Augustan History*. Thus 'Aelius Spartianus'[17] and 'Vulcacius Gallicanus'[18] both announce a programme of *Lives* of all who have worn the purple, from Caesar onwards. 'Lampridius' states an intention of dealing with the Gordians, Claudius, Aurelian, Diocletian

16. See *Heliogabalus*, 35.6, p. 316 below.
17. *Aelius*, 1.7, p. 88 below.
18. *Avidius*, 3.3, p. 151 below.

and Maximian, and four rivals of Constantine.[19] But there is no trace in the work as it survives of these intentions having been fulfilled. As it is, the first four authors are represented as responsible for various biographies in an extraordinarily sporadic fashion. 'Spartianus' is credited with the *Hadrian*, *Aelius*, *Didius Julianus*, *Severus*, *Niger*, *Caracallus* and *Geta*. 'Capitolinus' starts with *Antoninus*, *Marcus* and *L. Verus*, then *Pertinax*, *Albinus* and *Macrinus*, and finally the emperors of the year 238. 'Lampridius' has only four *Lives* to his name, *Commodus*, *Diadumenus*, *Heliogabalus* and *Severus Alexander*, although the last of these is twice as long as any other biography in the entire work. As for 'Vulcacius Gallicanus' – labelled 'V.C.', *vir clarissimus* or 'Right Honourable', the title of senatorial rank – he is assigned only one *Life*, the *Avidius Cassius*, in spite of his ambitious programme.

These and other problems are placed in a new light if we accept Dessau's explanation – that the *Augustan History* is in reality the work of a single author, writing a good many years later than is claimed. Dessau drew attention to two lengthy sections in the work which bear a close resemblance to passages in the writings of Aurelius Victor and Eutropius, published in A.D. 360 and 369 respectively.[20] He noted, further, a whole host of anachronisms and allusions which can best be explained by dating the work to the age of Theodosius the Great. Since 1889 debate on Dessau's thesis has been continuous, but recently there has been considerable progress towards agreement. This has come about not least from the annual *Colloquia* devoted to the subject, organized by Professors Andreas Alföldi and Johannes Straub, the ultimate aim being the publication of an historical commentary. To be sure, the eminent historian A. H. M. Jones could write, as recently as 1964, that 'there is no

19. *Heliogabalus*, 35.6, p. 315f. below. For the apparent productions of 'Capitolinus', see *Maximini*, 1.3.

20. Victor, *de Caes.*, 20 (cf. *Severus*, 17.5–19.3, pp. 217–19, below); Eutropius, 8.11.1–14.2 (cf. *Marcus*, 16.3–18.1, pp. 124–6, below).

reason for doubting that [it] could have been written at the date its authors profess to have written it'.[21] But most students of the subject will prefer the authority of Sir Ronald Syme, who, in a number of works, particularly *Ammianus and the Historia Augusta* (1968) and *Emperors and Biography* (1971), has reinforced the original arguments of Dessau. As far as the names 'Aelius Spartianus', 'Julius Capitolinus' and the rest are concerned, it is reasonable to assume that the author thought of multiplying or sub-dividing himself into six at a late stage, and labelled the various *Lives* with authors' names in haphazard fashion.[22] Similarly, many if not all the allusions to 'contemporary' events may have been inserted as an afterthought, rather carelessly, with the intention of misleading.

What of the reliability of the work for the historian? There is no doubt that this is very varied. The 'major' biographies in the first half, those of the emperors themselves of the second and early third centuries (Hadrian, Pius, Marcus Aurelius and Lucius Verus, Commodus, Pertinax, Didius Julianus, Severus and Caracalla, and, in part, Elagabalus – but not Macrinus) are in the main sound and contain a great deal of authentic information, much of it not provided by any other literary sources but confirmed by epigraphic evidence.[23] But the 'minor', 'secondary' or 'subsidiary' *Lives* of other figures in this period, heirs to the throne or junior emperors, and usurpers (Aelius, Avidius Cassius, Niger, Albinus, Geta and Diadumenianus),

21. *The Later Roman Empire*, Blackwell, 1964, vol. 3, p. 1, n. 1, basing himself on the conservative position adopted by A. Momigliano, *Journal of the Warburg and Courtauld Institutes*, 1954, pp. 22ff., and still largely maintained by that scholar.

22. Syme, *EB*, pp. 73ff.

23. e.g. the information that Hadrian built the Wall in Britain (*Hadrian*, 11.2, p. 68f below), recorded by no other ancient writer, but amply attested by epigraphic and archaeological evidence; or the careers of Pertinax and Didius Julianus prior to their accession.

together with the *Life* of the emperor Macrinus contain very little that is neither fictional nor a reworking of material already transmitted in the biography of the relevant emperor.[24] After the *Heliogabalus* (as the *Augustan History* prefers to call Elagabalus), which itself descends into fiction at a point about half-way through, the remainder of the *Augustan History* is of very dubious quality. There is a thin substratum of fact, derived from Herodian, Dexippus and the brief Latin chroniclers, but otherwise, as in the 'secondary' *Lives*, fiction predominates. Much of the fiction consists of faked documents, such as speeches and letters. As long ago as 1870 it was shown that all the documents in the *Avidius Cassius*, while purporting to be speeches or letters by Marcus Aurelius, Lucius Verus, Faustina or Cassius himself, were the work of a single writer.[25] And it is now accepted that all the documents in the *Augustan History* are faked by the author, except for the 'acclamations of the Senate' at the end of the *Commodus*.

These documents in the *Commodus* are explicitly ascribed by the author to the writings of Marius Maximus. Maximus is known from Ammianus Marcellinus, who couples him with Juvenal, in a scathing passage, as the favourite reading-matter of the decadent aristocracy of fourth-century Rome.[26] And a Scholiast on Juvenal, writing at about the same time as Ammianus, quotes a story which evidently derives from a *Life of Nerva* by Maximus.[27] In the *Augustan History* he is named no fewer than thirty-one times, and he is credited with biographies of Trajan, Hadrian, Pius, M. Aurelius, Commodus, Pertinax, Severus and Elagabalus. There seems little doubt that he is the same man as the consul of A.D. 223, L. Marius Maximus, whose long and distinguished career in the late second and early third

24. See esp. Syme, *EB*, pp. 54ff.
25. C. Czwalina, *De epistolarum actorumque quae a Scriptoribus Historiae Augustae proferuntur fide atque auctoritate*, I.
26. Ammianus, 28.4.14.
27. *Schol. in Juvenalem*, 4.53, quoted below, p. 32.

centuries is known in detail from several inscriptions and papyri, and from a mention in Cassius Dio. It seems that Maximus wrote a continuation or sequel to Suetonius' *The Twelve Caesars*, when, after the murder of Elagabalus, it was possible for the first time to tackle a second twelve emperors.[28] He was well placed to have had access to information, and, if the *Augustan History* may be believed, he wrote at inordinate length, quoting documents copiously.[29] But there is some dispute as to whether the *Augustan History* relied wholly or mainly on Marius Maximus for the sound information in the 'major' *Lives*. For one thing, the *Life of Macrinus* in the *Augustan History* ought to have been exceptionally accurate and detailed if the author had used a biography by Maximus as his source, for the latter had been appointed prefect of Rome by Macrinus. Yet the *Macrinus* in the *Augustan History* is one of the worst and least reliable biographies in the series.[30] Argument about the use made of Maximus, and indeed about the quality of Maximus' *Caesars*, is, however, unlikely to be productive in the absence of new evidence.

There are certainly signs, as already mentioned, that the author used further sources, some of them not named, such as Victor and Eutropius, and others that he does name, e.g. Herodian and Dexippus. Since Herodian's *History* survives complete, it is possible to trace its use in the *Augustan History* and it can be seen that it has been quarried extensively, especially from the *Macrinus* onwards, although reworked and adapted in a perverse and idiosyncratic fashion. In citing

28. See Birley, *Severus*, pp. 308ff.

29. See e.g. *Quadrigae tyrannorum*, 1.1–2; *Commodus*, 18.2ff, pp. 176–8, below; *Pertinax*, 2.8, 15.8, pp. 180, 191, below.

30. See Syme, *AHA*, pp. 89ff., *EB*, pp. 30ff., who argues that the *Augustan History*'s principal source in the 'main' *Lives*, from Hadrian to Caracalla, was an unknown biographer ('Ignotus'), with Marius Maximus used only to add spice here and there. I prefer to regard Maximus as the main source.

Herodian, the name Arrianus is sometimes given. At first sight this is a slip of the pen, but it is quite possible that it is deliberate, stemming from an attempt to multiply his authorities by an author who is at pains throughout to emphasize that he is a scholar, engaged in laborious research – not for him the grandiose style of famous historians; he aims to produce plain facts, dug out from various sources, books in Greek and Latin, private journals, even coins.[31] It is not surprising therefore that as well as genuine sources such as Maximus, Herodian and Dexippus, he also cites a whole series of bogus authors.[32] The majority appear in the second half of the work, when his genuine authorities were in any case petering out, but several appear in the first half: Apollonius, 'the Syrian Platonist', Aemilius Parthenianus, 'author of *Lives of the Usurpers*', Aelius Maurus, 'freedman of Hadrian's freedman Phlegon', Aelius Cordus, later called Junius Cordus, the only one of these bogus authorities to be cited frequently, Aurelius Victor, 'surnamed Pinio', and Lollius Urbicus, 'author of a history of his own time'.

These bogus authors are part of the same picture as the bogus historical characters and the faked documents with which the biographies are heavily larded. The bogus names begin in the *Cassius*, where the usurper's father is named Avidius Severus and given a career quite different from that of Cassius' real father Heliodorus, who had in fact already been named in the *Hadrian*. No doubt the author was unaware of the connection. 'Of course,' as he admits in the *Cassius*, 'not much can be known about men whose lives no one dares to render famous, because of those by whom they were overcome[33].' This is a theme to which he returns several times, for example at the beginning of the *Niger*: 'It is unusual and difficult to set down a proper account of those whom the victory of others has made

31. See esp. *Tyranni triginta*, 33.8; *Aurelian*, 1–2; *Probus*, 2.1–2.
32. See esp. R. Syme, *HAC*, 1973.
33. *Avidius Cassius*, 3.1, p. 150f below.

into usurpers . . . not much care is spent in research on their ancestry and life, since it suffices to mention their presumption, the war in which they were defeated, and their punishment.'[34] These considerations do not, of course, deter the author from pressing on: the 'minor' *Lives* are his own special innovation.

Names, both bogus and genuine, are an obsession with the author[35] (not least in the rather feeble way that he plays on the meaning of names like Verus, Severus, Pertinax, Avidius).[36] In the case of two names in particular this has led him to a serious distortion of the facts. The first concerns the nomenclature of Hadrian's first choice as heir. It is perhaps desirable to set out the names of this man and of his son, as supplied by other evidence.[37] In A.D. 136 Hadrian adopted Lucius Ceionius Commodus, who thereupon changed his name to Lucius Aelius Caesar. Soon after this man's death, on 1 January A.D. 138, his own young son, also Lucius Ceionius Commodus, was adopted by Antoninus, together with Marcus Annius Verus. The two adoptive sons of Antoninus were now known as Lucius Aurelius Commodus and Marcus Aurelius Verus; and they retained these names until the death of Antoninus in A.D. 161. Marcus Aurelius then assumed the name Antoninus, gave up the name Verus and passed it on to his adoptive brother. The latter thus became Lucius Aurelius Verus, dropping the name Commodus. From A.D. 161, therefore, Marcus was Marcus Aurelius Antoninus and Lucius was Lucius (Aurelius) Verus. For some reason the author of the *Augustan History* was convinced that the name Verus had been borne by the family of the Ceionii, and hence applies it to L. Aelius Caesar, both before and after his adoption. This is simply a mistake: there is no other evidence that L. Aelius Caesar was

34. *Pescennius Niger*, 1.1–2, p. 225 below; cf. also *Macrinus*, 1.1ff., p. 268 below.

35. See esp. Syme, *AHA*, pp. 165ff., *EB*, pp. 1ff.

36. See e.g. *Avidius Cassius*, 1.7, 3.4; *Pertinax*, 1.1, pp. 150–51, 179, below.

37. *PIR²*, C 605, 606.

17

ever called Verus. Secondly, the author was convinced that Lucius Verus also had the name Antoninus. And he either believed, or pretended to believe, that Severus' younger son Geta had it as well. In fact no other evidence exists that either was ever called Antoninus. But the 'name of Antoninus' is a favourite theme in this work.[38]

The *Augustan History* can hardly be called literature of high quality, but its strange character and the controversy and mystery surrounding its author have given it a justified reputation as a literary curiosity. Who the author was and why he composed the work will presumably never be known.[39] Some have seen in it a work of propaganda, aimed at promoting the cause of the pagan aristocracy of Theodosian Rome. It may be more illuminating to think of the author as a hoaxer or joker[40], concealing his identity and giving the work the appearance of a collection preserved from an earlier age, purely to amuse himself and perhaps a small circle of friends by mystifying others. The popularity of Marius Maximus' biographies may have led him to attempt to go one better, by including biographies of minor figures and by taking the series on beyond the point where Maximus ended. Perhaps the recent publication of Ammianus' annalistic history in continuation of Cornelius Tacitus spurred him on to produce a rival work, imperial biographies in the manner of Tacitus' contemporary, Suetonius Tranquillus.

However that may be, the plan was carried out in a slapdash and hasty fashion. The author himself makes a remarkable statement in the latter part of the work:

38. See Syme, *EB*, pp. 78ff.

39. For parallels one might consider Chatterton, and Macpherson's Ossian; or 'Richard of Cirencester'.

40. His humour may not perhaps be immediately apparent, but it is there all right, in the 'minor' *Lives* in particular – humour of the sly, tongue-in-cheek variety.

For my part I feel that I have promised facts, not eloquence: indeed, I am not writing, but dictating, these books which I have been publishing on the *Lives* of the *principes* – and dictating with such haste that if I myself promise something or you request it, I press on so fast that I do not have the chance of drawing breath.[41]

Even without this admission, signs of impatience and carelessness may be detected, indeed they appear early in the work. Half way through the *Hadrian* he breaks off the narrative account of Hadrian's travels to turn to the more congenial theme of the emperor's artistic capacities.[42] Half way through the *Marcus* he clearly found himself in a mess, possibly because he had too much material for his needs (in Marius Maximus' two-volume biography?[43]), and because he had already chopped up his source to construct separate biographies of Marcus' co-emperor Lucius Verus and of the usurper Avidius Cassius.[44] His solution was to turn to Eutropius for a brief survey of Marcus' reign as sole emperor after Verus' death. But when he came to the end of this he seems to have found that he had achieved too abrupt a conclusion, and thus, after throwing in a scandalous story, went back to start with the death of Verus again. In the *Pertinax*, the desire for brevity is manifest. Twice he explicitly resists quoting documents from Maximus' biography of that emperor: their length was excessive, he explains.[45] He had, of course, just transcribed the tedious and repetitive 'acclamations of the Senate' from Maximus' *Life of Commodus*, and he was probably beginning to find the consular biographer, whom he was much later to call 'the most verbose of all men', *homo omnium verbosissimus*,[46] far too long-winded for his purpose. In the *Severus* this urge to compress struck

41. *Tyranni triginta*, 33.8.
42. p. 72 below.
43. *Avidius Cassius*, 9.5, p. 156 below.
44. See Birley, *Severus*, pp. 318ff.
45. *Pertinax*, 2.8, 15.8, pp. 180, 191 below.
46. *Quadrigae tyrannorum*, 1.2.

again. 'But since it is tedious to follow up minor details,' he suddenly announces, after a few particularly muddled pages, 'this man's great deeds were the following'[47] – and he then gives an almost verbatim extract from Aurelius Victor's *Caesares*,[48] summarizing the entire reign. Once again, this procedure seems to have brought him to the end of his subject's life a little too rapidly, and he provides several more pages of padding. After the *Severus*, he could at last spread his wings, with biographies of no fewer than five figures of whom virtually nothing can have been known in late fourth-century Rome: Severus' rivals Niger and Albinus and his younger son Geta, and the short-lived emperor Macrinus and his son. Only Caracalla (whom he calls Caracallus, among other names) may have been better known, and the author devoted most of that biography to a detailed account of the murder of Geta and its aftermath. Finally, in the first half – where he was still competing with Marius Maximus – there was Elagabalus, the perverted Syrian youth. The first part of this *Life* is relatively factual. Then, duty done, and the amazing emperor duly flung into the Tiber, he settles down to amuse himself: '... concerning his life, many obscene items have been put in writing, but since they are not worthy of record I have decided that I should relate the things that are relevant to his extravagance.'[49] Some mildly obscene items do slip in, to be sure, but for the most part it is innocent fantasy: the excesses of the most extravagant and exquisite hedonist the world had ever seen.

The earliest use made of the *Augustan History,* indeed the only use made of it in antiquity (and by the same token this is the true *terminus ante quem* for its composition) was by Q. Aurelius Memmius Symmachus, consul in A.D. 485, father-in-law of Boëthius and the author of a *Roman History*

47. *Severus*, 17.5, p. 217 below.
48. See now, reinforcing Dessau's case, A. Chastagnol, *HAC*, 1966/7, pp. 53ff.
49. *Heliogabalus*, 18.4, p. 304 below.

in seven books. But the work became exceedingly popular in the early Middle Ages, and seventeen manuscripts exist of varying completeness and accuracy, all deriving ultimately from the earliest copy, a ninth century codex.[50]

In making the present translation I have naturally benefited from that in the bilingual Loeb edition by D. Magie[51] (much of the first volume of which was prepared by A. O'Brien-Moore[52]). But I have preferred to work from the improved Latin text in the Teubner edition of E. Hohl,[53] taking into account subsequent emendations. The work is not a choice specimen of Latin prose. As Sir Ronald Syme puts it, the author

was not an elegant exponent. His normal language is flat and monotonous. But uneven, and significantly so. For this author is erudite, a fancier of words, and a collector. Hence many rarities, or even inventions, to the profit of the lexicographer. Two contrasted types of vocabulary may here suffice. First, when depicting the measures of a military disciplinarian, he brings in technical terms redolent of the camp. Second, archaism, preciosity, and flowery words.[54]

This provides a challenge for the translator. It would clearly have been a hopeless task to try to turn it into a literary masterpiece, and so my aim has been to provide as literal a version as possible. There is a danger with such an approach of sinking into translationese. I cannot claim to have avoided this danger completely; the friendly but firm persuasion of Mrs Betty Radice, Advisory Editor to the Penguin Classics series, has eliminated some of the grosser specimens. With two particular expressions I have been forced to abandon any attempt at

50. cf. A. R. Birley, *Latin Biography*, pp. 113ff., for references.
51. 3 vols., 1921, 1924, 1932.
52. See Magie, vol. 1, p.v.
53. 2 vols., reprinted with addenda and corrigenda, 1965.
54. Syme, *EB*, p. 251, with references to three words in the *Pescennius* (*buccellatum*, *papilio* and *stellatura*); and to a collection of choice vocabulary in *AHA*, p. 130, n. 1.

translation: I have not translated *princeps* at all, and I have rendered *respublica* 'republic' throughout. Admittedly, in the period here covered, *princeps* means 'emperor' and *respublica* means 'the state'. But the author was very much of an antiquarian in his politics as in much else, and *princeps* and 'republic', unsatisfactory though they may be, seem to convey something of the author's attitude better than the alternatives. The notes are far from comprehensive,[55] but are intended, together with the stemmata of the imperial families and the chronological table, to provide the reader less familiar with the historical background with the necessary minimum assistance.[56] More extensive annotation would have been inappropriate. As the author said (more than once): *longum est omnia persequi.*[57]

55. Except of course in the *Lives* of Nerva and Trajan, which, it must be emphasized once more, are *not* from the *Augustan History*, but compiled by myself from various sources, all of which are indicated in the notes to these *Lives*.

56. I was obliged to make use of the first half of the *Augustan History* a good deal in my biographies of *Marcus Aurelius*, 1966, and *Septimius Severus*, 1971, and for this reason have given fairly frequent references to these works in the notes. It may be mentioned here that I have standardized some of the spellings of proper names (e.g. Daphne for Dafne), but not all.

57. *Probus*, 2.5. The same thought is expressed many times in the second half of the work; cf *Severus*, 17.5 (cited above, p. 20). I cannot conclude this introduction without a word of gratitude to Professors Syme, Alföldi and Straub, the former for introducing me to the *Augustan History*, and the two latter for their kindness in inviting me to the *Colloquia*.

ABBREVIATIONS

Birley, *Marcus Aurelius*	A. Birley, *Marcus Aurelius*, Eyre & Spottiswoode, 1966.
Birley, *Severus*	A. Birley, *Septimius Severus the African Emperor*, Eyre & Spottiswoode, 1971.
CIL	*Corpus Inscriptionum Latinarum*, Prussian Academy, 1863ff.
Degrassi	A. Degrassi, *I Fasti Consolari dell' Impero Romano*, Edizioni di Storia e Letteratura, 1952.
HA	*Historia Augusta*.
HAC	*Bonner Historia-Augusta-Colloquia*, Habelt, 1963ff.: the year given refers to the year of the *Colloquium,* not to the year of publication.
Hohl	E. Hohl, *Scriptores Historiae Augustae*, Teubner, 1965.
ILS	H. Dessau, *Inscriptiones Latinae Selectae*, Weidmann, 1892–1916.
JRS	*The Journal of Roman Studies*, Society for the Promotion of Roman Studies, 1910ff.
Magie	D. Magie, *The Scriptores Historiae Augustae*, Heinemann, 1921–1932.
PIR²	E. Groag, A. Stein, L. Petersen, *Prosopographia Imperii Romani*, 2nd ed., de Gruyter, 1933ff.: entries are cited by letter and number, not page.
Smallwood	E. M. Smallwood, *Documents Illustrating the Principates of Nerva, Trajan and Hadrian*, Cambridge University Press, 1966.

Syme, *AHA*	R. Syme, *Ammianus and the Historia Augusta*, Oxford University Press, 1968.
Syme, *EB*	R. Syme, *Emperors and Biography. Studies in the Historia Augusta*, Oxford University Press, 1971.
Syme, *Tacitus*	R. Syme, *Tacitus*, Oxford University Press, 1958.

CHRONOLOGICAL TABLE
OF EMPERORS, A.D. 96–222

A.D.

96	18 September	Murder of DOMITIAN
		Accession of NERVA
97	27 October	Adoption of M. Ulpius Traianus (Trajan) by Nerva
98	28 January	Death of Nerva
		Accession of TRAJAN
117	9 August	Supposed adoption of P. Aelius Hadrianus (Hadrian) by Trajan
	11 August	Death of Trajan
		Accession of HADRIAN
136	December ?	Adoption of L. Ceionius Commodus by Hadrian, as L. Aelius Caesar
138	1 January	Death of L. Aelius Caesar
	25 February	Adoption of T. Aurelius Antoninus by Hadrian; adoption of Marcus and Lucius by Antoninus
	10 July	Death of Hadrian
		Accession of ANTONINUS PIUS
161	7 March	Death of Antoninus Pius
		Accession of MARCUS AURELIUS, who confers equal powers on LUCIUS VERUS
169	January	death of Lucius Verus
175	spring	AVIDIUS CASSIUS hailed emperor in east
	summer	Death of Cassius
177	1 ? January	COMMODUS made co-emperor
180	17 March	Death of Marcus Aurelius
		COMMODUS sole emperor

A.D.

192	31 December	Murder of Commodus
		Accession of PERTINAX
193	28 March	Murder of Pertinax
		Accession of DIDIUS JULIANUS
	9 April	SEPTIMIUS SEVERUS hailed emperor on Danube
	spring	PESCENNIUS NIGER hailed emperor in east
		D. Clodius Albinus made Caesar by Severus
	1 June	Death of Didius Julianus
194		Defeat and death of Pescennius Niger
195	December ?	CLODIUS ALBINUS hailed emperor in west
197	19 February	Defeat and death of Albinus
198	28 January	CARACALLA made co-emperor
209		GETA made co-emperor
211	4 February	Death of Severus
		CARACALLA and GETA joint emperors
	late December	Murder of Geta
217	8 April	Murder of Caracalla
		Accession of MACRINUS
218	spring ?	Macrinus' son DIADUMENIANUS made co-emperor
	16 May	ELAGABALUS hailed emperor
	8 June	Defeat of Macrinus
221	26 June	Alexander made Caesar and adopted by Elagabalus
222	12 March	Murder of Elagabalus
		Accession of SEVERUS ALEXANDER

LIVES
OF NERVA
AND TRAJAN

Compiled by Anthony Birley

NERVA*

A FTER the murder of Domitian, Marcus Cocceius Nerva
obtained the imperial power. His family came from
Narnia in Umbria,[1] and his father was a jurist,[2] although a less
celebrated one than his paternal grandfather Nerva, who was
consul under Tiberius.[3] His grandfather's grandfather was
consul five years before the battle of Actium [36 B.C.] and then
proconsul of Asia.[4] Nerva's mother was Sergia Plautilla,
daughter of Octavius Laenas, an ex-consul.[5] His mother's
brother was Octavius Laenas who married Rubellia, great-
granddaughter of Tiberius.[6] A kinswoman of his married Otho
Titianus, brother of the emperor Otho.[7]

Nerva was born at Narnia on the sixth day before the Ides
of November when Gallus and Nonianus were the consuls [8
November, A.D. 35].[8] About his upbringing and early life

* For a modern account of Nerva see especially Syme, *Tacitus*, pp.
1ff., 627ff. The bare details are furnished by *PIR*[2], C 1227.

1. *Epitome de Caesaribus*, 12.1.

2. Frequently cited in the *Digest*: *PIR*[2], C 1226.

3. Frequently cited in the *Digest*: *PIR*[2], C 1225; cf. esp. Tacitus,
Annals, 6.26.

4. *PIR*[2], C 1224.

5. *ILS*, no. 281.

6. *ILS*, no. 952.

7. Suetonius, *Domitian*, 10.3, refers to the murder of Salvius Coccei-
anus, nephew of Otho; Syme, *Tacitus*, p. 628, conjectures that this
person's mother was a Cocceia, probably Nerva's sister.

8. The year is given by *Epitome*, 12.11 – see Syme, *Tacitus*, p. 653,
n. 5; the month by various sources including *ILS*, no. 5285.

nothing has come down to us. Among other posts, he was honorary city prefect during the Latin festival and led a squadron of Roman knights at their ride past, as one of the six men. He held several priesthoods, being augur, *sodalis Augustalis*, and a Palatine *salius*. He served as urban quaestor.[9] As praetor designate he was honoured by Nero with triumphal decorations, together with Tigellinus the prefect of the guard and Petronius Turpilianus, an ex-consul. Nerva and Tigellinus were honoured by the erection of statues in the palace too, as well as the ones in triumphal dress in the Forum. At this time Nero was investigating the conspiracy of Piso.[10] He was consul for the first time with the emperor Vespasian as his colleague, the latter holding office for the third time [A.D. 71]. This was a great mark of distinction for Nerva, since Vespasian did not share the *fasces* with any other private citizen when he was emperor, while he was consul seven times with his son Titus as his colleague. He was consul a second time with Domitian, when Domitian held his fifteenth consulship [A.D. 90], the year after the attempted usurpation of Saturninus had been crushed.[11]

The Greek writer Philostratus states that Nerva was banished by Domitian to Tarentum, along with Orfitus and Rufus, who were sent to islands. He also says that Apollonius of Tyana, the philosopher, was accused of conspiracy against Domitian together with Nerva and the other two.[12] But this story is not very probable. Suetonius for his part says that Domitian in his early youth had been debauched by Nerva.[13] Martial the writer of epigrams praises Nerva for his quiet way of life – this was before he became emperor – and for his poetry, saying that he

9. *ILS*, no. 273 = Smallwood, no. 90. The *sodales Augustales* conducted the worship of the deified Augustus; the *salii*, or 'leaping priests', served the god Mars.

10. Tacitus, *Annals*, 15.72.

11. Degrassi, pp. 20–23, 27; Saturninus: Dio 67.11.1, etc; *PIR²*, A 874.

12. Philostratus, *Vita Apollonii*, 7.8, 11.

13. Suetonius, *Domitian*, 1.1.

was the Tibullus of the age, although modest about his own ability.[14]

Nerva became emperor on the fourteenth day before the Kalends of October when Valens and Vetus were the consuls [18 September, A.D. 96].[15] It is said that those who conspired against Domitian first offered the imperial power to a number of other men, but that they refused it, thinking that it was a trick. Then they went to Nerva, since he was from a most noble family and of a very amiable disposition. They persuaded him the more readily since an astrologer had once foretold that he would be emperor. Indeed, Domitian, who took careful note of the horoscopes of the leading men, and put to death not a few of them, even though they were not hoping for the imperial power, had intended to kill Nerva too, and would have done so just before his own death, had not one of the astrologers who was a friend of Nerva told Domitian that Nerva was fated to die within a few days in any case. Domitian therefore spared him, not wishing to be guilty of this further murder, seeing that Nerva was fated to die already.[16]

At first there was a rumour that Domitian was still alive and would appear and Nerva was very much afraid, and became pale and could scarcely stand up. But Parthenius the chamberlain reassured him. When he went to the Senate he was congratulated by all, except by Arrius Antoninus, an ex-consul, a shrewd man and a very close friend of his, who commented sagely on the lot of emperors, saying that he congratulated the Senate and people and provinces, but not Nerva himself. It was quite sufficient for him to have escaped the designs of bad *principes*, rather than to take up the weight of so great a burden, and not only submit himself to inconvenience and danger but to the judgement of enemies and friends alike. For the friends, reckoning that they deserved everything, if they did

14. Martial, 8.70; cf. 9.26.
15. Smallwood, no. 27a, etc.
16. Dio, 15.5–6 (abbreviated).

not extract a particular favour, were worse than actual enemies.[17] Now this Antoninus was the maternal grand-father of Antoninus, surnamed Pius, who afterwards became emperor.[18]

Everyone rejoiced at first that liberty had been restored. Because of the hatred for Domitian his images, many of them of silver and of gold, were melted down and large sums of money were obtained from this. The many arches that had been erected in his honour were torn down. Nerva did not permit anyone to make gold or silver statues in his own honour. He set free all who were on trial for treason and recalled the exiles. Further, he put to death all the slaves and freedmen who had conspired against their masters and prohibited that class of person from making complaints against their masters. No one was permitted to accuse anyone of treason or of adopting the Jewish way of life; and Nerva wiped out the abuses in the collection of the Jewish tax. Many of the informers were put to death, including Seras the philosopher.[19] Others who are named as having been informers were Armillatus, Demos-thenes, and Latinus, a principal actor; Marius Maximus writes that those men had been powerful under Domitian.[20]

But so much disturbance was created by the fact that every-one was now accusing everybody else that Fronto, the consul, is said to have remarked that it was a bad thing to have an emperor under whom no one was allowed to do anything but worse to have one under whom anyone was allowed to do anything. Nerva, on hearing this, is said to have ordered that this state of affairs should cease.[21] Once when Junius Mauricus, a Stoic who had been exiled by Domitian and had now returned, was dining with Nerva, and next to Nerva at the

17. *Epitome*, 12.2–3.
18. *HA, Antoninus Pius*, 1.4, p. 96 below.
19. Dio, 68.1.1–2,2.1.
20. *Schol. in Juvenalem*, 4.53 (Wessner, p. 57).
21. Dio, 68.1.3.

table was Veiento, who had been consul under Domitian and had persecuted many by secret accusations, and was now actually leaning on Nerva's shoulder, they were talking about Catullus Messallinus. Now Catullus had been blind and his loss of sight had increased his cruel disposition, so that he knew neither fear nor shame nor pity, and thus was often used by Domitian to aim at honest men, like a weapon which flies blindly and unthinkingly to its mark. When everyone had been talking of his villainy and murderous decisions, Nerva said: 'I wonder what he would be doing now if he had survived Domitian?' Mauricus replied: 'He would be dining with us.'[22]

Nerva himself swore an oath in the Senate that he would not put any senator to death, and he kept the oath even though there were plots against him.[23] Calpurnius Crassus, a descendant of the famous Crassi of old, plotted against him together with others, making vast promises to the soldiers. Nerva had them sit next to him at a spectacle (they did not know that they had been found out) and gave them swords, ostensibly to see if they were sharp but in reality to show them that he did not care even if he died there and then. After this Crassus confessed his plans and was banished to Tarentum, together with his wife, although the senators criticized Nerva for his leniency.[24] Crassus was put to death many years later, soon after the accession of Hadrian, on a charge of attempted usurpation.[25] As for Verginius Rufus, although he had several times in the past been saluted as emperor, Nerva did not shrink from having him as his colleague in the consulship. During his consulship, however, Rufus broke his leg and died in the same year, being then very old.[26]

22. Pliny, *epist.* 4.22.4–5 (whence *Epitome*, 12.5).
23. Dio, 68.2.3.
24. Dio, 68.3.2, *Epitome*, 12.6.
25. *HA, Hadrian*, 5.6, p. 62 below.
26. Dio, 68.2.4; Pliny, *epist.*, 2.1, etc.

Nerva ruled so well that he once remarked: 'I have done nothing of any sort that would make it impossible for me to lay down the imperial power and return to private life in safety.'[27] To those who had been deprived of their property without cause under Domitian he gave back all that was still to be found in the treasury. To very poor Romans he granted allotments of land worth sixty million sesterces, putting some senators in charge of their purchase and distribution. When he ran short of funds, he sold a great deal of clothing and many gold and silver vessels, and furnishings, both his own and those belonging to the imperial residence, and many estates and houses; everything in fact except what was indispensable. But he did not haggle over the price. He abolished many sacrifices, many horse-races and some other spectacles, in an attempt to reduce expenditure as much as possible. Moreover, he did nothing without the advice of the leading men,[28] and appointed a commission of five men to reduce public expenditure.[29] Among his various laws were those prohibiting the castration of any man and prohibiting any man to marry his own niece.[30]

He reduced the tribute, which had been increased by Domitian, back to its former level,[31] and he exempted close relations from the five per cent tax on inheritance.[32] He gave assistance to communities that were afflicted,[33] and he took away from the Italians the burden of supplying the public posting-service with vehicles.[34] He also initiated a scheme for assisting the sons and daughters of poor parents in the towns of Italy, at public

27. Dio, 68.3.1.
28. Dio, 68.2.1–3.
29. Pliny, *Paneg.*, 62.2; *epist.*, 2.1.9.
30. Dio, 68.2.4.
31. *Epitome*, 12.4.
32. Pliny, *Paneg.*, 37.6.
33. *Epitome*, 12.4.
34. Smallwood, no. 30.

expense, which Trajan later completed.[35] When there was a flood of the Tiber, he took steps to restore the damage.[36] He also made repairs to the amphitheatre.[37] The only building which bears his name is the Forum Transitorium, between the Forum of Augustus and the Temple of Peace, although this had been begun by Domitian.[38] He ordered that the Flavian House on the Palatine, where Domitian had had his residence, should be called the 'House of the People'.[39] The stage actors, which Domitian had banned, by request of the people he permitted to return. But later, Trajan banned them once more.[40]

But after he had ruled for only one year, he was placed in the greatest danger on account of the praetorian guards. For they had been angered at the murder of Domitian and they were incited to mutiny against Nerva by Casperius Aelianus, whom he had made prefect of the guard (he had formerly been prefect under Domitian, as well), and they demanded that Nerva should hand over to them those who had killed Domitian. Nerva was besieged in the palace, arrested and kept in custody. Full of consternation and sick with fear, he said repeatedly that he would rather die than besmirch his imperial authority by betraying those who were responsible for conferring it upon him. He bared his collar-bone and offered his throat to the soldiers. But he accomplished nothing and the soldiers ignored him. Petronius and Parthenius were handed over, the former being killed by a single blow, but Parthenius had his private parts torn off and thrust into his mouth, before they strangled him. Casperius forced Nerva to go before the people and render thanks to the soldiers for 'having killed the most wicked and sinful of men.'[41]

35. *Epitome*, 12.4.
36. *Epitome*, 13.12.
37. *CIL*, VI, no. 37137.
38. Victor, *de Caes.*, 12.2; Suetonius, *Domitian*, 5.1.
39. Pliny, *Paneg.*, 47.4.
40. Pliny, *Paneg.*, 46.2.
41. Dio, 68.3.3; *Epitome*, 12.6–8; Pliny, *Paneg.*, 6.1.

At this time then, when things were in a perilous state and the republic seemed to be tottering,[42] a laurelled letter came from Pannonia, announcing a victory over the Germans. Nerva took the laurels to lay them in the lap of Jupiter, and when he came out he said in a loud voice: 'May good fortune attend the Senate and people of Rome and myself, I hereby adopt Marcus Ulpius Traianus.' Later he and Trajan took the title Germanicus on account of the German victory. After this, in the Senate, he appointed him Caesar and then gave him the *imperium* and the tribunician power. Then he sent a message written in his own hand to Trajan, who was at that time governing Upper Germany, in which he wrote: 'May the Danaans by thy shafts requite my tears.'[43] He also presented him with a precious jewel, a diamond, which Trajan later gave to Hadrian.[44]

Thus Trajan became Caesar and later he became emperor, although Nerva had relatives living. But he did not esteem kinship above the safety of the republic, nor was he less inclined to adopt Trajan because he was a Spaniard instead of an Italian, inasmuch as no foreigner had previously held the imperial power. For he believed in looking at a man's ability rather than at his nationality;[45] although some say that, with the backing of Licinius Sura, Trajan actually seized the power,[46] even if he appeared to be reluctant.[47] Pliny the younger says that it would have been wanton and tyrannical of Nerva not to have adopted the one man who, all were agreed, would have become emperor even if he had not been adopted[48], thus showing that Nerva could hardly have avoided choosing Trajan. For Trajan

42. Pliny, *Paneg.*, 6.3.
43. Pliny, *Paneg.*, 8.2–3; Dio, 68.3.4. The quotation was from Homer (*Iliad*, 1.42).
44. *HA, Hadrian* 3.7, p. 60 below.
45. Dio, 68.4.1–2.
46. *Epitome*, 13.6.
47. Pliny, *Paneg.*, 5.6.
48. Pliny, *Paneg.*, 7.6.

at that time was commanding numerous legions, very close to Italy.[49]

Soon after this, Nerva became consul again, for the fourth time, with Trajan as his colleague, holding his second consulship.[50] Less than thirty days later he died.[51] Provoked by anger, he was rebuking a certain Regulus in a loud voice, when he was overcome by sweating. Then he became cold again and the excessive shivering of his body brought on a fever, and not long afterwards he expired at his villa in the Gardens of Sallust, in his sixty-third year,[52] having ruled for one year, ten months and nine days.[53] His body was carried to the sepulchre of Augustus by the Senate, the same honour which Augustus himself had been given.[54] The Senate later deified him at the request of Trajan, and built a temple in his honour.[55] There was a festival to celebrate his birthday, which is still in existence.[56]

He was handsome in appearance,[57] with a rather large nose.[58] But as emperor he was feeble in health, being old and rather weak, and he used to vomit up his food.[59] He was somewhat inclined to be a heavy drinker of wine, as was Trajan.[60]

49. As legate of Upper Germany: Dio, 68.3.4; *HA, Hadrian*, 2.5., p. 58 below.

50. Smallwood, p. 2.

51. Dio, 68.4.2.

52. *Epitome*, 12.10–11.

53. Dio, 68.4.2.

54. *Epitome*, 12.12.

55. Eutropius, 8.1.2; Pliny, *Paneg.*, 11.1.

56. *CIL* I, 2nd ed., nos. 255, 276f.

57. Julian, *Caesares*, 311A.

58. Nerva's coins illustrate this.

59. Dio, 68.1.3.

60. Victor, *de Caes.*, 13.10.

TRAJAN*

TRAJAN's family originally came from Tuder in Umbria,[1] but his ancestors settled at Italica in Spain.[2] His father Ulpius Traianus was made consul by Vespasian, having commanded a legion in the Jewish war, and was later made a patrician and given triumphal honours.[3] His mother was Marcia and his sister Ulpia Marciana,[4] who married Matidius Patruinus[5] and had a daughter Matidia.[6] Matidia married Vibius Sabinus[7] and her daughter Sabina married Hadrian, the son of Trajan's cousin through his mother.[8] Trajan's wife was Pompeia Plotina.[9]

Trajan was born at Italica on the fourteenth day before the Kalends of October[10] when Torquatus and Antoninus were the consuls [18 September A.D. 53],[11] although others say it was in a different year.[12] As a young man he served for a long time

---

* The best modern account of Trajan will be found in Syme, *Tacitus*, pp. 10ff., 86ff., 217ff.

1. *Epitome*, 13.1.
2. Victor, *de Caes.*, 13.1; Eutropius, 8.2.1; Appian, *Iberica*, 38.
3. *ILS*, no. 263; Josephus, *Jewish War* 3. pp. 289ff., etc.
4. Inscriptions and coins attest the names of his sister; that of his mother is deduced.
5. *CIL*, VI, no. 2056.
6. Inscriptions and coins.
7. *CIL*, XI, nos. 5383, 8020.
8. *HA, Hadrian*, 1.2, 2.10, pp. 57, 58 below.
9. *Epitome*, 42.41.
10. Pliny, *Paneg.*, 92.4; *epist.* 10.17.2, etc.
11. Eutropius, 8.5.2.
12. Dio, 68.6.3.

as a military tribune and was in the Syrian army when his father was governor of that province.[13] Later, after his praetorship, he commanded the legion VII Gemina in Tarraconensis and led the legion with great speed against Antonius Saturninus, when Saturninus rebelled against Domitian. However, he arrived after the rebellion had been crushed.[14] Then he served in other expeditions of Domitian.[15] He was consul for the first time with Acilius Glabrio [A.D. 91].[16] When Nerva became emperor he appointed Trajan governor of Upper Germany, and soon afterwards adopted him. While he was in Germany, according to some he seized the imperial power, with the encouragement of Licinius Sura, and others say that all were agreed that he would have become emperor even if he had not been adopted by Nerva. At any rate, he was adopted by Nerva as his son and took the name of Nerva, but not Cocceius, so that he was known as Marcus Ulpius Nerva Traianus Caesar and received the *imperium* and the tribunician power.[17]

Before he became emperor, he had a dream of the following kind. He thought that an old man in a purple-bordered toga and clothing and with a crown on his head, as the Senate is portrayed in pictures, impressed a seal upon him with a signet ring, first on the left side of his neck and then on the right.[18] He received the news of Nerva's death at Colonia Agrippinensis [Cologne] from his kinsman Hadrian, and at once was made emperor.[19] He sent a letter to the Senate, written in his own hand, in which he declared that he would not slay or disfranchise any good man and confirmed this by oaths not only at this time but later as well.[20] But he sent for Casperius Aelianus

13. Pliny, *Paneg.*, 14.1, 15.1–3.
14. Pliny, *Paneg.*, 14.2–4.
15. Pliny, *Paneg.*, 14.5.
16. Degrassi, p. 27.
17. p. 36 above.
18. Dio, 68.5.1.
19. *HA, Hadrian*, 2.6, p. 58 below; *Epitome*, 13.3.
20. Dio, 68.5.2.

and the praetorians who had mutinied against Nerva, pretending that he was going to employ them for some purpose, and then made away with them.[21] When he first handed to the man who was to be his prefect of the guard the sword which the prefect was required to wear at his side, he bared the blade and holding it up said: 'Take this sword, in order that, if I rule well, you may use it for me, but if ill, against me.'[22] Some say that this prefect was Attius Suburanus, whom he later made a senator and consul twice.[23] Marius Maximus says that prefects of the guard were replaced by sending a freedman to them with the broad stripe of senatorial rank.[24]

He did not return to Rome at first, but remained with the armies, and travelled through Pannonia to Moesia.[25] On his route back to Rome he conducted himself like a private citizen, and walked on foot.[26] At Rome he greeted the senators who awaited him with a kiss.[27] Then he walked to the palace, with the same modest demeanour as if it had been a private house.[28] When his wife Plotina first entered the palace, she turned around to face the steps and the people and said: 'I enter here such a woman as I would wish to be when I leave.'[29] He gave largess to the people and a donative to the soldiers.[30] His father Nerva, he deified.[31]

But after a short stay at Rome he began his first expedition, against the Dacians.[32] For Decebalus the Dacian king had

21. Dio, 68.5.4.
22. Dio, 68.16.1²; Victor, *de Caes.*, 13.9; Pliny, *Paneg.*, 67.8.
23. Victor, *de Caes.*, 13.9; *ILS*, no. 5035.
24. *HA, Severus Alexander*, 21.4.
25. Pliny, *Paneg.*, 12ff.
26. Pliny, *Paneg.*, 20.
27. Pliny, *Paneg.*, 23.1.
28. Pliny, *Paneg.*, 23.6.
29. Dio, 68.5.5.
30. Pliny, *Paneg.*, 25.2.
31. Pliny, *Paneg.*, 11.1–3; Eutropius, 8.1.2.
32. Dio, 68.6.1.

defeated Domitian previously[33] and Trajan saw that the power and pride of the Dacians were increasing.[34] There were various battles in which many Romans were killed, but when Trajan was approaching the Dacian king's residence, Decebalus sent envoys, called cap-bearers, who were to request that Trajan meet Decebalus and were to say that Decebalus would do all that Trajan commanded. Instead, Trajan sent his friend Licinius Sura, and Claudius Livianus, the prefect of the guard, to meet Decebalus. But the king was afraid and would not meet them. Then Laberius Maximus captured Decebalus' sister and Trajan recovered the standard of the legion lost under Domitian when Cornelius Fuscus the prefect of the guard had been slain by the Dacians. Decebalus came to Trajan, therefore, and fell on the ground before him, threw away his arms and did obeisance. He agreed to surrender his arms, engines and engine-makers, demolish the forts, give back the deserters and withdraw from captured territory, and become an ally of the Roman people. Trajan left garrisons all over Dacia and returned to Rome, where he held a triumph and was given the title Dacicus.[35]

But when it was announced to Trajan that Decebalus was breaking the treaty in various ways, the Senate again declared him a public enemy and Trajan once more conducted the war against him in person instead of entrusting it to legates.[36] At first Decebalus sued for peace again, but he could not be persuaded to surrender both his arms and himself, and openly collected troops and summoned the surrounding peoples to his aid.[37] He sent deserters into Moesia to see if they could make away with Trajan, but one of them was arrested and revealed the entire plot under torture. Then Decebalus seized the general

33. Dio, 67.6.1–4.
34. Dio, 68.6.1.
35. Dio, 68.9.1–10.2 (abbreviated); Maximus: PIR², L 9.
36. Dio, 68.10.3–4 (abbreviated).
37. Dio, 68.11.1.

Longinus who was sent as an envoy, after Decebalus had pretended that he wanted to offer submission. But Longinus drank poison and died.[38] Trajan now built a bridge over the Danube, with twenty piers of dressed stone, each one hundred and fifty feet in height and sixty feet wide.[39] Having crossed the Danube by this bridge he conducted the war with prudence and safety rather than with haste, and after a hard struggle defeated the Dacians.[40] Decebalus committed suicide and his head was cut off and brought to Trajan at Ranisstorum. Trajan sent the head to Rome,[41] where it was hurled down the Gemonian Steps.[42] Decebalus' treasures were discovered too, although he had hidden them beneath the river Sargetia. For Bicilis, a Dacian noble, who was captured, revealed where they were hidden.[43] Dacia was made into a Roman province, and Trajan brought into it, to cultivate the fields and inhabit the cities, countless settlers from all over the Roman world, for Dacia had been drained of its manpower during the long war.[44] When Trajan returned to Rome he gave spectacles lasting for one hundred and twenty-three days, during which eleven thousand animals, both wild and tame, were slain, and ten thousand gladiators fought.[45]

At this same time Cornelius Palma the governor of Syria subdued the part of Arabia around Petra and made it a Roman province.[46] Trajan honoured Palma with a second consulship and a statue, and he gave like honours to Sosius Senecio and Publilius Celsus, for he esteemed these three men above the

38. Dio, 68.11.3–12.4 (abbreviated).
39. Dio, 68.13.1.
40. Dio, 68.14.1.
41. Dio, 68.14.3; Ranisstorum: M. Speidel, *JRS* 1970, 142ff., for the remarkable funerary inscription of Decebalus' captor.
42. Smallwood, no. 20, A.D.106.
43. Dio, 68.14.4–5.
44. Eutropius, 8.2.2, 8.6.2.
45. Dio, 68.15.1.
46. Dio, 68.14.5.

rest.[47] But no one was so close a friend of his as Licinius Sura, to whom he gave a third consulship.[48] Sura used to compose Trajan's speeches for him.[49] When Sura died, Trajan bestowed upon him a public funeral and a statue. He had attained to such a degree of wealth and pride that he had built a gymnasium for the people of Rome.[50] And Trajan built baths in his honour.[51] So great was the friendship and confidence which he showed towards Trajan and Trajan towards him that, although he was often slandered, as naturally happens in the case of all those who possess any influence with the emperors, Trajan never felt any suspicion or hatred towards him. On the contrary, when those who envied Sura became very insistent, the emperor went uninvited to his house to dinner and having dismissed all his bodyguards, first called Sura's doctor and caused him to anoint his eyes, and then his barber, whom he caused to shave his chin, and after doing this he next took a bath and had dinner. Then on the following day he said to his friends who were in the habit of constantly disparaging Sura: 'If Sura had wanted to kill me, he would have killed me yesterday.' Thus his confidence was strengthened by his knowledge of Sura's conduct rather than by the conjectures of others.[52]

He often went to call on his friends, to greet them, when they were sick or were celebrating festivals, and accepted their invitations to dinner and invited them back in return. Often he would ride in their carriages.[53] His association with the people was marked by affability and his relations with the Senate by dignity, so that he was loved by all and feared by no one, except the enemy. He joined others in the hunt and in banquets, as well as in their labours and plans and jokes. Often he would

47. Dio, 68.16.2; see Smallwood, pp. 5ff., A.D.109, 107 and 113.
48. Smallwood, no. 5, A.D.107.
49. Julian, *Caesares*, 327A.
50. Dio, 68.15.3².
51. *Epitome*, 13.6.
52. Dio, 68.15.4–6 (abbreviated).
53. Eutropius, 8.4.

take three others into his carriage and he would enter the houses of citizens, sometimes even without a guard, and enjoy himself there.[54] His friends blamed him for being too accessible, but he replied that, as emperor, he behaved towards private citizens in the manner in which, as a private citizen, he had wanted emperors to behave towards him.[55]

Those who conspired against him he brought before the Senate and had punished, including Calpurnius Crassus and Laberius Maximus, of whom the latter had commanded armies for him. But he only sent them into exile on islands and did not kill them.[56] He had taken an oath that he would not shed blood and he made good his promise by his actions in spite of the plots formed against him. For by nature he was not at all inclined to duplicity or guile or harshness, but he loved, greeted and honoured the good, and the others he ignored. Moreover he became milder as he grew older.[57]

He is said to have chosen as his procurators the sort of men whom most of his subjects chose to try their cases in preference to anyone else, although free to take them to any court they wished.[58] But when certain of his procurators were causing trouble in the provinces by their unjust conduct, to the extent that one was said to ask every rich man: 'Why are you rich?'; another: 'Where do you get it from?'; and a third: 'Put down what you have got', his wife Plotina tackled him and reproached him for neglecting his own good name. As a result she made him detest unjust exactions, and he used to call the fisc a spleen, because when it grows the other parts of the body waste away.[59] But as for the city magistrates and the governors of provinces, he was less diligent in keeping check on them than Domitian

54. Dio, 68.7.3.
55. Eutropius, 8.5.1.
56. Dio, 68.16.2; *HA, Hadrian,* 5.5–6, p. 62 below.
57. Dio, 68.5.3.
58. Pliny, *Paneg.,* 36.5.
59. *Epitome,* 42.21.

had been, with the result that a great number of them were charged with crimes of every kind.[60]

He spent vast sums of money both on war and on the works of peace. While making very many urgently needed repairs to roads and harbours and public buildings he drained no one's blood for any of these undertakings. He was so high-minded and generous that after embellishing the Circus, which had crumbled away in many places, he merely inscribed on it a statement that he had made it adequate for the Roman people.[61] However, his name was inscribed on so many buildings that he was called a creeper that grows on walls.[62] For he also built libraries and, in the Forum named after himself, he erected an enormous column to serve both as a monument to himself and as a record of his work in the Forum. For the whole of that area had been hilly and he had had it excavated to a depth equal to the height of the column, thus making the Forum level.[63] During his reign there was a flood of the Tiber, much more destructive than the one under Nerva, with great damage to the adjacent buildings. He gave assistance to deal with all this and laid down that no buildings should be constructed to a height greater than sixty feet, since they might easily collapse and the expense in such cases would be damaging.[64] He also cut a canal to drain the Tiber.[65] Such was his concern for the corn-supply that he made a new harbour at Ostia,[66] and he was said to have let the sea into the shore and moved the shore out to sea.[67] And he made new harbours at Centumcellae[68] and at Ancona too.[69]

60. Suetonius, *Domitian*, 8.2 (adapted).
61. Dio, 68.7.1–2.
62. *Epitome*, 41.13.
63. Dio, 68.16.3; cf. Smallwood, no. 378a.
64. *Epitome*, 13.12–13.
65. Pliny, *epist.*, 8.17.2.
66. Smallwood, nos. 384–5.
67. Pliny, *Paneg.*, 29.2.
68. Pliny, *epist.*, 6.31.15.
69. Smallwood, no. 387.

Besides this, he built new baths at Rome, on the Oppian Hill, a new aqueduct, and a *naumachia*, which were all opened when Palma, for the second time, and Calvisius Tullus were the consuls [A.D. 109].[70] He built a new road too, from Beneventum to Brundisium, which was named the *via Traiana* in his honour.[71] In the provinces he constructed a great many buildings as well.[72]

He instituted the post of prefect of vehicles, to take charge of the imperial post, so that imperial messages might be carried more rapidly.[73] He made a number of improvements in the law. Anonymous accusations were prohibited.[74] Fathers who maltreated their sons were obliged to emancipate them and lose their rights over their inheritance.[75] Free-born children who had been exposed at birth and brought up by their finders were permitted to claim their freedom without having to pay the cost of their maintenance.[76] He also tightened up the regulations concerning guardians.[77] He laid down that public holidays did not apply to the army.[78] Where soldiers' wills were technically invalid because of ignorance on the part of the testators, he ruled that the wishes of the soldiers must be paramount.[79] He laid down punishments for those who mutilated their sons in an attempt to prevent them from being conscripted into the army.[80] He did in fact raise two new

70. Smallwood, no. 22. The *naumachia* was an artificial lake on which mock naval battles were held.

71. Smallwood, no. 400a.

72. Victor, *de Caes.*, 13.4; Eutropius, 8.2.2; Smallwood, nos. 389, 392, 394ff.

73. Victor, *de Caes.*, 13.5; Smallwood, no. 267a.

74. Pliny, *epist.*, 10.97.

75. *Digest*, 37.12.5.

76. Pliny, *epist.*, 10.66.

77. *Digest*, 26.7.12.1, 27.1.17, 41.4.2.8.

78. *Digest*, 2.12.9.

79. *Digest*, 29.1.1. preface and 24; 29.1.24.

80. *Digest*, 49.16.4.12.

legions, II Traiana and XXX Ulpia Victrix.[81] Defendants who were condemned in absence were given the right to a retrial.[82] He made further exemptions from the five per cent tax on inheritances[83] and he completed the child-welfare programme initiated by Nerva.[84] He compelled candidates for office at Rome to invest one third of their estate in Italian land, thinking it unseemly that they should treat Rome and Italy not as their native country but as a mere inn or lodging-house for them on their visits. As a result of this the price of land in Italy increased.[85]

It was a fault in him that he was a heavy drinker and also a pederast. But he did not incur censure, for he never committed any wicked deed because of this. He drank all the wine that he wanted and yet remained sober, and in his relations with boys he harmed no one.[86] It is reported that he tempered his wine-bibbing by ordering that his requests for drink should be ignored after long banquets.[87]

Both his wife Plotina and his sister Marciana received the title Augusta[88] and when Marciana died she was deified. Her daughter Matidia was then made Augusta also.[89] His grand-niece Vibia Sabina, the daughter of Matidia, he gave in marriage to Hadrian, his kinsman, although not very eager for the match, at the urging of Plotina, according to Marius Maximus.[90] His real father Traianus he deified.[91] He himself held four

81. Dio, 55.24.4.
82. *Digest*, 48.19.5.
83. Pliny, *Paneg.*, 37ff.
84. Smallwood, nos. 435–8: this is the *alimenta* system (see e.g. *Cambridge Ancient History XI*, 1936, pp. 210ff.).
85. Pliny, *epist.*, 6.19.4.
86. Dio, 68.7.4.
87. Victor, *de Caes.*, 13.10.
88. Smallwood, no. 106.
89. Smallwood, nos. 22, 108, 134 (A.D.112).
90. *HA, Hadrian*, 1.2, 2.10, pp. 57, 61f. below.
91. Smallwood, no. 133.

consulships as emperor.[92] The title of 'Father of the Fatherland' he accepted after a short interval.[93]

After he had ruled for fifteen years, he made another expedition, against the Armenians and the Parthians. His pretext was that the Armenian king had not obtained his crown from Trajan but from the Parthian king. But his real reason was desire for glory. After he had set off and had got as far as Athens an embassy from the king of the Parthians, Osroes, met him and asked for peace, proffering gifts. For the king had become terrified when he learned of Trajan's advance, because Trajan was accustomed to make good his threats by his deeds. So he implored him not to make war and at the same time he asked that Armenia be given to Parthamasiris. For he too was a son of Pacorus, like Axidares, whom Osroes had deposed on the grounds that he was not satisfactory either to the Romans or to the Parthians. Trajan did not accept the presents and did not give any reply except to say that friendship was determined by deeds and not by words, and that he would do what was fitting when he reached Syria. This being his intention, he proceeded through Asia and Lycia, into Syria. When he reached Antioch, Abgarus of Osrhoëne sent gifts and a message of friendship, but he did not come himself, for he feared both Trajan and the Parthians alike.[94]

After spending the winter at Antioch,[95] Trajan set out for Armenia. The satraps and princes came to meet him with gifts, one of which was a horse that had been taught to do obeisance, kneeling on its forelegs and placing its head beneath the feet of whoever stood near.[96] Parthamasiris wrote to Trajan, calling himself king, but when there was no reply he wrote again,

92. Smallwood, pp. 3ff., A.D. 100, 101, 103, 112.

93. Pliny, *Paneg.*, 21.1–4.

94. Dio, 68.17.1–18.1 (abbreviated).

95. John Malalas (sixth-century chronicler from Antioch in Syria), p. 272.

96. Dio, 68.18.2.

omitting this title and asking that Junius Homullus, the governor of Cappadocia, be sent to him, as if he wished to make some request through him. Trajan therefore sent the son of Homullus to him and he himself captured Arsamosata, without a battle. Then he came to Satala and rewarded Anchialus, king of the Heniochi and Machelones, with gifts. At Elegeia he received Parthamasiris, seated upon a tribunal in the camp. Parthamasiris saluted him, took his crown off and laid it at Trajan's feet, and then stood in silence, expecting to receive it back. At this the soldiers shouted aloud and acclaimed Trajan as *imperator*. This terrified the king, who thought it was meant as an insult and was a sign of impending doom. He turned as if to flee but as he was surrounded he begged that he might speak to Trajan in private. But he obtained nothing there, and left the camp in a rage. Trajan summoned him back and ordered him to say what he wanted in the hearing of all. Then Parthamasiris declared that he had not been defeated but had come of his own accord, believing that he should not be wronged and that he should receive back the kingdom, as Tiridates had from Nero. But Trajan replied that he would surrender Armenia to no one, for it belonged to the Romans and would have a Roman governor. He allowed Parthamasiris to depart, together with his Parthian companions,[97] and appointed Catilius Severus to govern Armenia together with Cappadocia.[98] But Parthamasiris was killed on his journey, even though Trajan had given him an escort of cavalry.[99]

When Trajan had conquered the whole country of the Armenians and had won over many of the kings too, some of whom he treated as friends, since they submitted of their own accord, and others of whom he subdued without a battle, the Senate bestowed upon him the title of Optimus, 'best of

97. Dio, 68.19.1–20.4 (abbreviated).
98. Smallwood, no. 197.
99. Arrian, *Parthica*, fr.39 (Roos); Fronto, *Principia Historiae*, p. 15 = Haines, II, pp. 212f.; Dio, 68.20.4.

emperors'.[100] This title, which had been given to him before because of his excellence and the love which all had for him, he now consented to accept.[101] He always marched on foot with the infantry and he dealt with the ordering and disposition of the soldiers throughout the whole campaign, leading them sometimes in one order and sometimes in another; and he forded all the rivers that they did. Sometimes he even caused his scouts to circulate false reports, so that the soldiers might at the same time practise military manoeuvres and become fearless and prepared for any dangers. From Armenia he moved into Mesopotamia and captured Nisibis and Batnae, after which he was given the title Parthicus.[102] Then, leaving garrisons behind him, he came to Edessa and met Abgarus, who had failed to meet him before. Now, partly through fear of Trajan and partly through the persuasions of his son Arbandes, a handsome youth who was in favour with Trajan, Abgarus came to meet him on the road. He entertained Trajan at a banquet and during the dinner brought in his son to perform a barbarian dance.[103]

Then Trajan returned to Antioch for the winter, and during the winter there was a very serious earthquake there and countless numbers perished in the destruction. He himself escaped through the window of the room in which he was staying, and the consul Pedo was killed.[104] But in spite of this, at the beginning of spring[105] he hastened into the enemy's country again, bringing the boats which had been constructed in the forests around Nisibis to the Tigris on wagons. The Romans crossed over the Tigris as well, and conquered the whole of Adiabene.[106] Then they advanced as far as Babylon, without

100. Dio, 68.18.3²; 23.1.
101. Pliny, *Paneg.*, 2.7, 88.4–10; Smallwood, nos. 99–101.
102. Dio, 68.23.1–2.
103. Dio, 68.21.1–2 (abbreviated: A.D.115).
104. Dio, 68.24.1–25.5 (abbreviated).
105. A.D.116, evidently.
106. Dio, 68.26.1–4 (abbreviated).

meeting any resistance.[107] After this he entered Ctesiphon and when he had taken possession of the place he accepted the title Parthicus, which had already been offered to him. He wanted to go down to the mouth of the Tigris and see the ocean, and when he got there and saw a ship sailing to India, he said: 'I should certainly have crossed over to the Indians too, if I were still young.' For he was very interested in the Indians and regarded Alexander as having been fortunate. Yet he himself used to say that he had advanced further than Alexander and wrote this to the Senate, even though he was unable to retain all the territory which he had conquered.[108] For he made two new provinces, Mesopotamia and Assyria,[109] and he was granted the honour of celebrating a triumph over as many peoples as he pleased, since on account of the large number of peoples which he named in his frequent letters, they were unable always to understand or even use the names correctly.[110]

But he was destined never to return to Rome and even to lose what he had conquered previously. For while he was sailing down to the ocean and returning from there, all the districts that had been conquered were thrown into upheaval and rebelled, and the garrisons that he had left there were either expelled or slain. Trajan learned of this when he was at Babylon, where he had gone to sacrifice to the spirit of Alexander, and because of its fame. He sent Maximus and Lusius Quietus against the rebels; Maximus was killed but Lusius recovered Nisibis and sacked Edessa, in addition to other successes. Then Erucius Clarus and Julius Alexander captured and burned Seleucia too. In the meantime, the Jews also, in Egypt, Cyrenaica and Cyprus, rose in rebellion, and Lusius was

107. Dio, 68.26.4².
108. Dio, 68.28.2–29.1.
109. Eutropius, 8.3.2, 8.6.2 (Armenia had already been declared a province).
110. Dio, 68.29.2.

sent to subdue them as well. Trajan now feared that the Parthians would rebel as well, and decided to give them a king. So he came to Ctesiphon and summoning everyone together appointed Parthamaspates king over the Parthians and placed the crown upon his head.[111] On his way back to Syria, Trajan attempted to capture Hatra, but the place was too difficult to besiege, because it lies in such barren country.[112] So Trajan desisted and departed, and soon after his health began to fail.[113]

He had intended to make another expedition into Mesopotamia, but his disease was afflicting him sorely and he set out to sail back to Italy.[114] Trajan himself thought that he had been poisoned, but others say that he had suffered a stroke and that part of his body was paralysed. When he reached Selinus in Cilicia, which was afterwards called Traianopolis, he suddenly expired, having reigned nineteen years, six months and fifteen days.[115] It was given out that he had adopted his kinsman Hadrian, then governor of Syria, as his son and made him Caesar, although some say that Plotina's party concealed his death and got an actor to impersonate him, speaking in a tired voice.[116] Certainly, one of Trajan's freedmen, Phaedimus, who had been in close attendance on him, died only a few days after him, although he was young, and his remains were not brought to Rome for thirteen years: hence it might be thought that he had been put to death because he knew too much.[117] After his death Trajan was deified and a triumph was celebrated for him

111. Dio, 68.29.3–30.3.
112. Dio, 68.31.1–4 (abbreviated).
113. Dio, 68.32.1.
114. Dio, 68.33.1.
115. Dio, 68.33.2–3.
116. HA, Hadrian, 4.10, p. 61f below.
117. Smallwood, no. 176: see Syme, Tacitus, p. 240, n. 7 for the interpretation of the inscription.

by Hadrian, who conducted an effigy of Trajan through the streets of Rome.[118] His ashes were placed in an urn at the foot of his column.[119]

118. *HA, Hadrian,* 6.1 and 3, p. 63 below.
119. Dio, 69.2.3; *Epitome,* 13.11; Eutropius, 8.5.2.

THE
AUGUSTAN
HISTORY

*The lives of various emperors and usurpers from the deified
Hadrian to Numerian, composed by various hands*

HADRIAN*

BY AELIUS SPARTIANUS

Hadrian's family derived originally from Picenum but his more recent ancestors were from Spain – at least, Hadrian himself in his autobiography records that his ancestors were natives of Hadria who had settled at Italica in the time of the Scipios.[1] Hadrian's father was Aelius Hadrianus, surnamed Afer, a cousin of the Emperor Trajan. His mother was Domitia Paulina, born at Gades [Cadiz]; his sister was Paulina, who was married to Servianus; and his wife was Sabina.[2] His great-great-great-grandfather Maryllinus was the first member of the family to be a senator of the Roman people. Hadrian was born on the ninth day before the Kalends of February [24 January] when the consuls were Vespasian for the seventh time and Titus for the second [A.D. 76].

In his tenth year he lost his father and had Ulpius Traianus (Trajan), then of praetorian rank, his cousin and the future emperor, and Acilius Attianus,[3] as his guardians. He immersed himself rather enthusiastically in Greek studies – in fact he was so attracted in this direction that some people used to call him a 'little Greek'. In his fifteenth year he returned to his home

* The best modern account of Hadrian is to be found in Syme, *Tacitus*, esp. pp. 236ff., 481ff.

1. A small town near Seville, in the Spanish province of Baetica, Italica was founded by Scipio Africanus in 206 B.C. (Appian, *Iberica*, 38).

2. See genealogical table A.

3. Reading Acilium Attianum in preference to the MS's 'Caelium Tatianum'. P. Acilius Attianus (*PIR*², A 45), a fellow-townsman of Trajan and Hadrian, rose to be prefect of the guard by A.D. 117.

town, and at once began military training.⁴ He was keen on hunting, so much so as to arouse criticism, hence he was taken away from Italica by Trajan and treated as his son. Soon after, he was appointed a member of the Board of Ten (*decemvir litibus iudicandis*),⁵ and this was followed by a commission as tribune in the legion II Adiutrix. After this he was transferred to Lower Moesia – it was, by this time, the very end of Domitian's principate. In Lower Moesia he is said to have learned that he would be emperor from an astrologer, who told him the same things which, he had found out, had been predicted by his great-uncle Aelius Hadrianus, a man skilled in astrological matters. When Trajan was adopted by Nerva, Hadrian was sent to give the army's congratulations, and was then transferred to Upper Germany. It was from this province that he was hurrying to Trajan to be the first to announce Nerva's death, when he was detained for some while by Servianus, his sister's husband, delayed by the deliberate breaking of his carriage. Servianus incited Trajan against Hadrian by revealing to him what he was spending and the debts he had contracted. But he made his way on foot and arrived before Servianus' emissary (*beneficiarius*).⁶ He was in favour with Trajan, and yet he did not fail, making use of the tutors assigned to Trajan's boy favourites, to . . .⁷ with the encouragement of Gallus. Indeed, at this time, when he was anxious about the emperor's opinion of him, he consulted the 'Virgilian oracle' and this is what came out:

4. Presumably in the local para-military youth organization (*iuventus*).
5. The *decemviri* were future senators, who carried out duties in the law-courts at Rome. Hadrian's career as given here is confirmed by an inscription erected in his honour at Athens in A.D.112 (Smallwood, no. 109), with a few extra items.
6. A soldier seconded for special duties on an officer's staff.
7. The MSS are defective here.

But what's the man, who from afar appears,
His head with olive crown'd, his hand a censer bears?
His hoary beard, and holy vestments bring
His lost idea back: I know the Roman king.
He shall to peaceful Rome new laws ordain:
Call'd from his mean abode, a scepter to sustain.[8]

Others said that this oracle came to him from the Sibylline verses. He also had a forecast that he would soon become emperor in the reply emanating from the shrine of Jupiter Niceforius, which Apollonius of Syria, the Platonist, has included in his books.[9]

Finally, when Sura[10] gave his support, he at once returned into fuller friendship with Trajan, receiving, as his wife, Trajan's niece (his sister's daughter) – Plotina being in favour of the match, while Trajan, according to Marius Maximus, was not greatly enthusiastic. He served his quaestorship when the consuls were Trajan for the fourth time and Articuleius [A.D. 101]; during his tenure of office he gave attention to his Latin, and reached the highest proficiency and eloquence after having been laughed at for his somewhat uncultivated accent while reading an address of the emperor in the Senate. After his quaestorship he was curator of the *Acts of the Senate*, and followed Trajan to the Dacian Wars in a position of fairly close intimacy; at this time, indeed, he states that he indulged in wine too, so as to fall in with Trajan's habits, and that he was very richly rewarded for this by Trajan. He was made tribune of the plebs when the consuls were Candidus and Quadratus, each for the second time [A.D. 105]; he claims that in this magistracy he was given an omen that he would receive perpetual tribunician power, in that he lost the cloaks which the tribunes of the plebs used to wear in rainy weather, but which the emperors never wear. (For which reason even today

8. Virgil, *Aeneid*, 808–812 (Dryden's translation).
9. Presumably a bogus author: see p. 16 above.
10. L. Licinius Sura (*cos. III ord.* 107: *PIR²*, L 253).

emperors appear before the citizens without a cloak.) In the second Dacian expedition Trajan put him in command of the legion I Minervia and took him with him; and at this time, certainly, his many outstanding deeds became renowned. Hence, having been presented with a diamond which Trajan had received from Nerva, he was encouraged to hope for the succession. He was made praetor when the consuls were Suburanus and Servianus, each for the second time[11], and he received four million sesterces from Trajan to put on games. After this he was sent as a praetorian governor to Lower Pannonia; he restrained the Sarmatians, preserved military discipline, and checked the procurators who were overstepping the mark. For this he was made consul [A.D. 108].

While holding this magistracy, he learned from Sura that he was to be adopted by Trajan, and was then no longer despised and ignored by Trajan's friends. Indeed, on the death of Sura, Trajan's intimacy with him increased, the reason being principally the speeches which he composed for the emperor. He enjoyed the favour of Plotina too, and it was through her support that he was appointed to a governorship at the time of the Parthian expedition. At this period, at any rate, Hadrian enjoyed the friendship of Sosius Senecio, Aemilius Papus and Platorius Nepos[12] from the senatorial order, and, from the equestrian order, of Attianus, his former guardian, Livianus

11. An error: the year is presumably 107, when the consuls were Sura III and Senecio II. Suburanus was cos. II in A.D.104, Servianus in 102. See Smallwood, pp. 3ff.

12. I follow H. G. Pflaum, *HAC*, 1966, p. 148 in his restoration of the text. Q. Sosius Senecio (*cos. II ord.* 107) was a prominent figure under Trajan. A. Platorius Nepos (*cos.* 119), perhaps a Spaniard, was the man responsible for building Hadrian's Wall in Britain. Papus, another Spaniard, is not known to have been prominent in public life.

and Turbo.[13] He got a guarantee that he would be adopted
when Palma and Celsus[14] – who were always his enemies and
whom he subsequently attacked himself – fell under suspicion
of plotting a usurpation. His appointment as consul for the
second time [A.D. 118], through the favour of Plotina, served to
make his adoption a completely foregone conclusion. Widespread rumour asserted that he had bribed Trajan's freedmen,
had cultivated his boy favourites and had had frequent sexual
relations with them during the periods when he was an inner
member of the court. On the fifth day before the Ides of August
[9 August A.D. 117], while governor of Syria, he received his
letter of adoption, and he ordered the anniversary of his adoption to be celebrated on that date. On the third day before the
Ides of the same month [11 August] the death of Trajan was
reported to him; he decreed that the anniversary of his accession
should be celebrated on that day.

There was of course a persistent rumour that it had been in
Trajan's mind to leave Neratius Priscus[15] and not Hadrian as
his successor, with the concurrence of many of his friends, to
the extent that he once said to Priscus: 'I commend the provinces to you if anything should befall me.' Many indeed say that
Trajan had it in mind to die without a definite successor,
following the example of Alexander the Macedonian; and
many say that he wanted to send an address to the Senate, to
request that if anything should befall him the Senate should
give a *princeps* to the Roman republic, adding some names
from which it should choose the best man. There are not
lacking those who have recorded that it was through Plotina's

13. Ti. Julius ... Claudius Livianus (*PIR*², C 913) was prefect of the
guard under Trajan (cf. p. 41 above) Q. Marcius Turbo, a native of
Epidaurus in Dalmatia, was to hold the same office soon after Hadrian's
accession: see Syme, *JRS*, 1962, pp. 87ff.

14. A. Cornelius Palma (*cos. II ord.* 109) and L. Publilius Celsus (*cos.
II ord.* 113).

15. L. Neratius Priscus (*cos.* 97) was a leading jurist. But the story is
dubious: see Syme, *Tacitus*, pp. 233f.

party, Trajan being already dead, that Hadrian was received into adoption; and that a substitute impersonating Trajan spoke the words, in a tired voice.

When he gained the imperial power he at once set himself to follow ancestral custom, and gave his attention to maintaining peace throughout the world. For those nations which Trajan had subjugated were defecting, the Moors were aroused, the Sarmatians were making war, the Britons could not be kept under Roman control, Egypt was being pressed by insurrection, and, finally, Libya and Palestine were exhibiting the spirit of rebellion.[16] He therefore gave up everything beyond the Euphrates and Tigris, following the example of Cato, as he said, who declared the Macedonians to be free because they could not be protected.[17] Parthamasiris,[18] whom Trajan had made king of the Parthians, he appointed as king over the neighbouring peoples, because he saw that he did not carry great weight among the Parthians.

So great in fact was his immediate desire to show clemency that, when in his first days as emperor he was warned by Attianus, in a letter, that Baebius Macer[19] the prefect of the city should be murdered in case he opposed his rule, also Laberius Maximus, who was in exile on an island, and Frugi Crassus,[20] he harmed none of them; although subsequently, without an order from Hadrian, a procurator killed Crassus when he left the island, on the grounds that he was planning a *coup*. He gave a double donative to the soldiers, to mark the opening of his reign. He disarmed Lusius Quietus,[21] taking away from him the

16. Egypt, Libya (Cyrenaica) and Palestine were all affected (with Cyprus) by the Jewish revolt of A.D. 115–17. See p. 51f above.

17. In 167 B.C.

18. An error: the correct name was Parthamaspates (p. 52 above).

19. A friend of the younger Pliny (*epist.*, 3.5, 4.9.16ff., 4.12.4).

20. See pp. 33, 44 above.

21. A Moorish chieftain promoted to high command by Trajan, he served in both Dacian and Parthian wars (*PIR*², L 439, and cf. p. 51 above).

Moorish tribesmen whom he had under his command, because he had come under suspicion of aiming for the imperial power, and Marcius Turbo was appointed, when the Jews had been suppressed, to put down the rising in Mauretania.[22] After this he left Antioch to inspect the remains of Trajan, which were being escorted by Attianus, Plotina, and Matidia, and, placing Catilius Severus[23] in command of Syria, he came to Rome by way of Illyricum. In a letter sent to the Senate – and it was certainly very carefully composed – he requested divine honours for Trajan; and for this he obtained unanimous support; in fact, the Senate spontaneously decreed many things in honour of Trajan which Hadrian had not requested. When he wrote to the Senate he asked for pardon because he had not given the Senate the right of deciding about his accession to the imperial power, explaining that he had been hailed as emperor by the soldiers in precipitate fashion because the republic could not be without an emperor. When the Senate offered to him the triumph which belonged of right to Trajan, he refused it for himself, and conveyed the effigy of Trajan in the triumphal chariot, so that the best of emperors, even after his death, might not lose the honour of a triumph. He deferred the acceptance of the title of Father of the Fatherland, which was offered him straightaway, and again later, because Augustus had earned this title at a late stage.[24] He remitted Italy's crown-gold and reduced it for the provinces, while he did indeed make a statement, courting popularity and carefully worded, about the problems of the public treasury.

Then, hearing of the uprising of the Sarmatians and Roxalani, he made for Moesia, sending the armies ahead.[25] He placed

---

22. Thought to have been provoked by Quietus' treatment.
23. *PIR*², C 558, and see p. 49 above.
24. Augustus received the title in 2 B.C. Hadrian took it in A.D.128.
25. This resumes the narrative from the end of chapter 5.

Marcius Turbo in command of Pannonia and Dacia for the time being, conferring the insignia of the prefecture on him after his post in Mauretania. With the king of the Roxolani, who was complaining about the reduction of his subsidy, he made peace, after the matter had been examined.

Nigrinus had plotted to murder Hadrian while he was making sacrifice, Lusius being a fellow-conspirator, and many others, although Hadrian had actually intended Nigrinus as his own successor.[26] Hadrian escaped death; and as a result, on the orders of the Senate, Palma was killed at Tarracina, Celsus at Baiae,[27] Nigrinus at Faventia and Lusius on a journey – against Hadrian's will, as he himself says in his autobiography. Hadrian immediately came to Rome, to counteract the very harsh impression of him that was created by his allowing four ex-consuls to be killed at one and the same time (having entrusted Dacia to Turbo, dignifying him with the title of the Egyptian prefecture to give him more authority)[28] and, to check the rumour about himself, he gave the people a double largess, in person, even though three gold pieces a head had already been distributed in his absence. In the Senate too, having made excuses for what had been done, he swore that he would never punish a senator except by a vote of the Senate. He instituted a regular posting-service run by the fisc, so that magistrates should not be burdened by this task. Moreover, overlooking nothing to gain favour, he remitted to private debtors in the city and in Italy an immense amount of money which was owed to the fisc, and huge sums from the arrears in the provinces too: the forms were burnt in the Forum of the

26. C. Avidius Nigrinus (*PIR*², A 1408) was stepfather of L. Ceionius Commodus: see p. 83 below and genealogical table E. (Lusius is Lusius Quietus.)

27. See p. 61 above.

28. This repeats, with slightly different wording, what has just been said a little earlier: but this is hardly evidence for the use of two separate sources, merely for carelessness.

Deified Trajan, to strengthen general confidence. As for the
property of the condemned, he ordered that it should not go
to the private fisc, the whole sum being collected by the public
treasury. To the boys and girls to whom Trajan, too, had
granted support-payments, he gave an increased bounty. As
for senators who had become bankrupt through no fault of
their own, he made a grant to bring their property up to the
requirements of the senatorial register, in accordance with the
number of their children – in such a way that he paid out to
many without deferment until the term of their life was
measured out.[29] He bestowed a great deal of largess to enable
not only his friends but a great many others too, far and wide,
to fulfil the demands of public office. A number of women he
assisted with expenses to keep up their position in life. He put
on a gladiatorial show lasting for six successive days and put a
thousand wild beasts into the arena on his birthday. He admitted all the leading men from the Senate into close association
with the emperor's majesty. Circus-games, except those
decreed in honour of his birthday, he refused. Both before the
people and in the Senate he frequently stated that he would so
administer the republic that it would know that the state
belonged to the people and was not his property.

When he himself had been consul for a third time [A.D. 119]
he appointed a great many to third consulships, while he bestowed the honour of a second consulship on an immense
number.[30] Although he held his own third consulship for only
four months, he did in fact administer justice on many occasions during that period. He always attended the regular

29. I read *numero* after *liberorum* as the best way of making sense of
the passage.

30. This statement appears to be incorrect: the only men known to
have been given a third consulship were M. Annius Verus in A.D.126
(p. 108 below) and his brother-in-law L. Julius Ursus Servianus in A.D.
134 (p. 66 below). Only five second consulships are known. See
Smallwood, pp. 7ff.

meetings of the Senate when he was in the city or near it. He greatly exalted the rank of the Senate, restricting his creation of new senators: when he made Attianus, who had been prefect of the guard, a senator with honorary consular rank, he made it clear that he had no greater honour that could be conferred upon him. He did not allow Roman knights to sit in judgement on senators, either in his absence or even if he was present. For it was then the custom that when the *princeps* tried cases, he should call both senators and Roman knights to his council and give a decision based on his consultation with them all. Finally, he denounced the *principes* who had shown no deference towards the senators. On his brother-in-law Servianus – to whom he showed such deference that he always went to meet him as he came from his bedroom – he bestowed a third consulship, but not with himself as colleague, so that he would not take second place in senatorial precedence, as Servianus had been consul twice before Hadrian. Servianus did not request it and Hadrian granted it without any urging on his part.

In the meantime, however, he abandoned many provinces[31] annexed by Trajan and, against the wishes of all, demolished the theatre which Trajan had built on the Campus Martius. These things seemed all the harsher because Hadrian pretended that everything that he saw to be unpopular had been secretly enjoined upon him by Trajan. When he could not endure the power of Attianus, his prefect and former guardian, he attempted to slay him, but was deterred because he was already labouring under the odium incurred by the killing of the four ex-consuls – the decision for whose deaths he of course tried to shift back on to Attianus' shoulders. Since he could not give Attianus a successor because he did not ask for one, he brought it about that he did request it; and as soon as he requested it he transferred the power to Turbo. At this time also, in fact, he

31. Armenia, Mesopotamia and Assyria, and part of Lower Moesia.

appointed Septicius Clarus as successor to Similis, the other prefect.[32]

Having removed from the prefecture the very men to whom he owed the imperial power, he made for Campania, and gave support to all its towns by benefactions and largess, attaching all the leading men to his friendship. At Rome, of course, he frequently attended the official functions of the praetors and consuls, was present at friends' banquets, visited them twice or three times a day when they were sick, including some who were Roman knights and freedmen, revived them with sympathetic words and supported them with advice, and always invited them to his own banquets. In short, he did everything in the style of a private citizen. On his mother-in-law he bestowed special honours, with gladiatorial games and other ceremonies.[33]

After this, setting out for the Gallic provinces, he gave support to all the communities with various forms of generosity. From there he crossed into Germany and, while he was eager for peace rather than for war, he trained the soldiers as if war were imminent, instilling into them the lessons of his own endurance; and he himself supervised the military life among the maniples,[34] cheerfully eating camp fare out of doors – bacon fat, cheese and rough wine – after the example of Scipio Aemilianus, Metellus and his own progenitor Trajan, giving rewards to many and honours to a few, so that they would be able to put up with the harsher conditions that he was imposing.

32. C. Septicius Clarus, friend of the younger Pliny and of Suetonius (mentioned below, p. 69), and dedicatee of the former's letters and the latter's *The Twelve Caesars*. Ser. Sulpicius Similis is known to have governed Egypt before promotion to the guard.
33. To mark Matidia's death in A.D.119; see Smallwood, no. 114 (Hadrian's funeral speech from December of that year).
34. The term is used anachronistically, for the maniple was superseded by the cohort, as a subdivision of the legion, in the late 2nd century B.C.

For he did in fact take army discipline in hand. After Caesar Octavianus it had been sinking, owing to the lack of attention given by previous *principes*. He set in order both the duties and the expenditure, never allowing anyone to be absent from camp without proper authorization, since it was not popularity with the soldiers but just conduct that won commendation for tribunes. He encouraged others by the example of his own good qualities, too: he would walk as much as twenty miles in armour; he demolished dining-rooms in the camps, and porticoes, covered galleries and ornamental gardens; frequently he would wear the humblest clothing – putting on an ungilded sword-belt, fastening his cloak with an unjewelled clasp, and only reluctantly permitting himself an ivory hilt to his sword. He would visit sick soldiers in their quarters, would choose the site for camp himself, and he would not give the vine-staff to anyone who was not robust and of good reputation, nor would he appoint anyone tribune who did not have a full beard or was not of an age to assume the powers of the tribunate with prudence and maturity; and he would not allow a tribune to accept any presents from a soldier. He cleared out every kind of luxury from all sides. Finally, he improved their arms and equipment. As regards soldiers' age, too, he pronounced that no one should serve in camp contrary to ancient usage either at a younger age than his strength called for or at an age more advanced than humanity would permit. It was his practice always to be acquainted with them and to know their unit. Besides this, he made an effort carefully to familiarize himself with the military stores, examining the provincial revenues in expert fashion too, so that if there was any particular deficiency anywhere he could make it good. But he strove, more than all emperors, never at any time to buy or to maintain anything that was unserviceable.

Having completely transformed the soldiers, in royal fashion, he made for Britain, where he set right many things and – the first to do so – drew a wall along a length of eighty miles to

separate barbarians and Romans.[35] Septicius Clarus, prefect of
the guard, and Suetonius Tranquillus, director of his correspondence, he replaced, because they had at that time behaved
in the company of his wife Sabina, in their association with her,
in a more informal fashion than respect for the court household
demanded.[36] He would have dismissed his wife too, for being
moody and difficult – if he had been a private citizen, as he
himself used to say. He did not investigate his own household
only, but those of his friends as well, to the extent that he
searched out all their secrets by means of commissary agents,[37]
and his friends were not aware that their private lives were
known by the emperor until the emperor himself revealed the
fact. With reference to this it is not displeasing to insert an epi-
sode which shows that he learned a great deal about his friends.
The wife of a certain man wrote to her husband that he was so
preoccupied with pleasures and the baths that he did not want
to come back to her. Hadrian had found this out through commissary agents, and when the man asked for leave, he reproached him about the baths and pleasures. To this the man
replied: 'Surely my wife didn't write to you as well what she
wrote to me!' In fact this practice has been regarded as a very
bad fault in Hadrian; added to this are the assertions about his
passion for adult males and the adulteries with married women
in which he is said to have been involved; and there is the
further assertion that he did not keep faith with his friends.

After settling matters in Britain he crossed to Gaul, disturbed
by the rioting at Alexandria. This arose on account of Apis,[38]

35. This is the sole ancient literary evidence for Hadrian having built
the Wall. His visit was evidently in A.D. 122.

36. Syme, *Tacitus*, pp. 778ff., discusses the question of where and
when the dismissal took place. Suetonius is, of course, the biographer.

37. The so-called *frumentarii*, whose functions might be compared to
those of the secret police in modern states, seem to have been reorganized
for this purpose by Hadrian.

38. The sacred bull of the Egyptians.

who, when he had been rediscovered after many years, provoked quarrels among the peoples as to which one ought to house him, all of them keenly competing. At the same time he built a basilica at Nemausus [Nîmes] in honour of Plotina, a remarkable construction.[39] After this he made for the Spains and wintered at Tarraco [Tarragona], where he restored the temple of Augustus at his own expense. All the Spaniards had been summoned to an assembly at Tarraco and were 'jokingly expressing reluctance' – to use Marius Maximus' actual words – over conscription. To the Italici[40] he gave some strong advice, to the others he spoke cautiously and with circumspection. At this time, actually, he came into very grave danger, not without glory; while he was taking a stroll among the trees at Tarraco, a slave of his host madly rushed at him with a sword. He took hold of him and handed him over to the attendants who ran up, and, when it was established that he was mad, he gave him over to doctors to be treated, he himself being in no way agitated.

During this period, and frequently at other times, in a great many places where the barbarians are separated off not by rivers but by frontier-barriers, he set them apart by great stakes driven deep into the ground and fastened together in the manner of a palisade.[41]

He appointed a king for the Germans, suppressed revolts among the Moors, and earned public thanksgivings from the Senate. A war with Parthia was getting under way at this period, and it was checked by Hadrian's personal discussion of the matter.[42]

39. After her death (Dio, 69.10.3). Plotina was probably from a Nemausus family.

40. Perhaps an abbreviated form of *Italicenses*, i.e. citizens of his home town Italica; see Syme, *JRS*, 1964, pp. 142ff.

41. In particular, in Upper Germany.

42. The author's desire for compression has caused him to omit mention of Hadrian's journey from Spain to Syria.

After this he sailed along the coast of Asia and past the islands
to Achaia, and undertook the Eleusinian rites, following the
example of Hercules and Philip; he conferred many benefits on
the Athenians and took his seat as president of the games.[43]
During this stay in Achaia, care was taken, they say, that when
Hadrian was present none should come to a sacrifice armed,
whereas generally many used to carry knives. Afterwards he
sailed to Sicily, where he climbed Mount Etna to see the sunrise, which is many-coloured, it is said, like a rainbow. Thence
he came to Rome and from there crossed to Africa and bestowed
a great many favours on the African provinces.[44] Hardly any
other *princeps* has travelled so quickly across so much territory.
Finally, when he had returned to Rome from Africa, he set out
at once for the east, travelling by way of Athens. There he
dedicated the public works which he had initiated among the
Athenians, such as the shrine to Olympian Jupiter and the altar
to himself.[45] In the same manner, as he journeyed through Asia,
he consecrated temples to his own name. Then he received
slaves from the Cappadocians for service in the camp. To the
toparchs[46] and kings he made offers of friendship – even to
Osroes, the king of the Parthians, as well: his daughter, whom
Trajan had captured, was sent back to him, and the throne
which had been seized at the same time was promised.[47] When
certain kings had come to him, he acted in such a way that
those who had not been willing to come regretted it, especially
in the case of Pharasmanes,[48] who had haughtily ignored his
invitation. Indeed, as he went round the provinces, he inflicted
punishments on procurators and governors in accordance with
their actions, with such severity that he was believed to have

43. In March A.D.125.
44. His visit can be dated to summer A.D.128: Smallwood, no. 328.
45. This stay was from September A.D.128 to March 129.
46. District governors.
47. See p. 104 below.
48. King of the Hiberi in the Caucasus region.

been inciting the accusers personally. During this period he held the people of Antioch in such hatred that he wanted to split off Phoenice from Syria, so that Antioch would not be called the metropolis of so many cities. At this time too, the Jews set a war in motion, because they were forbidden to mutilate their genitals.[49] But on Mount Casius, when he had ascended by night for the sake of seeing the sunrise, a rainstorm arose while he was sacrificing and a thunderbolt descended, blasting the sacrificial victim and the attendant.

Having travelled through Arabia he came to Pelusium,[50] and rebuilt Pompey's burial mound in a more magnificent fashion. Antinous, his favourite, he lost during a voyage along the Nile, and he wept for him like a woman. There are varying rumours about this person, some asserting that he had devoted himself to death for Hadrian's sake, others – what both his beauty and Hadrian's excessive sensuality make obvious. The Greeks, to be sure, consecrated him a god at Hadrian's wish, asserting that oracles were given through him – Hadrian himself is talked about as their author.[51]

Certainly he was excessively keen on poetry and literature. In arithmetic, geometry, and painting he was highly skilled – while as for his expertness in playing the cithara and in singing, he used to boast of it. In his sensual pleasures he was immoderate for he even composed a great deal of verse – about his favourites. Hadrian was most skilled with weapons and most expert in military science; he also wielded gladiatorial weapons. He was in one and the same person both stern and cheerful, affable and harsh, impetuous and hesitant, mean and generous, hypocritical

49. i.e. carry out circumcision. This version differs from that of Dio (69.12–14), who ascribes the outbreak of rebellion to Hadrian's foundation of a pagan city at Jerusalem. In any case, the war did not become serious until A.D. 132, whereas the context of this statement places it in 130.

50. A.D. 130.

51. Here the narrative suddenly breaks off, as if the author had tired of it (see p. 19 above).

and straightforward, cruel and merciful, and always in all things changeable. His friends he enriched, even those who did not ask him, while to those who did ask he would refuse nothing. Yet this same man listened readily to whatever was whispered about his friends, and thus almost all, even the closest and even those whom he had raised to the highest honours, he regarded as being in the category of enemy in the sequel – for example Attianus and Nepos and Septicius Clarus. For Eudaemon,[52] formerly his accomplice in gaining the imperial power, he reduced to poverty; Polemaeanus[53] and Marcellus[54] he compelled to suicide; Heliodorus[55] he provoked by a highly defamatory letter; Titianus[56] he suffered to be accused and convicted of a plot to seize the imperial power, and to be proscribed; Ummidius Quadratus[57] and Catilius Severus and Turbo he assailed harshly; in order to prevent Servianus, his sister's husband, from surviving him, he compelled him to commit suicide, although the man was already in his ninetieth year; finally he assailed his freedmen and a number of soldiers. Although he was very practised as a writer of prose and verse and very skilled in all the arts, yet he always mocked the teachers of all the arts on the grounds that he was more learned than they, and despised and humiliated them. With these same

52. Valerius Eudaemon, appointed prefect of Egypt by Antoninus Pius.

53. Reading *Polemaeanum* instead of the MS's *Polyaenum*. Perhaps a son of Ti. Julius Aquila Polemaeanus, colleague of Avidius Nigrinus as consul in A.D.110 and a native of Ephesus (*PIR*², J 168).

54. C. Quinctius Certus Poblicius Marcellus, governor of Syria A.D.132.

55. *PIR*², A 1405: C. Avidius Heliodorus, father of Avidius Cassius. But Heliodorus was still in office as prefect of Egypt when Hadrian died.

56. Probably a confusion with the Titianus who is referred to in the *Life* of Antoninus, p. 101 below: *PIR*², A 1305 (T. Atilius Rufus Titianus).

57. C. Ummidius Quadratus (*cos.* 118). His son was to marry M. Aurelius' sister.

professors and philosophers he often competed, taking turns
to publish books or poems. Once, indeed, a word used by
Favorinus[58] was criticized by Hadrian. Favorinus yielded,
which provoked some very agreeable amusement. He was
wrong to concede to Hadrian, his friends charged him, over a
word which reputable authors had used. 'You don't give me
good advice, my friends,' said Favorinus, 'when you don't
allow me to believe the man who possesses thirty legions to be
more learned than anyone else!'

So eager for widespread renown was Hadrian that he entrusted some books he had written about his own life to his
educated freedmen, ordering them to publish them under their
own names; for Phlegon's books too are said to have been in
fact by Hadrian.[59] He wrote *catacannae*, some very obscure
books in imitation of Antimachus.[60] To the poet Florus,[61] who
wrote to him:

> I do not want to be Caesar,
> To walk about among the Britons,
> To endure the Scythian hoar-frosts,

he wrote back:

> I do not want to be Florus,
> To walk about among taverns,
> To lurk about among cook-shops,
> To put up with the round insects.

---

58. *PIR²*, F 123: a prominent rhetorician, native of Arles, a friend of
Plutarch and Aulus Gellius, and frequently mentioned by Lucian,
Philostratus and others.

59. As Syme points out, this passage reveals that the author 'was
familiar with the notion of literary impersonation – who more so?' (*EB*,
p. 19, n. 5).

60. An epic poet from Colophon, flourished about 400 B.C. The term
catacanna is obscure: it apparently means a fruit-tree onto which stocks
of different kinds have been grafted.

61. *PIR²*, A 650: P. Annius Florus.

Besides this he loved the old style of speaking; and he made debating-competition speeches. He preferred Cato to Cicero, Ennius to Virgil, Coelius[62] to Sallust, and pronounced opinions on Homer and Plato with the same cocksureness. In astrology he regarded himself as such an expert that late on the Kalends of January he would write down what might happen to him during the whole year. In fact, he wrote down for the year when he died what he was going to do up to the very hour of his death. But although he was ready to criticize musicians, tragedians, comedians, grammarians, rhetoricians and orators, yet he both honoured and made rich all who professed the arts – although he always goaded them by his questioning. While he was himself responsible for many of them leaving his company in dejection, he used to say that he took it hardly if he saw anyone dejected. He treated with the greatest friendliness Epictetus[63] and Heliodorus and philosophers, and, not to mention all of them by name, grammarians, rhetoricians, musicians, geometricians, painters and astrologers. Favorinus was conspicuous above the rest, as many assert. Teachers who appeared to be unfit for their profession he enriched and honoured, and then dismissed from their posts.

Men whom he had treated as his enemies when a private citizen he merely ignored as emperor – so that, after his accession, he said to one man whom he had regarded as a mortal foe: 'You have escaped!' To those whom he personally called up for military service he always presented horses, mules, clothing, expenses and their entire equipment. He frequently sent Saturnalia and Sigillaria[64] presents to friends when they were not expecting them, and he himself gladly accepted

62. L. Coelius Antipater, an historian who lived in the second century B.C.

63. The lame, Stoic, ex-slave, whose *Discourses* still survive.

64. The Saturnalia was a festival lasting several days, beginning on 17 December; the last days were called the Sigillaria, when presents, especially little images (*sigilla*), were exchanged.

presents from them, and gave others in return. To detect frauds
on the part of caterers, when he was giving banquets with
several tables, he ordered that dishes from other tables, including each of the bottom tables, should be set before himself.
He surpassed all kings by his gifts. Often he bathed in the public
baths, even when everyone was present, as a result of which the
following bathing-joke became well-known: on one occasion
he had seen a certain veteran, known to him in military service,
rubbing his back and the rest of his body on the wall; he asked
why he had the marble scrape him, and when he learned that
this was done for the reason that he did not have a slave, he
presented him both with slaves and with the cost of their
maintenance. But on another day when several old men were
rubbing themselves on the wall to arouse the emperor's
generosity, he ordered them to be called out and to rub each
other down in turn. He was, indeed, a most ostentatious lover
of the common people. So fond was he of travelling that he
wanted to learn further, at first hand, about everything that he
had read concerning the different parts of the world. His endurance of the cold and bad weather was such that he never
covered his head. On many kings he conferred a great deal, but
from most of them he actually purchased peace; by not a few
he was despised, but to many he gave huge favours – to none
greater than to the king of the Hiberi, to whom he presented an
elephant and a quingenary cohort,[65] in addition to magnificent
gifts. When he himself, too, had received huge gifts and
presents from Pharasmanes, including gold-embroidered
cloaks, he sent into the arena three hundred criminals clad in
gold-embroidered cloaks in order to ridicule the king's presents.

When he sat in judgement he had on his council not only his
friends and *comites*[66] but jurists too, and, in particular, Juventius

65. i.e. a cohort 500 strong, reading *quingenariam*.
66. The post of *comes*, 'companion' (of the emperor), was becoming
formalized at this time and evidently meant something like 'imperial
staff officer'.

Celsus,[67] Salvius Julianus,[68] Neratius Priscus, and others, all of whom, however, the Senate had recommended. Among other decisions he ruled that in no community should a house be demolished for the purpose of transporting cheap building material to another city. To the children of the proscribed he granted one twelfth of their property. He did not accept charges of *maiestas*.[69] Legacies from persons unknown to him he refused, and he did not accept them from persons he did know if they had sons. On treasure-trove, he stipulated as follows, that if anyone found anything on his own property he might take possession of it himself; if anyone found anything on someone else's property he should give half to the owner; if anyone found anything on public land he should share it equally with the fisc. He prohibited the killing of slaves by their owners and ordered that they should be sentenced by judges if they deserved it. He prohibited the sale of a male or female slave to a pimp or gladiatorial trainer without cause being given. Bankrupts, if their status made them legally responsible, he ordered to be flogged in the amphitheatre, and let go. Workhouses for slaves and freedmen he abolished. He divided public baths between the sexes. In cases where a slave-owner had been murdered in his house he ruled that not all the slaves should be put to the torture but only those who were in a position to have some knowledge through having been in the vicinity.

In Etruria he held the *praetura* while emperor. In the Latin towns he was *dictator* and aedile and *duumvir*, at Neapolis [Naples] he was *demarchus*, in his own home town *quinquennalis*,

67. PIR², J 882: P. Juventius Celsus (*cos. II ord.* 129), frequently cited in the *Digest*.

68. Another celebrated lawyer, L. Octavius Cornelius P. Salvius Julianus (*cos. ord.* 148), still a young man in Hadrian's reign: Smallwood, no. 236.

69. i.e. *lèse majesté*, or high treason, a charge that first became common under Tiberius.

and, likewise, *quinquennalis* at Hadria – as it were, in his other
home town – and at Athens, *archon*.[70] In almost all the cities he
built something and gave games. He never called a single wild-
beast-hunter or actor away from Rome. At Rome, after other
enormous delights, he presented the people with spices in
honour of his mother-in-law, and in honour of Trajan he
ordered that balsam and saffron should flow over the steps of
the theatre. He put on plays of every kind, in the ancient fashion,
in the theatre, and he had the court players perform in public.
In the circus he slew many wild beasts and often a hundred
lions. He frequently put on military Pyrrhic dances for the
people, and he often watched the gladiators. Although he built
countless buildings everywhere, he himself never inscribed his
own name on them except on the temple of his father Trajan.
At Rome he restored the Pantheon,[71] the Saepta,[72] the Basilica
of Neptune, very many sacred buildings, the Forum of Augustus and the Baths of Agrippa, and dedicated all of them in the
names of their original builders. He also built a bridge named
after himself and the tomb next to the Tiber, and the shrine of
the Bona Dea. With the help of the architect Decrianus he also
moved the Colossus,[73] held in an upright position, from the
place where the Temple of the City is now – so vast a weight
that he provided twenty-four elephants for the work. When he
had consecrated this statue to the Sun, after removing the face
of Nero to whom it had previously been dedicated, he undertook to make another one of a similar kind, for the Moon,
under the direction of the architect Apollodorus.[74]

70. All these posts are local magistracies in different towns.

71. Still standing, with the inscription of its original builder, M.
Agrippa.

72. The voting-enclosure in the Campus Martius.

73. A statue set up by Nero, over 100 feet high, representing himself.

74. *PIR*², A 922: a Syrian, who had built Trajan's Danube bridge (p.
42 above) and new Forum at Rome. He was banished and then put to
death by Hadrian (Dio, 69.4.1).

In conversation even with people of the humblest class he acted very much as an ordinary citizen, denouncing those who, as if they were preserving the *princeps'* high eminence, would begrudge him this pleasure in human nature. At Alexandria, in the Museum,[75] he propounded many debating questions to the professors and himself solved what he had propounded. Marius Maximus says that he was cruel by nature, and that the reason why he performed many acts of kindness was that he feared that the same thing might befall him as happened to Domitian.[76] Although he did not love inscriptions on public works, he named many cities Hadrianopolis, even Carthage for example, and part of Athens. He called countless aqueducts by his own name as well. He was the first to establish the post of Treasury Counsel (*advocatus fisci*). His memory was vast, his capability boundless; for he both dictated his speeches, and made his replies to everything, in person. Many of his jokes still survive, for he was also very witty. Hence the following story has also become well known: when he had refused a request to a certain grey-haired man, and the same man petitioned again, but with dyed hair, Hadrian replied: 'I have already refused this to your father.' In the case of a great many persons he repeated, without a *nomenclator*,[77] names which he had heard a single time and in a group on the same occasion, so that he corrected the *nomenclatores*, who would quite often make mistakes. He could also say the names of the veterans whom he had at any time discharged. Books, immediately he had read them – and ones which were in fact not known to most people – he could repeat from memory. At one and the same time he wrote, dictated, listened and conversed with his friends – if it

75. An academy and research institution founded by Ptolemy I (305–283 B.C.).

76. Assassinated 18 September A.D. 96 (p. 31 above).

77. A slave whose special duty was to tell his master the names of people presented to him.

can be believed. He had as comprehensive a knowledge of all the public accounts as any thrifty head of a family has of his private household. Horses and dogs he loved so much that he set up tombs for them.[78] He built the town of Hadrianotherae[79] in one place because there he had had a successful hunt and had once killed a bear.

In all trials he always continued his investigations, scrutinizing everything, until he found the truth. He did not want his freedmen to be known in public nor to have any power over himself, his maxim being to blame all earlier *principes* for the vices of their freedmen – all freedmen of his own who boasted of their influence over him were punished. Hence, too, there survives the following story concerning slaves, stern to be sure, but almost humorous. On one occasion he had seen a slave of his walk away from his presence between two senators, so he sent someone to give him a box on the ear and tell him: 'Do not walk between men whose slave you can yet be.' Among foods he particularly loved the *tetrafarmacum*,[80] which consisted of pheasant, sow's udder, ham and pastry.

During his times there were famines, plague and earthquakes, all of which he dealt with as far as he could, and he aided many communities which had been devastated by them. There was also a flood of the Tiber. He gave Latin rights[81] to many communities, to many he remitted their tribute.

The expeditions under him were in no case major ones; the wars too were brought to completion almost without com-

78. See Smallwood, no. 520, for the verse epitaph on his horse, Borysthenes.

79. In Bithynia.

80. See also p. 92 below.

81. A kind of half-way stage to full Roman citizenship: in Latin communities the annual magistrates acquired full citizenship on election. (Hadrian appears to have introduced an enhanced form, *Latium maius*, whereby all members of town councils became full citizens.)

ment.[82] By the soldiers he was greatly loved on account of his great attention to the army, and at the same time because he was very generous towards them. The Parthians he retained in a state of friendship, because he took away from them the king that Trajan had imposed. He allowed the Armenians to have a king, whereas under Trajan they had had a legate. He did not exact from the Mesopotamians the tribute which Trajan had imposed. He kept the Albani and Hiberi on very friendly terms, because he bestowed bounties on their kings, although they had scorned to come as suppliants to him. The kings of the Bactrians sent ambassadors to him, to request friendship.

He very often appointed guardians. Discipline in civilian affairs he maintained no differently from in the military sphere. He ordered senators and Roman knights always to wear the toga in public unless they were returning from a banquet; he himself, when he was in Italy, always appeared in the toga. When receiving senators coming to a social occasion he stood up, and he always reclined at table either clad in a Greek cloak or with his toga let down. He determined the costs of a social occasion with the diligence of a judge and reduced them to the ancient level. He prohibited vehicles with heavy loads from entering the city and did not permit horses to be ridden in towns. He allowed no one unless ill to bath in public before the eighth hour. He was the first to have Roman knights as *ab epistulis* and *a libellis*.[83] Those men whom he saw to be poor and blameless he enriched of his own accord, while he regarded with actual hatred those who had become rich through cunning means. Roman rites he most carefully observed, foreign ones he despised. He always carried out the duties of the *pontifex*

82. This is misleading: the Jewish war of A.D.132–5 was quite serious (see Dio, 69.12–14).

83. Respectively 'Chief Secretary' and 'Secretary for Petitions'. But the statement is mistaken, as a knight was already *ab epistulis* under Domitian, Nerva and Trajan (Smallwood, no. 270).

maximus.[84] He frequently heard lawsuits at Rome and in the provinces, taking on to his council the consuls and praetors and the best senators. He drained the Fucine Lake. He appointed four consulars as judges for the whole of Italy. When he came to Africa, on his arrival, it rained for the first time for five years, and for this reason he was esteemed highly by the Africans.

However, after traversing all parts of the world bare-headed and often in severe rainstorms and frosts he contracted an illness which confined him to bed. Having become anxious about a successor, at first he thought about Servianus, whom, in the sequel, as we have said, he compelled to die. Fuscus[85] he held in the greatest abhorrence, on the grounds that he had been aroused by prophecies and presentiments to hope for the empire. In the case of Platorius Nepos – whom Hadrian had formerly esteemed so very highly that when he came to him when he was ill and was refused admission no punishment was inflicted – he was led on by suspicions; it was likewise with Terentius Gentianus,[86] and in his case hatred was the more violent because at this time he could see that the man was esteemed by the Senate. All, in the end, whom he had considered for the imperial position, he detested as though they were emperors-to-be.

In fact he restrained all the force of his innate cruelty up to

84. These two sentences look suspiciously like inventions by the author. All emperors were pontifex maximus – until Gratian, who laid down the office in A.D.382 (Zosimus, 4.36.5). As for the phrase 'foreign ones he despised', this is difficult to reconcile with his amply attested interest in the Eleusinian mysteries (cf. p. 71 above) and it may reveal the author's attitude to the 'foreign rites' of the Christians.

85. His grand-nephew Cn. Pedanius Fuscus Salinator: genealogical table A.

86. Son of the prominent Trajanic marshal Terentius Scaurianus, D. Terentius Gentianus (*cos.* 116) had apparently become consul before he was thirty (Smallwood, no. 237).

the time when he almost met his end at his Tiburtine villa,
through a haemorrhage. Then, casting aside restraint, he compelled Servianus to die, on the grounds that he was an aspirant
for the empire – because he had provided a banquet for the
royal slaves, because he had sat on a royal seat, placed next to
the bed, because he, a ninety-year-old, had stood up and gone
to meet the soldiers on guard-duty. Many others were put to
death, either openly or by craft. At this time, indeed, Sabina his
wife died, not without a rumour that poison had been given
her by Hadrian.

  Then he determined to adopt Ceionius Commodus, son-in-
law of Nigrinus the former conspirator – Commodus' recommendation to him being his beauty. So he adopted Ceionius
Commodus Verus, against the wishes of all, and named him
Aelius Verus Caesar.[87] On the occasion of the adoption he gave
circus-games and bestowed a donative on the people and the
soldiers. He honoured Commodus with the praetorship and at
once placed him in charge of the Pannonian provinces; and the
consulship, together with the expenses thereof, was decreed
for him.[88] The same Commodus he designated to be consul a
second time [A.D. 137]. When he saw that he was by no means
healthy, he used very often to say: 'We have leaned against a
falling wall and we have lost the 300 million sesterces that we
gave the people and the soldiers to mark the adoption of Commodus.' Commodus, indeed, because of his health, could not
even make his speech of thanks to Hadrian for his adoption in
the Senate. Finally, having taken too copious a dose of medicine, his condition began to worsen and he died in his sleep – on
the very Kalends of January [1 January A.D. 138]; hence
mourning was prohibited by Hadrian on account of the vow-
taking.

  87. There is an error over the name: Ceionius Commodus was never
called Verus (see p. 17f above). Nigrinus; stemma E.
  88. Incorrect: he had been praetor in A.D. 130 and was already consul
in 136, before his adoption in the same year (*PIR*², C 605).

Aelius Verus Caesar being dead, Hadrian, afflicted by the most wretched health, adopted Arrius Antoninus who was afterwards called Pius; and in the same law laid down that Antoninus should adopt two sons, Annius Verus and Marcus Antoninus.[89] These are the two who subsequently governed the republic as the first joint Augusti. Antoninus, indeed, is said to have been named Pius because he used to support his father-in-law with a hand when worn out by age; although others say that this surname was given him because he had rescued many senators from Hadrian when he was already acting cruelly; and others say that it was because he bestowed great honours on Hadrian after his death. A great many were grieved that the adoption of Antoninus had been carried out, especially Catilius Severus, the prefect of the city, who had designs on the imperial power for himself. When this fact was made known, he was given a successor and deprived of his office.

Hadrian, however, now moved with extreme disgust for life, ordered a slave to stab him with a sword. When this was known and had come to the attention of Antoninus, he, as Hadrian's son, and the prefects, went in to Hadrian and begged him to endure the necessity of the disease with equanimity; Antoninus told him that he would be a parricide if, having himself been adopted, he allowed him to be killed. Hadrian was angered by them and ordered the person responsible for informing them to be killed (he was however saved by Antoninus). He at once wrote his will; however, he did not lay aside the business of the republic. After making his will he did in fact attempt to kill himself again; when the dagger was taken from him he became more violent. He sought poison from a doctor, who killed himself to avoid giving it.

89. There is a hopeless confusion over the names here: the adoptive sons of Antoninus were Marcus Annius Verus and Lucius Ceionius Commodus the younger (see p. 17f above).

At that time a certain woman arrived who said she had been warned in a dream to recommend Hadrian not to kill himself, because he was going to have good health; and that because she had not done this she had gone blind. However, she said, she had been ordered again to say the same things to Hadrian and to kiss his knees; and she was to recover her sight if she did this. When she had done this in accordance with the dream, she did recover her eyesight, after washing her eyes with water from the sanctuary from which she had come. There came also from Pannonia a certain old man to the fevered Hadrian, and touched him, whereupon the man recovered his eyesight and the fever left Hadrian; although Marius Maximus records that these things were faked.

After this Hadrian made for Baiae, Antoninus being left at Rome to rule. When he made no progress there, he summoned Antoninus and passed away in his presence, at Baiae itself, on the sixth day before the Ides of July [10 July A.D. 138]. Unseen by all,[90] he was buried at Cicero's villa at Puteoli. Shortly before the time of his death he compelled Servianus to die – in his ninetieth year, as was said above, so that he would not outlive him and, as he thought, become emperor – and also, for slight reasons, ordered the killing of a great many persons, whom Antoninus saved. He is said, as he was actually dying, to have composed these verses:

> Little charmer, wanderer, little sprite,
> Body's companion and guest,
> To what places now will you take flight,
> Forbidding and empty and dim as night?
> And you won't make your wonted jest!

He did compose such verses as these, and Greek ones too, that were not much better. He lived sixty-two years, five months and seventeen days and ruled for twenty years and four months. In stature he was tall, in appearance elegant; his hair was curled

90. *invisus omnibus* could also mean 'hated by all'.

on a comb and his beard was full, to cover the natural blemishes on his face; his figure was robust. He rode and walked a very great deal, and always practised with weapons and with the javelin. He also hunted, and on many occasions killed a lion with his own hand; but once when hunting he broke his collarbone and a rib. He always shared the hunt with friends. When entertaining guests he always put on tragedies, comedies, Atellan farces, Sambuca players,[91] readers or poets, to fit the occasion. He completed the building of his Tiburtine villa[92] in wonderful fashion, in such a way that he inscribed the most famous of names of provinces and places there, and called them, for example, Lycium, Academia, Prytanium, Canopus, Poecile and Tempe. So that he might omit nothing, he even made a Lower World.

He had the following signs of death. On his last birthday [24 January A.D. 138], when he was commending Antoninus, his bordered toga fell down of its own accord and uncovered his head. The ring, on which his own portrait was carved, of its own accord slipped from his finger. On the day before his birthday somebody came to the Senate wailing; Hadrian was as much moved in his presence as if he were speaking about his own death, for no one could understand his words. Again, when he meant to say in the Senate: 'After my son's death', he said: 'After my death'. Besides this, he dreamed that he was overcome by a lion.

Many things were said against him by many people when he was dead. The Senate wanted his acts to be made invalid, and he would not have been deified if Antoninus had not asked. Finally, Antoninus built a temple for him at Puteoli, instead of a tomb, and established a quinquennial contest and *flamines* and

91. The Sambuca was a triangular stringed instrument with a shrill tone.

92. Substantial remains of Hadrian's great villa still survive at Tibur, the modern Tivoli, close to Rome.

sodales[93] and many other things which appertain to the honouring of a divinity. As was said above, many think that is why
Antoninus was called Pius.

93. Both the *flamen* and the *sodales* were priests chosen from the
senatorial class to conduct the worship of deified emperors – *sodales
Augustales* for Augustus, *Flaviales* for Vespasian, *Hadrianales* for Hadrian,
and so on.

AELIUS*

BY AELIUS SPARTIANUS

To Diocletian Augustus, his Aelius Spartianus, greeting.
I have it in mind, Diocletian Augustus, greatest among
so many *principes*, to bring to the cognizance of your Divinity,
not only those who have held the place of *princeps* in that
position which you maintain, as I have done as far as the Deified
Hadrian, but also those who have either been called by the
name of Caesar but have not been *principes* or Augusti; or who
in any other fashion whatsoever have come either to the fame
or the hope of the imperial power. Of these one must speak
especially of Aelius Verus, who was the first to receive only
the name of Caesar, being taken by Hadrian's adoption into
the family of the *principes*. Since there is very little to be
said, nor should the prologue be of too disproportionate a
size in relation to the play, I shall now speak about the man
himself.

Ceionius Commodus, who was also called Aelius Verus –
whom Hadrian adopted when his age was becoming burdensome, being laid low by distressing diseases, having by now
traversed the world[1] – had nothing memorable in his life except
that he was the first who was only called Caesar, and called
this not in the will, as was formerly the custom, nor in that
manner in which Trajan was adopted, but almost in the manner
in which in our times Maximian and Constantius were named

* Most of this *Life* is fictional, except where it consists of material
from the *Hadrian* or *Verus* (or their sources), reworked.
1. cf. *Hadrian*, 23.1 (p. 82 above).

Caesars[2] by Your Clemency, as what one might call sons of
principes, designated because of their virtue as heirs of the
August Majesty.

Since there must be some discussion about the name of the
Caesars in the *Life* of this one in particular, who acquired only
this name, the most learned men and the most scholarly think
that he who was first so called was named Caesar either from
killing in battle an elephant (which in the language of the Moors
is called *caesai*), or because he was born when his mother was
dead and her stomach was cut open (*caeso*), or because he rushed
forth from his mother's womb with a thick growth of hair
(*caesaries*), or because he had grey eyes (*oculis caesiis*) and super-
human energy. However this may be, certainly it was a happy
necessity which resulted in the growth of a name so distinguished and one that shall endure for as long as the eternal
universe.

This man, therefore, with whom this discourse deals, was
first called Lucius Aurelius Verus,[3] but on being adopted by
Hadrian was transferred into the family of the Aelii, that is
Hadrian's family, and was called Caesar. His father was
Ceionius Commodus, whose name some have recorded as
Verus, others as Lucius Aurelius, many as Annius.[4] His ancestors
were all most noble, their origin for the most part being in
Etruria or at Faventia.[5] Of his family, of course, we shall treat
more fully in the *Life* of Lucius Aurelius Ceionius Commodus
Verus Antoninus, his son, whom Antoninus was ordered to
adopt. For that work, which handles a *princeps* about whom
there is more to be said, should contain everything which
pertains to the family tree. Aelius Verus, then, was adopted by
Hadrian at the time when, as we said earlier, his powers were

2. In A.D.285 and 293 respectively.
3. He was never called Aurelius or Verus: see p. 17f above.
4. A confusion: see p. 17f above.
5. cf. *Verus*, 1.9 (p. 138 below).

declining and he was thinking about the successor that was
needed; and he was at once made praetor and set over the
Pannonians as general and governor. Presently he was created
consul and, because he had been made deputy emperor, he was
designated to a second consulship. Largess was given to the
people on account of his adoption, too, and three hundred
million sesterces were bestowed on the soldiers.[6] Circus games
were put on, and nothing was omitted which might bring
about repeated public rejoicing. He had such great influence
with Hadrian, the *princeps*, that, in addition to the affection
displayed in the adoption, by which he was seen to be working
in harness with him, he alone obtained everything that he
desired, even by letter. Even in the province of which he was
given charge he did not fall short. Through a well-conducted –
or rather, a fortunate – campaign, he gained the reputation, if
not of an outstanding, at least of an average general.

However, he had such wretched health that Hadrian at once
regretted the adoption and would have removed him from the
imperial family – since he frequently considered other men – if
he had happened to live on. Finally, it is said by those who have
set down Hadrian's life in writing with some degree of accuracy
that Hadrian knew Verus' horoscope, and that the reason why
he adopted him, a man whom he had appraised as being little
fitted to rule the republic, was to satisfy his own pleasure, and,
as some say, an oath which was reported to have existed between himself and Verus, on secret terms. Marius Maximus
describes Hadrian as having been skilled in astrology, to such
an extent, he says, that he knew everything about himself, and
thus that he wrote down in advance his future actions for every
day up to the hour of his death.[7] Besides, it is established that
he often said of Verus:

6. cf. *Hadrian*, 23.13 (p. 83 above).
7. cf. *Hadrian*, 16.7 (p. 75 above).

> This youth (the blissful vision of a day)
> Shall just be shown on earth, and snatch'd away.[8]

These verses he was once reciting when strolling in a little garden; one of the literary men whose brilliant company he used to enjoy was present, and wanted to add:

> The Gods too high had raised the Roman state,
> Were but their gifts as permanent as great.[9]

Hadrian is reported to have said: 'The life of Verus does not accord with these lines,' adding:

> Full canisters of fragrant lillies bring,
> Mix'd with the purple roses of the spring:
> Let me with fun'ral flow'rs his body strow;
> This gift which parents to their children owe,
> This unavailing gift, at least I may bestow![10]

At this time, in fact, he is said to have remarked with a laugh: 'I have adopted a god, not a son.' Now, however, when one of the literary men who was present was consoling him and saying: 'What if the grouping of the stars has not been correctly calculated in the case of this man – whom we believe will live?', Hadrian is reported to have replied: 'It is easy for you to say that, who are looking for an heir for your own estate, not for the republic.' From this it is apparent that at the end of his life he had it in mind to choose another and to withdraw this man from public life. But fate assisted his plans. Aelius had returned from his province and had prepared, either on his own, or making use of the directors of the secretariat or teachers of oratory, a very fine speech – which is read even today – by which he was to render thanks to Hadrian his father on the Kalends of January. He took a draught of medicine which he judged would help him, and died on the very Kalends of

8. Virgil, *Aeneid*, 6.869f. (Dryden's translation).
9. Virgil, *Aeneid*, 6.870f. (Dryden's translation).
10. Virgil, *Aeneid*, 6.883ff. (Dryden's translation).

January. Hadrian ordered that he should not be mourned, since the taking of the vows came at the same time.[11]

He was a person of joyous life, and well educated; to Hadrian, as the malicious say, more acceptable for his beauty than for his character.[12] He was not long at the court. In his private life, although he was by no means deserving of praise, yet he could hardly be faulted, and he was mindful of his own family. Elegant, graceful and of a royal beauty, he had a face that commanded respect; his eloquence was somewhat lofty; he had the capacity to compose verses readily; and he was not lacking in talent for public affairs as well. Many of his pleasures are recorded by those who have written his life, and they were in fact not disreputable: rather they took somewhat unusual directions. He is said to have personally invented the *tetrafarmacum*, or rather *pentepharmacum*, which Hadrian always subsequently enjoyed, that is, sow's udder, pheasant, peacock, ham in pastry and wild boar. Marius Maximus gives a different description of this kind of food, calling it not *pentefarmacum* but *tetrafarmacum*, as we ourselves, too, have set down in our *Life* of Hadrian.[13] Another kind of pleasure is also recorded which Verus had devised: for he had made a bed with four high cushions, closed in on all sides with a fine net; this he used to fill with rose-petals from which the white part had been removed, and lying with his concubines he used to cover himself, anointed with Persian perfumes, with a coverlet made of lilies. Indeed, not a few repeat the story that he even made couches and tables of roses and lilies, which of course had been cleaned. These things, although they lacked propriety, were nonetheless unlikely to cause public disaster. He is also reported to have known Ovid's books of *Amores* by heart, word for word; likewise, as is related by others, to have had Apicius'

11. cf. *Hadrian*, 23.16 (p. 83 above).
12. cf. *Hadrian*, 23.10 (p. 83 above).
13. cf. *Hadrian*, 21.4 (p. 80 above).

books[14] always by his bed and to have called Martial, the epi-
grammatic poet, his Virgil. Still more frivolous are the following items: that he frequently fastened wings onto his couriers,
like Cupids, and often called them after the names of the winds,
naming one Boreas, another Notus, and likewise Aquilo or
Circius and the other names, while making them run messages
without respite or humanity. To his wife, complaining about
his outside pleasures, he is reported to have said: 'Suffer me to
engage in my desires with other women: for "wife" is the
name of a duty, not of a pleasure.'

His son is the Antoninus Verus who was adopted by
Marcus[15] – or certainly with Marcus – and with the latter
wielded joint imperial power. They are the ones who were the
first pair to be named Augusti, and whose names are thus
inscribed in the consular Fasti, so that they are called not 'the
two Antonini', but the 'two Augusti'. (Such an effect did the
novelty and dignity of this fact have, that several consular
Fasti begin their lists of consuls with them.)

To mark his adoption Hadrian gave countless sums of money
to the people and the soldiers. But being a fairly acute person,
when Hadrian saw that his health was absolutely wretched, to
the extent that he could not even brandish a reasonably substantial shield, he is reported to have said: 'We have lost the
three hundred million sesterces that we have spent on the army
and the people, since we have leaned for long enough against
a falling wall and one which can scarcely sustain our own
weight, let alone the republic itself.'[16] Hadrian actually spoke
these words to his prefect, and the prefect repeated them and, as
a result, Aelius Caesar was every day increasingly burdened by

14. Evidently a reference to the fourth-century Roman cookery book
still extant. It is attributed to 'Apicius Caelius', which perhaps indicates
that the contents were associated with the notorious first-century
gourmet, M. Gavius Apicius (*PIR*², G 91).

15. This is inaccurate: see p. 17f above.

16. cf. *Hadrian*, 23.14 (p. 83 above).

anxiety, as happens to a person who has lost hope. Hadrian appointed a successor to his prefect who had made the matter known, wishing it to appear that he had modified his harsh words. But it did no good, for, as we have said, Lucius Ceionius Commodus Verus Aelius Caesar (for he was called by all these names) passed away, and was buried after an imperial funeral; and he had nothing of the royal rank except in death.

Hadrian mourned his death as a good father, not as a good *princeps*. When his friends anxiously inquired who could be adopted, Hadrian is reported to have told them: 'I had decided that even when Verus was still alive.' Thereby he referred either to his judgement or to his knowledge of the future. After Verus, in fact, Hadrian was long hesitant about what to do, and then adopted Antoninus, called by the surname of Pius. On him he imposed the extra condition that he should himself adopt Marcus and Verus as his sons, and should give his daughter to Verus, not Marcus. Hadrian did not live on very long, burdened by weariness and a varied set of diseases, often saying that a *princeps* ought to die when he was healthy, not when he was weak. He did, of course, order statues to be set up to Aelius Verus all over the world, of giant size, and temples to be built to him too, in a number of cities. Finally, out of respect for him, he gave Aelius' son Verus – who was after all his own grandson, and on the demise of Aelius had remained in Hadrian's own family – to Antoninus Pius to be adopted, together with Marcus (as we have already mentioned); and he would often say: 'Let the republic retain something of Verus at any rate.' This is in fact an argument against what has been intimated by very many authors about his having regretted the adoption, since the second Verus had nothing in his character apart from clemency that was capable of shedding lustre on the imperial family.

These are the facts which are worthy of being committed to writing on the subject of Verus Caesar. On him I did not keep silence for the reason that I have set myself the task of publishing one book each on all those who, after Caesar the dictator, that is the Deified Julius, have been called either Caesars or Augusti or *principes*, and those who have entered the imperial family by adoption, whether they were sanctified with the name of the Caesars as sons of emperors or as parents, satisfying my own conscience even if, to many, there may be no necessity to inquire into such things.

ANTONINUS PIUS*

BY JULIUS CAPITOLINUS

Titus Aurelius Fulvus Boionius Antoninus Pius on his father's side was of a family from Transalpine Gaul, from Nemausus [Nîmes] to be precise. His grandfather was Titus Aurelius Fulvus, who arrived by way of various offices at a second consulship and the city prefecture. His father was Aurelius Fulvus, who was consul himself as well, a stern and irreproachable man. His maternal grandmother was Boionia Procilla, his mother was Arria Fadilla, and his maternal grandfather was Arrius Antoninus, twice consul, a just man who commiserated with Nerva on the fact that he had begun to be emperor. Through his mother his half-sister was Julia Fadilla and his stepfather was Julius Lupus, an ex-consul. His father-in-law was Annius Verus and his wife was Annia Faustina. He had two male children and two female, through the elder of which his son-in-law was Lamia Silvanus, and through the younger Marcus Antoninus.[1]

Antoninus Pius himself was born on the thirteenth day before the Kalends of October when Domitian, for the twelfth time, and Cornelius Dolabella, were the consuls [19 September A.D. 86], at the Lanuvian villa. He was brought up at Lorium on the *Via Aurelia*, where he subsequently built a palace (of which the ruins still survive today). His boyhood was passed with his paternal grandfather, then with his mother's father, and he showed dutiful respect for all his relations; as a result he was

---

* There is no satisfactory modern account of Pius in English: for a sketch, see Birley, *Marcus Aurelius*, pp. 48ff.

1. See stemma, p. 318.

enriched by inheritance even from cousins and from his stepfather and many kinsmen. He was a man of striking appearance,
his natural capacities were brilliant and his character kindly.
His countenance was noble, his innate qualities were outstanding – he was a polished speaker and exceptionally learned.
A man of moderation, and a thrifty landowner, of mild disposition, with his own he was generous and he kept away from
what belonged to others. All these qualities were in balance and
without ostentation: in short he was praiseworthy in every
respect and, in the opinion of right-thinking men, was deservedly compared with Numa Pompilius. The surname Pius was
given to him by the Senate, either because he used to support
his father-in-law, by now tired and aged, with his hand at
Senate meetings – which, to be sure, is not sufficient proof of
great dutifulness, since it is more a case of the man who did not
do these things being undutiful; or because he had preserved
those whom Hadrian, during his ill-health, had ordered to be
killed; or because he decreed to Hadrian, against the efforts of
everyone, unlimited and boundless honours after his death; or
because, when Hadrian wanted to do away with himself, by
intense watchfulness and care he made it impossible for him to
carry that out; or because he was in fact most merciful by nature
and did no harsh deed in his own times. He also made loans at
four per cent, that is, at the minimum rate of interest, in order
to assist large numbers of people with his personal fortune. He
was a munificent quaestor, a distinguished praetor, and was
consul with Catilius Severus [A.D. 120]. Throughout the whole
of his life as a private citizen he lived for a large part of the time
on his estates; but he was well known everywhere. By Hadrian
he was chosen as one of the four ex-consuls under whose juris-
diction Italy was placed, to administer that part of Italy in which
he had most of his possessions; and thus Hadrian took into
consideration both the dignity of such a man and also his quiet
way of life.

During his administration of Italy, an omen of imperial rule occurred. He had ascended the tribunal, when, among other shouts of approbation, someone said: 'Augustus, may the gods preserve you!' The proconsulship of Asia he carried out in such a way that he was the only man to excel his grandfather. In his proconsulship, too, he received an omen of empire, in this manner: for although the priestess at Tralles customarily greeted the proconsuls by this title, to him she said, not 'Hail proconsul!' but 'Hail emperor!' At Cyzicus also a crown was transferred from an image of a god to his statue. After his consulship a marble bull was suspended in his garden, its horns attached to the crown of a tree; a thunderbolt from a clear sky struck his house without damaging it; in Etruria storage jars which had been buried were found above the ground again, and swarms of bees clustered on his statues all over Etruria; and in a dream he was frequently warned to include Hadrian's image among his household gods.

While he was setting out for his proconsulship he lost his elder daughter. Many things were said about his wife because of her excessive frankness and the levity of her way of life. After the proconsulship he often spoke at meetings of Hadrian's council, at Rome, on all matters about which Hadrian consulted him, always putting forward the more merciful judgement.

Now the manner of his adoption is reported as follows: when Aelius Verus whom Hadrian had adopted and named Caesar died, a regular meeting of the Senate was being held; to it came Arrius Antoninus,[2] supporting the steps of his father-in-law; and he is said to have been adopted by Hadrian for this reason. This cannot possibly have been the sole reason for his adoption; nor ought it to have been, especially as Antoninus had always carried out public office well and had showed himself to be a conscientious and serious man in his proconsulship. Accordingly, when Hadrian had announced that he wished to adopt him, he was given time to consider whether he wished to go through with adoption by Hadrian. The law issued for

2. The author confusingly but legitimately (p. 318) call him Arrius here.

the adoption was framed in such a way that he should himself
adopt M. Antoninus, the son of his wife's brother, and L. Verus
(who was subsequently called Verus Antoninus), son of Aelius
Verus[3] who had been adopted by Hadrian. He was adopted on
the fifth day before the Kalends of March [25 February A.D.
138], while rendering thanks in the Senate for Hadrian's having
had such an opinion of him. He was made a colleague of his
father both in the proconsular *imperium* and in the tribunician
power. It is reported that his first comment, when he was being
reproved by his wife for being insufficiently generous to his
own people in some small matter, was: 'Foolish woman, after
moving over to the imperial position we have lost what we had
before!' He gave a largess to the soldiers and people from his
own funds, and also the sums that his father had promised. He
contributed a very great deal to Hadrian's public works, and of
the crown-gold that had been offered him on account of his
adoption, he remitted the whole amount to the Italians and
half to the provincials.

His father, as long as he survived, he obeyed most scrupu-
lously. But when Hadrian died at Baiae, he carried his remains
to Rome with piety and reverence, and placed them in the
Gardens of Domitia; also, with everyone opposing this, he
enrolled him among the deified emperors. His wife Faustina he
permitted to be named Augusta by the Senate, and he accepted
the name of Pius. The statues decreed to his father and mother
and grandfathers and brothers, who were already dead, he
gladly accepted. The circus-games set aside for his birthday he
did not refuse; other honours he rejected. He set up a most
magnificent shield and established priests in honour of Hadrian.

Having become emperor he did not appoint successors for
any of those whom Hadrian had promoted, and he was so
steadfast that he retained good governors in the provinces for
seven and even nine years each.[4] Through his legates he waged

3. See p. 17f above.
4. This statement is not borne out by the available evidence.

a number of wars. He conquered the Britons through his legate Lollius Urbicus (another wall, of turf, being set up when the barbarians had been driven back),[5] and compelled the Moors to sue for peace; and he crushed the Germans and Dacians and many peoples, including the Jews, who were rebelling, through governors and legates. In Achaia also, and in Egypt, he put down rebellions. He frequently curbed the Alani when they began disturbances.[6] He ordered his procurators to levy tribute in moderation, and he instructed the ones who exceeded the limit to render an account of their actions; nor did he ever take pleasure in any profit as a result of which a provincial was oppressed. Those making complaints against his procurators he listened to readily. For those whom Hadrian had condemned he sought pardon in the Senate, saying that Hadrian himself would have done this. He brought down the eminence of the imperial position completely to the level of the ordinary citizen. As a result he was the more esteemed, although the court servants objected, since, as he used to do nothing through intermediaries, they could neither intimidate people at any time, nor could they sell information, when it was not secret. To the Senate he deferred, as emperor, to the same extent as he had wished, when a private citizen, that deference should be shown him by another *princeps*. The title 'Father of the Fatherland', conferred by the Senate, which at first he had delayed taking, he accepted with a lengthy speech of thanks. In his third year as emperor he lost Faustina his wife, who was consecrated by the Senate; circus-games were voted to her and a temple and *flaminicae*, and statues of gold and silver. At this time also he himself agreed that her statue should be set up at all the circuses;

5. i.e. the Antonine Wall, between the Forth and Clyde. Q. Lollius Urbicus, a native of Numidia (modern Algeria), governed Britain from A.D.139–43 (*PIR²*, L 327).
6. None of these wars appears to have been very serious except for that in Mauretania, which reached its height in A.D.145.

and he undertook to erect the golden statue voted by the Senate.

At the request of the Senate he appointed M. Antoninus, then quaestor, to be consul. Annius Verus,[7] who was afterwards called Antoninus, he designated quaestor before the legal age. Nor did he decide anything about the provinces or about any matters unless he first brought it before his friends, and he composed his rescripts in accordance with their opinions. Indeed he was seen by his friends even wearing his ordinary clothes and performing various domestic duties. Certainly he ruled the people subject to him with such great care that he looked after everything and everyone as if they were his own. The provinces all flourished under him. Informers were stamped out. Confiscation of property was rarer than it had ever been, so that only one man was proscribed on a charge of attempted usurpation, namely Atilius Titianus, and it was the Senate that punished him – while Antoninus forbade it to investigate the man's accomplices and his son was always given help in every way.[8] Priscianus also perished, charged with attempted usurpation, but it was by his own hand. He forbade any investigation of this conspiracy.[9]

The style of life of Antoninus Pius was such that there was opulence without cause for reproof and frugality without meanness; his table was supplied by his own slaves, his own fowlers, fishermen and huntsmen. A bath-house which he had used he presented to the people without charge, and he did not change anything at all from his manner of life as a private

7. i.e. Lucius Commodus the younger: see p. 17f above for the muddle over names.

8. Evidently T. Atilius Rufus Titianus (*cos. ord.* 127): *PIR²*, A 1305. No details are known. The Titianus in *Hadrian*, 15.6 (p. 73 above) is probably this man, misplaced.

9. Cornelius Priscianus (*PIR²*, C 1418) was condemned in the Senate on 15 September A.D.145 for 'disturbing the peace of the province of Spain in hostile fashion'. Nothing more is known of the affair.

citizen. He took away the salaries of many people whom he saw were receiving them for doing nothing, saying that there was nothing meaner, or rather, more hard-hearted, than for a man to gnaw away at the republic who rendered it no service by his own work. For this reason also he reduced the salary of Mesomedes the lyric poet.[10] He had a first-class knowledge of the accounts of all the provinces and of the taxes. His private fortune he settled on his daughter, but he donated the interest on it to the republic. He sold the superfluous imperial goods and lands and lived on his own private estates, varying his stay according to the season. Nor did he engage on any expeditions – except that he set out to his own landed properties and to Campania – saying that the retinue of a *princeps*, even a very economical one, was burdensome to the provincials.

Yet he had immense authority among all nations, since he purposely resided in the city so that he could receive messengers from all sides the more rapidly, seeing that he was at the centre. To the people he gave largess, on the soldiers he bestowed a donative. He arranged for girls, called 'the Faustinians' in honour of Faustina, to receive state support.[11] Of his public works the following survive: at Rome, the temple of Hadrian dedicated in honour of his father, the Graecostadium, restored after a fire, the amphitheatre, which was repaired; the tomb of Hadrian, the temple of Agrippa and the Pons Sublicius; the restored Pharus; the harbour of Caieta; the restored port of Tarracina; the baths at Ostia; the aqueduct at Antium; the temples at Lanuvium. He also assisted many communities with money, either to erect new public buildings or to restore old ones; and he even gave financial aid to magistrates and senators of the city to help them to perform their duties.

10. A freedman of Hadrian, of Cretan origin; a few of his hymns (to the Sun, Nature, etc.) are preserved, three of them with the musical notation.

11. As an addition to the *alimenta* system founded by Nerva and Trajan (p. 47, n. 84 above).

Legacies from persons who had children he declined. He was the first to lay down that bequests made to avoid a penalty should not remain valid. He did not appoint a successor for any holder of judicial office who was good as long as the man was alive, except in the case of Orfitus, the prefect of the city, but Orfitus requested it himself. Gavius Maximus, the prefect of the guard, reached his twentieth year of service under him, a very stern man, who was succeeded by Tatius Maximus.[12] The latter's place, on his death, he filled with two prefects, Furius Victorinus and Cornelius Repentinus.[13] But Repentinus came under fire through a rumour that he had reached the prefecture by the agency of the *princeps'* concubine.[14] Under him no senator was executed, even to the extent that a confessed parricide was placed on a desert island – because natural law did not permit him to live. He relieved a scarcity of wine, oil and wheat at a loss to his own treasury by buying them and giving them free to the people.

During his time the following unpropitious events took place: the famine about which we have spoken; the collapse of the circus; an earthquake by which towns of Rhodes and Asia were destroyed – all of which he restored in wonderful fashion; and a fire at Rome which consumed 340 blocks or houses. The city of Narbo, the town of Antioch, and the forum at Carthage, were damaged by fire. There was an inundation of the Tiber and a comet appeared; also a child was born with two heads and a woman gave birth to quintuplets. In Arabia a crested serpent was seen, larger than the usual ones, which ate itself from the tail to the middle. There was also a pestilence in Arabia. In Moesia barley sprouted at the tops of trees. Besides these things, in Arabia, four lions became tame of their own accord and yielded to capture.

12. Gavius retired not earlier than A.D.156 when his successor, Tattius, was still in office as prefect of the watch: *PIR*², G 104.

13. *PIR*², C 1428, F 584.

14. Galeria Lysistrate, a freedwoman of his late wife: *ILS*, p. 1839.

King Pharasmanes came to Rome and deferred more to him than he had to Hadrian. He appointed Pacorus king of the Lazi. Merely by a letter he caused the king of the Parthians to desist from assaulting the Armenians. By his influence alone he brought king Abgarus back from the regions of the east. He settled the legal disputes of several kings. When the king of the Parthians asked to have back the royal throne which Trajan had captured, he flatly refused. He sent Rhoemetalces back to the Bosphoran kingdom after listening to the matter at issue between him and Eupator. He sent auxiliary soldiers into the Pontus [Black Sea] to help the Olbiopolitans against the Tauroscythae, and defeated the Tauroscythae – even making them give hostages to the Olbiopolitans. In fact no one has had so much authority among foreign nations as he, although he always loved peace, so much so that he often quoted Scipio's opinion, in which he used to state that he would rather save a single citizen than kill a thousand enemies.

The Senate decreed that the months of September and October should be named Antoninus and Faustinus, but Antoninus rejected that. His daughter Faustina's marriage,[15] when he gave her to Marcus Antoninus, he made most noteworthy, to the extent of a donative for the soldiers. Verus Antoninus[16] he made consul after his quaestorship. When he called for Apollonius, whom he had summoned from Calchis,[17] to come to the Tiberian Palace where he was staying, so that he might hand Marcus Antoninus over to him, Apollonius replied: 'A master ought not to come to a pupil, but a pupil to a master.' Antoninus laughed at him, saying: 'It was easier for Apollonius to come from Calchis to Rome than from his own house to the palace.' He took note of the man's greed over his fees as well. As one of the proofs of his dutifulness to his family

15. In A.D.145.
16. i.e. Lucius Commodus the younger: see p. 18 above.
17. This should be Chalcedon: *PIR*², A 929.

this also is related, that when Marcus was weeping for his fosterer who had died, and was being called on by the court servants to refrain from displaying affection, Antoninus' reply was: 'Let him be human, for neither philosophy nor imperial power takes away feelings.'

His prefects he both enriched and honoured with honorary consulships. If he convicted anyone for corrupt administration, he restored to their children their father's property, on condition that they restored to the provincials what their parents had taken. He was very prone to grant pardons. He put on games at which he showed elephants and corocottas and tigers and rhinoceroses, also crocodiles and hippopotami, and all the animals from all over the world. He even put on a hundred lions together with tigers at a single performance. His friends he treated no differently as emperor from when he was a private citizen, since they themselves never joined with the freedmen to sell false hopes of favours; and of course he treated his freedmen with very great strictness. He loved the arts of the stage-players; in fishing and hunting he took great pleasure, as he did in strolling with his friends and making conversation. He used to harvest the vintage with his friends like a private citizen. On rhetoricians and philosophers in all the provinces he bestowed both honours and salaries. Most have said that the speeches which have come down under his name are the work of others; Marius Maximus says that they were his own. Banquets, both private and public, he shared with his friends, and he never performed any sacrifice through a deputy, unless he was ill. When he was seeking honours for himself or his sons, he did everything as if he were a private citizen. He himself often went to his friends' banquets as well. Among other things too there is this outstanding piece of evidence of the way he behaved like an ordinary citizen. On a visit to Homullus' house, he admired the porphyry columns, and inquired where he had got them. Homullus replied: 'When you come to someone else's house, be deaf and dumb.' He took this in good part as he always did take the many jokes which Homullus made.[18]

He made many legal decisions, and used the legal experts Vindius Verus, Salvius Julianus, Aburnius Valens, Volusius Maecianus, Ulpius Marcellus and Diabolenus.[19] Rebellions, wherever they occurred, he suppressed, not ruthlessly, but with moderation and in a serious manner. He prohibited the burial of the dead inside cities. He set a limit to expenses for gladiatorial games. He mitigated the burden of the posting-service by very careful management. Everything that he did he accounted for, both in the Senate and by means of edicts.

He died in his seventieth year,[20] but was missed as though he were a youth. His actual death is described as being like this: after eating Alpine cheese at dinner rather greedily, he vomited in the night and on the next day was affected by fever. On the third day, when he saw that he was becoming worse, he commended the republic and his daughter to Marcus Antoninus in the presence of his prefects, and ordered that the golden statue of Fortune which used to be placed in the bedroom of the *principes* should be handed over to him. Then he gave the watchword to the tribune, 'Equanimity', and so, turning as if he would sleep, he gave up the ghost, at Lorium. While delirious in his fever he spoke of nothing except the republic and those kings with whom he was angry. His personal fortune he bequeathed to his daughter. Further, in his will, he bestowed suitable legacies on all his household.

He was of lofty stature and handsome. But since he was tall

18. Generally identified as M. Valerius Homullus (*cos. ord.* 152), although it might be preferable to postulate an homonymous father, as H. G. Pflaum suggests (*HAC*, 1964/65, pp. 147f.), on the grounds that a man consul in A.D. 152 would have been too young to be an intimate of Pius. See also the story in the *Marcus*, 6.9 (p. 114 below).

19. The last of these names is probably bogus. For this and the other five, see Pflaum, op. cit., pp. 148ff.

20. This should be 'seventy-fifth': he was born in September A.D. 86 and died in March 161.

and an old man and stooped, he used to be strapped up with linden-wood boards placed on his chest, so that he could walk in an upright posture. As an old man, too, before callers used to arrive, he ate dry bréad to keep up his strength. He had a hoarse voice, resonant too, but agreeably so. The Senate deified him, everyone competing in their efforts, for all praised his dutifulness, clemency, intelligence and purity. In addition, all the honours were decreed which had previously been conferred on the best *principes*. He merited both a *flamen* and circus-games and a temple, and *sodales Antoniniani*.[21] Alone among almost all *principes* he lived entirely free from the blood of either citizen or foe, so far as lay within his own power, and he was a man who was justly compared with Numa, whose good fortune, dutifulness, tranquillity and religious rites he always maintained.

21. See p. 87, n. 93 above.

MARCUS ANTONINUS
THE PHILOSOPHER*

BY JULIUS CAPITOLINUS

MARCUS ANTONINUS was a man who devoted himself
to philosophy throughout his life and he excels all the
principes in purity of character. His father was Annius Verus,
who died during his praetorship. His grandfather, Annius
Verus, was consul twice[1] and prefect of the city, and had been
enrolled among the patricians by the *principes* Vespasian
and Titus as censors.[2] His uncle was the consul Annius Libo[3]
and his aunt was Galeria Faustina Augusta. His mother was
Domitia Lucilla, daughter of the consul Calvisius Tullus,
and his maternal grandmother was Lucilla, daughter of
Domitius Tullus, twice consul.[4] His paternal great-grandfather,
Annius Verus, from the chartered town of Uccubi in Spain,
had been given the rank of praetor in the Senate. His step-
grandfather on his mother's side was Catilius Severus, twice
consul, and prefect of the city.[5] His paternal grandmother was
Rupilia Faustina, daughter of Rupilius Libo, an ex-consul.[6]

---

* For the background, see Birley, *Marcus Aurelius*.
1. Actually three times (A.D.97, 121, 126).
2. A.D.73–4.
3. *cos. ord.* 128.
4. I translate the text as restored by Syme, *Tacitus*, p. 793.
5. The meaning of *proavus* is normally 'great-grandfather', but
Catilius can hardly have been father of Calvisius Tullus; he might
however have been the second husband of Domitia Lucilla the elder.
6. Reading *Rupili Libonis* instead of *Rupili Boni*: see A. Birley,
Historia, 1966, pp. 249f. See stemma, p. 319, for further details of the
family.

Marcus was born at Rome on the sixth day before the Kalends of May at the family seat on the Caelian Hill, when his grand-father, for the second time, and Augur were the consuls [26 April A.D. 121]. His family, in tracing its origins, proved descent from Numa, as Marius Maximus informs us – and also descent from the Sallentine king Malemnius, son of Dasummus, who founded Lupiae. He was brought up partly in the place where he was born and partly in the house of his grandfather Verus, next to the Lateran Palace. He had a younger sister too, Annia Cornificia, and was to marry his first cousin, Annia Faustina. At the beginning of his life Marcus Antoninus was called after Catilius Severus, his step-grandfather on his mother's side. As a matter of fact, after his father died he was called Annius Verissimus by Hadrian, but when he took the toga of manhood he became Annius Verus. After his father's death he was adopted and brought up by his paternal grand-father.

He was serious-minded from his earliest childhood. But it was when he had grown out of the care of nurses that he was handed over to great teachers and came to know the tenets of philosophy. The teachers he had for his elementary education were Euphorio, a reading-master, Geminus, an actor, and the musician Andro, who was also a geometry-teacher. He was extremely generous to all these men, regarding them as the leaders of their particular professions. After this, for his secon-dary education, his teacher in Greek literature was Alexander of Cotiaeum,[7] and in Latin he was taught by Trosius Aper of Pola and Tuticius Proculus of Sicca.[8] The orators who taught him were the Greeks Aninius Macer, Caninius Celer[9] and Herodes Atticus,[10] and the Latin orator Cornelius

7. *PIR*², A 502.

8. See A. R. Birley, *HAC*, 1966/7, pp. 39ff. for these names.

9. *PIR*², C 388.

10. *PIR*², C 802: Ti. Claudius Atticus Herodes (*cos. ord.* 143), the celebrated Athenian millionaire sophist.

Fronto.[11] Of these, Fronto in particular received very favourable treatment – Marcus even asked the Senate to vote him a statue. Indeed, he advanced Proculus in his career as well, as far as a proconsulship, and he himself took over the burdensome expenses involved.

He took a passionate interest in philosophy even when still a boy: when he had entered his twelfth year he dressed himself in the philosopher's standard clothing and then began to practise endurance of hardship as philosophers do. He began to do his studies dressed in a Greek cloak and used to sleep on the ground. His mother had some trouble persuading him to sleep on a couch spread with skins. He had lessons from Apollonius of Chalcedon, the Stoic philosopher, as well, the teacher of that Commodus[12] whose kinsman it had been intended that Marcus should become. So great was his enthusiasm for philosophy, in fact, that even when he had been taken into the imperial family, he still used to go to Apollonius' house for instruction. He also attended the lectures of Sextus of Chaeronea (Plutarch's nephew), Junius Rusticus,[13] Claudius Maximus[14] and Cinna Catulus, all Stoics. He went to lectures by Claudius Severus[15] too, as he was interested in the Peripatetic School. But it was Junius Rusticus that he admired and imitated, a man distinguished in both his private and his public life, and an extremely experienced practitioner of the Stoic discipline. Marcus shared all his plans, both public and private, with Rusticus, and

11. *PIR*², C 1364: M. Cornelius Fronto (*cos*. 143), the most highly regarded Latin orator of the day, a native of Cirta (Constantine) in Numidia, remained Marcus' friend throughout his life and much of their correspondence is preserved.

12. i.e. L. Aelius Caesar.

13. *PIR*², J 814.

14. *PIR*², C 933.

15. *PIR*², C 1027: his son was to marry Marcus' eldest daughter (stemma, p. 320).

Rusticus always received the kiss of greeting before the prefects of the guard. Marcus made him consul a second time,[16] as well, and after his death he asked the Senate to decree statues to him. In fact he treated his teachers with such honour that he used to have gold portrait-busts of them in his private chapel and used to show respect for their tombs by personal visits, and by offering sacrifices and leaving flowers.

He also studied law, attending lectures by Lucius Volusius Maecianus.[17] In general, he devoted so much effort and hard work to his studies that his physical health was impaired; and this was the only respect in which one might find fault with his boyhood. He attended public schools of oratory too. Of his fellow-pupils from the senatorial order he was especially fond of Seius Fuscianus[18] and Aufidius Victorinus.[19] From the equestrian order his particular friends were Baebius Longus and Calenus. He was extremely generous to these friends and bestowed money on the ones whose station in life made it impossible for him to promote them to public office.

He was brought up under the close supervision of Hadrian, who used to call him Verissimus, as we mentioned above. Hadrian did him the honour of enrolling him in the equestrian order at the age of six and of admitting him to the college of Salian priests in his eighth year. During his time as a Salian he had an omen of empire. The Salians were all throwing their garlands onto the banqueting couch in the traditional way. The

16. In A.D.162. Rusticus was presumably from the family of the Stoic 'martyr' of the same name, put to death by Domitian in A.D. 93.

17. A jurist frequently cited in the *Digest*, he rose to be prefect of Egypt in A.D.160–61 and was later made a senator.

18. *cos. II ord.* 188, and prefect of Rome.

19. *PIR²*, A 1393 + add.: consul in A.D.155, *cos. II ord.* 183, C. Aufidius Victorinus was the son-in-law of Fronto, in whose correspondence he features.

other garlands landed in various places, but his own fell straight on the head of Mars, as if placed there by his hand. In this priestly college Marcus was in turn Leader of the Dance, Prophet and Master. As Master he initiated and dismissed many fellow-members, with no one to prompt him, as he had learned all the ritual chants by heart. He assumed the toga of manhood in his fifteenth year and at once was betrothed, at Hadrian's wish, to the daughter of Lucius Commodus. Not long after this he was prefect during the Latin Festival. While holding this position he deputized for the regular magistrates and performed very brilliantly, as he did at the banquets of the *princeps* Hadrian as well. After this he handed over to his sister everything that he had inherited from his father. His mother had asked him to share it, but he replied that he was quite satisfied with his grandfather's property and added that she could bestow her own estate on his sister too, so that she would not be worse off than her husband. He was in fact so good-natured that on occasion people could get him to attend hunts or to go to the theatre or watch the shows. Besides this he gave some attention to painting under the supervision of his teacher Diognetus. He loved boxing and wrestling, running and fowling, was a first-class ball-player and hunted as well. His enthusiasm for philosophy led him away from all these pursuits and made him an earnest and serious-minded person. Yet it never completely took away a certain warmth of manner, which he showed to his own household first of all, then to his friends and even to those he knew less well. He was austere but not obstinately so, retiring but not timid, serious but not gloomy.

This sums up his character at the time when Hadrian was looking for a successor to his rule after the death of Lucius Caesar. Marcus himself could not be regarded as suitable as he was only in his eighteenth year, so Hadrian adopted Antoninus Pius, the husband of Marcus' aunt. This adoption was made with the provision that Marcus should then adopt Lucius

Commodus[20]. On the very day that he was adopted he dreamed that he had shoulders of ivory and that when he was asked whether they were capable of bearing the weight he found that they were stronger than usual. In fact he was horrified rather than delighted on learning that he had been adopted by Hadrian, and he was reluctant to leave his mother's mansion when ordered to move to Hadrian's private house. His household staff asked him why he was so sad at being adopted into the royal family, and he listed the evils inherent in imperial power. It was at this time that he first began to be called Aurelius instead of Annius, since by the law of adoption he had passed into the Aurelian family, that is, the family of Antoninus. So in his eighteenth year he was adopted; and he was designated to be quaestor during the second consulship of Antoninus, who was now his father – at Hadrian's insistence he was granted special exemption from the age qualification. After his adoption into the imperial house, he still treated all his relations with the same respect that he had shown them when he was a commoner, and was also just as sparing and careful with his property as he had been when he belonged to a non-imperial family, wishing to model his actions, words and thoughts on his father's principles.

When Hadrian died at Baiae and Pius had set off to bring back his remains, Marcus was left at Rome and performed the religious rites for his grandfather; and, although quaestor, he presented a gladiatorial spectacle in his private capacity. After Hadrian's death, Pius immediately got his wife to ask Marcus if he would break off his betrothal to the daughter of Lucius Commodus and marry their own daughter Faustina (whom Hadrian had wanted to marry Commodus' son, even though he was badly matched in age). After thinking the matter over Marcus replied that he was willing. When this was arranged, Pius designated Marcus to be consul with himself [A.D. 139],

20. Another muddled idea, found in the *Aelius* 5.12 as well (p. 93 above).

even though he was still only quaestor, and also gave him the name of Caesar. During the period that Marcus was consul-designate, Pius created him one of the six leaders of the squadrons of Roman knights and took his seat beside him when he was holding his official games with his five colleagues. He ordered him to move to the Tiberian Palace, where, in spite of his objections, he provided him with the courtly trappings of his lofty station; and at the Senate's command he made him a member of the priestly colleges. He also designated him to be consul a second time at the same moment when the emperor himself entered on his fourth consulship [A.D. 145].

During this period, with honorific public duties to keep him busy, and having to take part in his father's activities so that he could be fitted to direct the government of the republic, he still worked very eagerly at his studies. Later he married Faustina,[21] and when they had a daughter[22] he was granted the tribunician power and proconsular *imperium* outside the city, with the right of bringing in five motions in the Senate. Pius valued him so highly that he did not lightly grant promotion to anyone without Marcus' consent. Marcus for his part deferred absolutely to his father. Even so, there were not lacking men who spread adverse rumours about him, in particular Valerius Homullus. This man saw Marcus' mother Lucilla praying in front of a statue of Apollo in her garden. 'That woman', he insinuated to Pius, 'is in the act of praying that you may bring your life to an end and her son become emperor.' This carried absolutely no weight with Pius: Marcus was so honourable and self-effacing while he was sharing part of the imperial power.

In fact, Marcus was so careful about his reputation that even as a boy he used to warn his procurators not to act in a high-handed way, and on several occasions he refused to accept legacies that were left to him and passed them on to the next of

21. A.D.145.
22. 30 November A.D.147.

kin. To sum up, during the twenty-three years that he spent in his father's house, he conducted himself so well that Pius' love for him increased every day, and Marcus was never apart from Pius during all those years except on two nights, on separate occasions. Hence when Antoninus Pius realized that the end of his life was at hand, he called his friends and prefects, commended Marcus to all of them and confirmed his nomination as successor to the empire. Straight after this he gave the tribune the watchword, 'Equanimity', and ordered that the golden statue of Fortune, which used to be kept in his bedroom, should be moved to Marcus' bedroom. Marcus handed over part of his mother's property to Ummidius Quadratus, the son of his sister, as the latter was now dead.[23]

After the death of the deified Pius, Marcus, being compelled by the Senate to take on the government of the state, nominated his brother as joint emperor with himself. He gave him the name of Lucius Aurelius Verus Commodus and the titles of Caesar and Augustus, and from that moment they began to govern the republic jointly. It was then that the Roman Empire first began to have two emperors, since Marcus had shared with another the powers that had been left to him alone. Presently he himself took the name Antoninus and, just as if he were the father of Lucius Commodus, gave him the name of Verus, adding the name Antoninus as well.[24] To Lucius, legally his brother, he betrothed his daughter Lucilla. In honour of this union they gave orders that new institutions of boys and girls, named after them, should be added to the state child-welfare scheme. When what had to be done in the Senate had been dealt with, they went to the camp of the guard together and promised the soldiers a bounty in honour of their joint accession, twenty thousand sesterces each for the other ranks, the rest proportionately more. They laid their father's body to

23. See stemma, p. 319.
24. On this error, see p. 17f, above.

rest in Hadrian's tomb with a magnificent ceremony. Presently, at a public holiday which followed, there was a formal funeral service. Both emperors gave addresses in praise of their father, from the rostra, and they appointed a *flamen* for him chosen from the family and Aurelian *sodales*[25] chosen from his closest friends.

Having acquired the imperial power, both conducted themselves so much like ordinary citizens that no one missed the leniency of Pius – for Marullus, a contemporary writer of farces, reprimanded them in satirical fashion without being punished. They gave funeral games for their father. Marcus was giving himself completely to philosophy too, aspiring to the affection of the citizens. But to interrupt the emperor's happiness and freedom from care, there was the first Tiber flood, which was the worst of their reign. This event damaged many buildings in the city, caused the death of a great many animals, and created a very serious famine. All these troubles Marcus and Verus dealt with by taking charge personally and being on the spot. There was at that time also a Parthian war, which Vologessus had prepared under Pius and declared in the time of Marcus and Verus; Attidius Cornelianus,[26] who was then governing Syria, was put to flight. There was too a threat of a British war, and the Catthi[27] had burst into Germany and Raetia. Calpurnius Agricola[28] was sent against the Britons, and Aufidius Victorinus against the Catthi. But to the Parthian war, with the agreement of the Senate, his brother Verus was sent; he himself remained at Rome, for the affairs of the city demanded an emperor's presence. Marcus actually accompanied Verus as far as Capua, with a retinue of friends from the Senate

25. See p. 87, n. 93 above.

26. *PIR*[2], A 1341.

27. Usually called Chatti, this German tribe lived in the Taunus mountains.

28. *PIR*[2], C 249. Five inscriptions in the north of England record his activities.

to do him honour, and the heads of all the departments of state were assigned to him as well. But when Marcus had returned to Rome and had learned that Verus was ill at Canusium [Canossa], he hastened to see him, after taking vows in the Senate; these, after he returned to Rome on hearing of Verus' crossing, he at once fulfilled.

Verus, of course, after he arrived in Syria, lived in luxury at Antioch and Daphne, although he was acclaimed *imperator* while waging the Parthian war through his legates. In the meantime, Marcus was at all hours watching over the business of the republic and patiently putting up with his brother's luxurious living, almost without reluctance, and willingly. In short, Marcus, based at Rome, both disposed and ordained everything which was necessary for the war.

Successes were achieved in Armenia by Statius Priscus, Artaxata being captured, and the name Armeniacus was conferred on each of the *principes*.[29] This Marcus through modesty at first refused; subsequently however, he accepted it. Moreover, when the war was almost ended, each was named Parthicus.[30] But that name, too, which was conferred upon him Marcus rejected at first, and afterwards accepted. Furthermore, the title 'Father of the Fatherland', which was conferred in his brother's absence, he delayed taking until the latter was present.[31] In the middle of the war, he conducted as far as Brundisium [Brindisi] both Civica, Verus' uncle, and his own daughter who was about to be married, in the care of her sister,[32] having endowed her with money, and sent them to Verus. He himself at once returned to Rome, recalled by the talk of those who were saying that Marcus wanted to lay claim to the glory of the war for himself when it was finished, and that for that reason he was setting out for Syria. To the proconsuls he

29. A.D.163: Priscus' career is given by *ILS*, no. 1092.
30. A.D.165.
31. A.D.166.
32. See Birley, *Marcus Aurelius* p. 174f.

wrote that no one should meet his daughter on her journey.

In the meantime he strengthened lawsuits for personal freedom by being the first to lay down that each and every citizen should declare his freeborn children before the prefects of the treasury of Saturn within thirty days, having given them a name. In the provinces he established the use of public registrars, before whom the same thing was to be done concerning births as before the treasury prefects at Rome. This was to ensure that if anyone born in a province should chance to be pleading a case to prove personal freedom, he might cite the evidence from this source.[33] He made this entire law dealing with declarations of freedom stronger, and brought in others dealing with money-lenders and public sales. He appointed the Senate to adjudicate in many legal inquiries and most particularly in cases which belonged to its own sphere. With regard to the status of the deceased, too, he ordered that investigations must be made within five years. Nor did any of the *principes* defer more to the Senate; and indeed, to show honour to the Senate, he delegated matters which had to be adjudicated to many ex-praetors and ex-consuls not holding office, so that their authority might increase through their administration of the law. Many of his friends he enrolled into the Senate with aedilician or praetorian rank. To many senators, who were poor through no fault of their own, he granted tribunician or aedilician rank. Nor did he enrol anyone into the senatorial order unless he knew him well personally. He also made the following concession to senators: whenever any of them was to be tried on a capital charge, he would make a secret investigation and only after that make it public; and he would not allow Roman knights to be present at such cases. Furthermore, whenever he was able, he always attended the Senate, even if

33. Although this information appears to be authentic, i.e. not invented by the author, it may be that he has misunderstood his source, for registration of births was introduced long before this. Perhaps M. Aurelius merely made some amendments to the regulations.

there were no motion before it, if he was at Rome; of course, if he wanted to bring some motion before it he came in person, even from Campania. Besides this, at elections he frequently attended right up to nightfall, and never left the Senate-House unless the consul had said: 'We do not detain you, Conscript Fathers.' He also appointed the Senate to hear appeals made from the consul.

To the judiciary he gave particular attention. He added court-days to the calendar, making two hundred and thirty days a year for pleading cases and judging lawsuits. He was the first to appoint a praetor for trusteeships – whereas previously applications for trustees had been made to the consuls – so that greater care might be taken over trustees. Concerning guardians, indeed, whereas previously they were only appointed under the Plaetorian Law[34] or in cases of wanton conduct or of madness, he so regulated matters that all youths should receive guardians without special reasons being given.

He also provided carefully for public expenditure, and he prohibited libels on the part of informers, the mark of infamy being placed on false accusers. Accusations which would swell the fisc he despised. He devised many wise measures dealing with the state child-welfare system. He appointed curators from the Senate for many communities, so as to extend senatorial functions more widely. During the time of famine he presented grain from the city to the Italian communities, and he took care of the grain-supply in general. He limited gladiatorial spectacles in every way. He also limited the amount that could be donated for theatrical performances, laying down that actors might receive five gold pieces each, but with the proviso that no producer might exceed an expenditure of ten gold pieces. The streets of the city too, and the highways, he maintained with the greatest care. He made serious provision for the

34. The *lex Plaetoria* of 192 B.C. or earlier was designed to protect those under 25 against fraud.

grain-supply. By appointing assize judges (*iuridici*) he took
thought for Italy, following that precedent by which Hadrian
had appointed men of consular rank to administer justice. He
took wise counsel for the Spaniards, worn out by the enrolment
of the Italic element, contrary to Trajan's instructions (. . .).[35]
Also, he made additional laws covering the five per cent tax on
inheritances, trusteeships for freedmen, property inherited
from the mother, and likewise on sons' succession to the
mother's share, and laying down that non-Italian senators
should have a quarter of their property in Italy.[36] Besides these
things, he gave the curators of regions and roads the power
either to punish those who had exacted anything from anyone
over and above his taxes, or to send them back to the city
prefect for punishment. In general, he restored the old laws,
rather than making new ones. He had with him prefects by
whose authority and legal opinion he always enunciated laws.
Moreover, he made use of Scaevola, a man particularly learned
in the law.[37]

Towards the people, indeed, he conducted himself no differently than is the case under a free state. He was in all matters a
very great influence for moderation, in deterring people from
evil and urging them to good deeds, generous in rewarding and
mild in granting pardon; and he made the bad good and the
good very good, even bearing with restraint criticism from
several quarters. Once he advised a certain Vetrasinus, a man of
abominable reputation, who was seeking office, to defend himself against the views of the people. Vetrasinus replied that he
saw that many men who had fought in the arena with him
were praetors, and Marcus took it with good grace. So as not

35. The MSS. are defective here and the sense cannot be recovered:
but it is doubtful whether this refers to recruitment into the army as
some have assumed: see Syme, *JRS* 1964, pp. 147ff.

36. Thus modifying a ruling of Trajan (p. 47 above).

37. *PIR*[2], C 681: the lawyer Q. Cervidius Scaevola, quoted frequently
in the legal sources; he was prefect of the watch in A.D.175.

to take an easy revenge on anyone, he did not order a praetor who had conducted certain affairs very badly to resign from his praetorship, but entrusted his administration of justice to a colleague. He never favoured the imperial treasury when adjudicating lawsuits about profits.

Indeed, although he was firm, he was also diffident. After his brother had returned from Syria victorious,[38] the title 'Father of the Fatherland' was decreed to both of them, since Marcus, in the absence of Verus, had conducted himself with great moderation towards all senators and all the people. Besides this, the civic crown was offered to both of them; and Lucius requested that Marcus should triumph with him. Lucius requested further that the sons of Marcus should be called Caesars.[39] But Marcus had such great moderation that, although he had triumphed together with Lucius, yet after Lucius' death he called himself Germanicus only, because he had won that name for himself in his own war. At the triumph, moreover, they let Marcus' children of both sexes ride with them, even the unmarried girls[40]. The games, too, which were decreed for the triumph, they watched in triumphal dress. Among other examples of his dutifulness this act of moderation must also be commended: he ordered mattresses to be laid below the tight-rope walkers after some boys had fallen. Hence a net is still stretched out under them today.

While the Parthian war was being waged, the Marcomannic war broke out[41]. For a long while it was held in check by the skill of the men on the spot, so that the Marcomannic war could be carried on when the eastern war had already been concluded. Although he had hinted about the war to the people

38. A.D.166.
39. The sons were Commodus and M. Annius Verus: see stemma, p. 320.
40. Presumably Fadilla and Cornificia: see stemma, p. 320.
41. The Marcomanni were a German people who inhabited what is now Bohemia and Moravia.

at the time of the famine, when his brother returned after five years he spoke on the question in the Senate, saying that both emperors were needed for the German war. So great, indeed, was the fear of the Marcomannic war that Antoninus summoned priests from all sides, performed foreign rituals and purified Rome in every way[42]; and, being delayed in his departure for the war, he likewise celebrated the *lectisternia* (feast of the gods) by the Roman ritual as well, for seven days. There was in fact so great a pestilence that corpses were carried out on wagons and carts. At this time, indeed, the Antonini ratified very strict laws on burials and tombs, whereby they forbade anyone to construct a tomb as he wished; and this is still in force today. The pestilence did in fact devour many thousands, including many of the leading men, for the most distinguished of whom Antoninus set up statues. So great too was his mercifulness that he ordered funeral ceremonies to be carried out for the common people at public expense. There was a trickster who, with certain accomplices, was looking for a chance of plundering the city, and made public speeches from the wild fig-tree in the Campus Martius. He said that fire would descend if he himself fell down from the tree and turned into a stork. At the appointed time, he fell down and let a stork out of a fold in his clothes. When the man was brought to him, and confessed, the emperor pardoned him.

Nevertheless, both the emperors set forth,[43] clad in the military cloak. Both the Victuali and Marcomanni were throwing everything into disorder, and other peoples as well, who had taken flight under pressure from the more distant barbarians, were going to make war unless they were allowed in. The emperors' departure produced no small gain, for, when they had come as far as Aquileia, most of the kings withdrew,

42. These rites were clearly performed on account of the plague, mentioned below, rather than because of 'the fear of the Marcomannic war'.

43. A.D. 168.

together with their peoples, and put to death those responsible for the disturbances. The Quadi,[44] moreover, having lost their king, said that they would not confirm the man who had been appointed until the choice had been approved by our emperors. Lucius, however, set out against his will, since a number of peoples were sending word to the emperors' legates asking pardon for their rebellion. Lucius for his part was of the opinion that they should return, because Furius Victorinus had been lost and part of the army had perished.[45] Marcus, on the other hand, believed that the barbarians were feigning both their retreat and other measures purporting to offer military security – to avoid being crushed by the weight of such great preparations; and he held that they must press on. Finally, having crossed the Alps, they proceeded a considerable distance and settled everything pertinent to the defence of Italy and Illyricum.[46] They decided, further, at Lucius' insistence, that letters should be sent ahead to the Senate, and that Lucius should return to Rome. Two days after they started the journey, Lucius, sitting in the carriage with his brother, was seized with apoplexy and died.[47]

*

Furthermore, it was Marcus' custom at the spectacles in the circus to read and to listen to and sign documents; and for this he is in fact said to have been frequently ridiculed by the people. The freedmen Geminus and Agaclytus had a very great deal of influence under Marcus and Verus. However, so great was Marcus' integrity that he both concealed and defended Verus' vices, although they strongly displeased him, and he deified

44. The eastern neighbours of the Marcomanni, and their main allies.
45. Very probably from the plague rather than from enemy action.
46. Probably a reference to the defensive zone known as the *praetentura Italiae et Alpium* (*ILS*, no. 8977).
47. In late December, A.D.168, or early in January 169. At this point the account is abruptly interrupted: see p. 19 above.

him when he died, and aided and advanced Verus' aunts and sisters[48] by decreeing them honours and salaries. Verus himself he honoured with many sacred rites, dedicating a *flamen* to him and *sodales Antoniniani*[49] and all the honours which deified emperors have. There is none among the *principes* who is not touched by some disagreeable rumour, and even Marcus met with the rumour that he had put Verus out of the way, either with poison – by cutting a sow's womb with a knife poisoned on one side, setting the poisoned part before his brother to eat and keeping the harmless part for himself – or, certainly, by means of the doctor Posidippus, who is said to have bled him at an inopportune moment.

Cassius defected from Marcus after Verus' death.[50]

Now so great was Marcus' kindness to his own family that while he conferred the insignia of every office on all his kinsmen, on his son – and it was Commodus, an accursed and impure son – he quickly conferred the name of Caesar and presently a priesthood, and straightaway the title *imperator* and a share in the triumph and the consulship. At this time, indeed, the emperor ran on foot in the Circus alongside the triumphal chariot, without his son . . .[51]

After the death of Verus,[52] Marcus Antoninus held sole possession of the republic, a much better man, and the more abundant in virtues since he was now hindered by none of Verus' faults, neither the simulated ones of contrived strictness – under which he laboured on account of his innate imperfection

48. See stemma, p. 321.

49. See p. 87, n. 93 above.

50. *PIR*², A 1402: C. Avidius Cassius rebelled in A.D.175 (see esp. p. 132f below). The item is of course completely misplaced here.

51. The MSS. are defective here: the reference is to the triumph in December A.D.176.

52. This paragraph and the beginning of the next are almost certainly borrowed directly from Eutropius, 8.11: see p. 12 above.

— nor the ones which used particularly to annoy Marcus Antoninus from the earliest period of his life, the principles or habits of a depraved mind. For Marcus himself had such great tranquillity that he never altered his expression either from grief or from joy, being dedicated to the Stoic philosophy which he had learned from the best masters and gathered together himself from every source. Hadrian had intended this same man as his successor, if his youthful age had not been an obstacle. This is indeed obvious from the fact that he selected Marcus as son-in-law for Pius, so that the Roman empire might eventually pass on to him, seeing that he was a man worthy of it.

After these things he administered the provinces with great moderation and benevolence. Against the Germans he waged a successful campaign. In particular, he carried out the Marcomannic war – a war that surpassed any that could be remembered – with both courage and success, and indeed this was at a time when a burdensome plague had destroyed many thousands, of civilians as well as soldiers. Thus, by wiping out the Marcomanni, Sarmatians, Vandals and Quadi at the same time, he freed the Pannonian provinces from servitude and celebrated a triumph at Rome with Commodus, whom he had already made Caesar – his son, as we have said. Moreover, when he had drained his entire treasury for this war, and would not contemplate imposing any extraordinary tax on the provincials, he held an auction, in the Forum of the Deified Trajan, of the imperial furnishings, and sold goblets of gold and crystal and fluorspar, and even royal vases, and his wife's silk and gold-embroidered clothing, in fact even jewels which he had discovered in large numbers in an inner sanctum of Hadrian's. This sale actually went on for two months, and so much gold was obtained that after conducting the remainder of the Marcomannic war in accordance with his decision, he afterwards gave the purchasers an option that if anyone wanted to return what he had bought and get the gold back, he should know that he might do so. Nor was he disagreeable to anyone who did or did not return what was bought. At that time he allowed the more prominent men to hold banquets in the same style that he himself used and with the same attendants. Concerning the public games, moreover, he was so generous that he put on a hundred lions simultaneously at a single performance, which were killed with arrows.

When therefore he had completed his rule, beloved by all, and was both named and loved by some as a brother, by others as a father, by others as a son, according to his own age, he brought his life to an end in his eighteenth year as emperor and the sixty-first[53] of his life. Such great love for him shone forth on the day of his royal funeral that no one thought he should be lamented, everyone being certain that having been lent by the gods he had gone back to the gods. Finally, before his funeral was held, as most say, Senate and people, not in separate places but sitting together – as was never done before or after this – declared him a propitious god. This man, certainly so great and of such character, and associated with the gods in life and in death, left one son, Commodus; and had he been fortunate he would not have left a son. It was not sufficient that people of every age, sex, status and rank, gave him divine honours – anyone who did not have a likeness of him in his own house who, because of his personal circumstances, either could or should have had one, was adjudged guilty of sacrilege. Indeed, even today in many houses statues of Marcus Antoninus stand among the household gods. Nor were there lacking men who, supposing that he foretold many things in dreams, prophesied future events and did so truthfully. Hence too a temple was established for him, and Antoninian priests were given him, both *sodales* and *flamines*,[54] and everything which ancient practice laid down for the consecrated.

Some say, and this seems plausible, that Commodus

53. An error: born in April A.D.121, he died in March 180, aged 58.
54. See p. 87, n. 93 above.

Antoninus his son and successor was not begotten by him but from an adulterous union, and they embroider such a tale with a story current among the common people.[55] Allegedly Faustina, Pius' daughter and Marcus' wife, had once seen gladiators pass by and was inflamed with passion for one of them. While troubled by a long illness she confessed to her husband about her passion. When Marcus had related this to the Chaldaeans, it was their advice that the gladiator be killed and that Faustina should wash herself from beneath in his blood and in this state lie with her husband. When this had been done the passion was indeed abated, but Commodus was born a gladiator not a *princeps*; for as emperor he put on nearly a thousand gladiatorial fights, with the people looking on (as will be shown in his *Life*). This, of course, is regarded as plausible for the reason that the son of so virtuous a *princeps* was of a character possessed by no gladiatorial trainer, no actor, no performer in the arena, indeed by no creature formed by the off-scourings of all dishonour and crime. Many relate, however, that Commodus was actually begotten in adultery, since it is reasonably well known that Faustina chose both sailors and gladiators as paramours for herself at Caieta. When Marcus Antoninus was told about her, so that he might divorce her – if not execute her – he is reported to have said: 'If we send our wife away, we must give back her dowry too' – and what dowry did he have but the empire, which he had received from his father-in-law when adopted by him at Hadrian's wish?

Yet so great is the power of a good *princeps*' way of life – righteousness, serenity and dutifulness – that scorn for no kinsman sullies his fame. In short, since he always maintained his own code of conduct and was not affected by anyone's whispered insinuations, neither his gladiator son nor his ill-famed wife harmed Antoninus. Even now he is held to be a god, as has ever seemed right and does now so seem to you yourself, Most

55. Some of this may be the author's invention, but similar material appears in Victor, *de Caes.*, 16.2.

Sacred Emperor Diocletian, who worship him among your deities, not as you do the others but in a special way, and who often say that you desire in your way of life and in your mercifulness to be such a one as was Marcus, even though in philosophy not even Plato, were he to come back to life, could resemble him. This of course is a brief and concise account.

But the deeds of Marcus Antoninus after his brother's death were as follows. First the body was conveyed to Rome and laid in the tomb of his ancestors: divine honours were decreed for him. Then, while rendering thanks to the Senate for deifying his brother, Marcus covertly indicated that all the war-plans by which the Parthians were overcome had been his own. Besides this, he made a further statement in which he indicated that now at last he would govern the republic, as it were from afresh, now that that person who seemed rather neglectful had been removed. Nor did the Senate take it otherwise than Marcus had spoken, so that he appeared to be rendering thanks that Verus had departed from life. Then he conferred rights, honours and money, in very great quantity, on all Verus' sisters and relatives and freedmen. For he cared a very great deal about his own reputation, inquiring about the truth of what each man said about him, and putting right whatever seemed to have been justly criticized.

When about to set off for the German war, and before the period of mourning had expired, he gave his daughter to Claudius Pompeianus, an Antiochene of advanced age, son of a Roman knight and not of sufficiently noble family (subsequently he made him consul twice)[56] – since his daughter was an Augusta and the daughter of an Augusta. But both Faustina and the girl who was being given in marriage regarded this wedding with reluctance.

*

56. Lucilla, widow of Verus, married Ti. Claudius Pompeianus (*cos. II ord.* 173): *PIR²*, C 973.

When the Moors were laying waste almost the whole of the Spanish provinces, successful campaigns were carried out by legates;[57] and when the Bucoli rebels had done many unpleasant things in Egypt they were given a hammering by Avidius Cassius[58] (who subsequently attempted a usurpation)[59].

*

Just before the actual day of his departure, while living in retreat at Praeneste [Palestrina], he lost his seven-year-old son, Verus Caesar by name, after an operation on a tumour under the ear. He mourned him for not longer than five days, and after comforting the doctors returned to affairs of state. Because the games of Jupiter Best and Greatest were in progress, he was unwilling for them to be interrupted by public mourning and ordered that statues only be decreed for his dead son, and a likeness in gold, to be carried in procession at the circus-games, and that his name should be inserted in the hymn of the Salii. As the plague was still very much unabated, he both revived the worship of the gods most zealously and trained slaves for military service (in the way it had been done during the Punic war), calling them the 'Volunteers', after the example of the *volones*.[60] He also armed gladiators and called them the 'Obedient'. Brigands, too, from Dalmatia and Dardania, he made into soldiers; and he armed the *diogmitae*.[61] He also hired auxiliary units of Germans to fight against the Germans. Besides this, he prepared legions with all care for the German, or Marcomannic, war[62]. So as not to burden the provincials, he

57. A.D.171.
58. A.D.172.
59. A.D.175.
60. Slaves who volunteered for military service in the Second Punic War (218–202 B.C.) were given this name.
61. Paramilitary police who served in cities of the Greek east.
62. He had raised two new legions, II and III Italica (Dio, 55.24.4), in A.D.165–6.

held an auction of court property, as we have said, in the Forum of the Deified Trajan, at which besides clothes and goblets and gold vases he even sold gold statues, together with paintings by great artists.

*

He wiped out the Marcomanni at their very crossing of the Danube, and restored the plunder to the provincials; all the peoples from the frontier of Illyricum as far as Gaul had conspired together, Marcomanni, Naristae, Hermunduri and Quadi, Suevi, Sarmatae, Lacringes and Buri, these and others, together with the Victuali, Osi, Bessi, Cobotes, Roxolani, Basternae, Halani, Peucini and Costoboci.[63] Meanwhile a Parthian war was threatening, and a British one.[64] So, with a great struggle on his own part as well, he conquered the toughest peoples; the soldiers followed his example, and the legates and the prefects of the guard commanded the army; and he received the surrender of the Marcomanni, a great many of whom were brought over into Italy.

Of course he always conferred with the leading men not only on matters of war but on civilian affairs as well, before he did anything. Indeed, this was always his particular saying: 'It is fairer that I should follow the advice of so many and such good friends, than that so many and such good friends should follow the wishes of a single man, myself.' To be sure, because he used to seem harsh, as a result of his philosophical principles, in his military endeavours and in his life as a whole he was heavily criticized; but he used to reply, either verbally or by letter to

63. The dislocation of the account that began with the death of Verus (cf. p. 123 above) has resulted in the omission of the most significant event of the war: the enemies of Rome had invaded Italy, besieging Aquileia (Lucian, *Alexander*, 48; Ammianus, 29.6.1), and Greece. This probably took place in A.D.170, while M. Aurelius was planning an offensive on the Danube. See Birley, *Marcus Aurelius*, pp. 222ff.

64. This sentence looks like a repetition, in error, from 8.6–7 (p. 116 above).

those who spoke ill of him. Many nobles died in the German or Marcomannic war (or rather, the war of many nations), to all of whom he set up statues in the Ulpian Forum. Hence his friends frequently tried to persuade him to leave the wars and come to Rome, but he was scornful and persisted, nor did he withdraw until he finished all the wars. He made provinces consular instead of proconsular, or proconsular or praetorian instead of consular, in accordance with the necessities of war. Disturbances among the Sequani, also, he checked by a rebuke and by his authority. The situation was dealt with in Spain too, where there had been trouble in Lusitania. To his son Commodus, who was summoned to the frontier,[65] he gave the toga of manhood, on account of which he distributed largess to the people, and designated him to be consul before the legal age.

If anyone was proscribed by the prefect of the city, he did not accept it with pleasure. He himself was very sparing with public money in giving largess – and this is related in praise rather than in criticism – but nevertheless he gave money to good men and brought assistance to towns on the brink of ruin; and he remitted tribute or taxes where necessity compelled. While absent he gave forceful instructions that the pleasures of the Roman people should be taken care of by the richer promoters of spectacles. For there was a rumour among the people, when he had removed the gladiators for the war, that he wanted to take away their pleasures and compel the people to take up philosophy. He had in fact ordered that the pantomimists should appear at a later hour and not for the whole day, so that merchandise might not be impeded. There was talk about the pantomimists loved by his wife, as we have said above. But he cleared her of all this in his letters. Marcus also prohibited riding and driving in carriages in towns. He reformed the morals of married women and of young noblemen, which were growing lax. The sacred rites of Serapis he cleared

65. A.D.175 (see p. 172 below).

away from the mixed ceremony of the Pelusia.[66] There was, to be sure, a rumour that certain men in the guise of philosophers had been causing trouble both to the republic and to private citizens. This he refuted.

Antoninus followed that custom of punishing all crimes with a lighter penalty than was usually inflicted by the laws, although sometimes he remained implacable against those who were clearly guilty, in the case of serious crimes. Capital cases involving persons of high status he took in person, and indeed with very great equity – so that he reprimanded a praetor who had heard the pleas of the defendants hastily, and ordered him to take the cases again, saying that it was important for the honour of the defendants that they should be heard by a man who was capable of judging on behalf of the people. Furthermore, he maintained equity even when dealing with enemy prisoners.

He settled countless numbers from foreign peoples on Roman soil. By his prayers he summoned a thunderbolt from heaven against a military device of the enemy, and similarly obtained rain for his men when they were suffering from thirst.[67] He wanted to make Marcomannia a province, and Sarmatia too, and he would have done so if Avidius Cassius had not at this very moment rebelled in the east.[68] Cassius called himself emperor, as some say, at the wish of Faustina, who was in despair about her husband's health. Others say that Cassius called himself emperor when a report of the death of Antoninus had been fabricated – since he called Marcus 'the deified'. Antoninus for his part was not much disturbed by the defection of Cassius, nor did he exhibit anger against his loved ones, but

66. A fertility cult of Egyptian origin, celebrated annually at Rome on 20 March.

67. The so-called 'lightning miracle' and 'rain miracle', both of which are depicted on the Aurelian Column (see Birley, *Marcus Aurelius*, plates 11 and 12).

68. A.D.175.

Cassius was declared a public enemy by the Senate, and his property was proscribed in the name of the public treasury. Having abandoned the Sarmatian and Marcomannic war, therefore, he set out against Cassius. At Rome, too, there were disturbances, caused by the fear that Cassius would arrive while Antoninus was away. But Cassius was immediately put to death and his head was brought to Antoninus. Marcus, however, did not rejoice at the death of Cassius and ordered his head to be buried. Maecianus, also, Cassius' son, to whom Alexandria[69] had been entrusted, the army killed. Cassius had even appointed his own prefect of the guard, who was put to death as well. Marcus forbade the Senate to inflict heavy penalties on those implicated in the rebellion; at the same time he requested that during the period of his principate no senator might be killed, so that his reign as emperor might not be defiled – even those who had been exiled he ordered to be recalled, although a very small number of centurions had been punished with death. He also pardoned the communities that had sided with Cassius; he even pardoned the people of Antioch, who had said many things against Marcus on Cassius' behalf. He did abolish both their spectacles and public assemblies, and public gatherings of all kinds, and dispatched a very severe edict against them. Moreover, a speech of Marcus, delivered among his friends – quoted by Marius Maximus – declares them to be rebels. Finally, he was not willing to visit Antioch when he set out for Syria. For, obviously, he did not want to visit Cyrrhus, Cassius' hometown. When he was at Alexandria, he acted mercifully towards the people there. Subsequently however he did visit Antioch. He conducted much business with kings and ratified peace; all the kings, and legates of the Persians,[70] coming to see him. He was greatly beloved by all the eastern provinces. In many of them he left the imprint of philosophy as

69. Cassius's daughter (PIR², A 512), rather than the city; for Maecianus: PIR², A 1406.

70. i.e. the Parthians: 'Persians' is used anachronistically.

well. Among the Egyptians he behaved like an ordinary citizen, and like a philosopher, in all the academies, temples and public places. Although the Alexandrians said many favourable things about Cassius, nevertheless he forgave them all, and left his daughter among them. He lost his own Faustina, who expired at the onset of a sudden illness in the foothills of Mount Taurus, at the village of Halala.[71] He requested the Senate to decree honours and a temple for Faustina, and likewise he praised her, even though she had a reputation for lack of chastity. Of these things Antoninus either was ignorant or feigned ignorance. He established new Faustinian girls[72] in honour of his dead wife, and rendered thanks that she had been deified as well, by the Senate. He had had her with him even in the campaigning season, and for this reason gave her the title 'Mother of the Camp'. He also made the village where Faustina died a colony, and built her a temple. But this temple was afterwards dedicated to Heliogabalus.[73] With this characteristic clemency he suffered Cassius to be killed, but did not order it. Heliodorus, the son of Cassius, was banished, and others of his children were exiled, but given a share of their property. In fact, Cassius' sons received more than half their father's estate and were given aid in the form of gold and silver, while the women were even given jewellery: indeed Alexandria, Cassius' daughter, and Dryantianus, his son-in-law, had the right of travelling freely, and were put in the care of an aunt's husband.[74] Indeed, he grieved that Cassius was dead, saying that he had wanted to complete his time as emperor without shedding any senatorial blood.

Having settled matters in the east he came to Athens. There he entered the initiation rites of Ceres,[75] so that he might prove

71. A.D. 176.

72. As part of the *alimenta* system (p. 47, n. 84).

73. See p. 260 below.

74. The lady would seem to be Claudia Helena (*PIR*², C 1097), wife of Claudius Titianus (*ib*. 1043) and aunt of Cassius' son-in-law Ti. Claudius Dryantianus Antoninus (*ib*. 859): see *PIR*², II, p. 166 (stemma).

75. i.e. the Eleusinian mysteries.

himself to be free of guilt, and went into the sanctuary alone. On his way back to Italy he suffered a very severe storm on the voyage. Reaching Italy by way of Brundisium, he both put on the toga himself and ordered the soldiers to wear it, nor were the soldiers under him ever clad in the military cloak. When he came to Rome, he held a triumph[76] and then set out for Lavinium. After this he took Commodus as his colleague in the tribunician power, gave largess to the people and marvellous shows; then he put right many civilian matters. He set a limit to the expenses of gladiatorial combats.[77] The saying of Plato was ever on his lips, that states flourished if either philosophers were rulers or the rulers were philosophers. He united his son in marriage with the daughter of Bruttius Praesens,[78] the wedding being celebrated in the manner of private citizens; and for this too he gave largess to the people.

Then he turned to finish off the war,[79] in the conduct of which he died. His son's character was already falling away from his own standards. For three years after this he waged war, with the Marcomanni, Hermunduri, Sarmatae and Quadi, and if he had survived for one year longer he would have made provinces out of them. Two days before he expired his friends were admitted to his presence, and he is said to have expressed to them the same opinion about his son as Philip did about Alexander, when he thought ill of him, adding that he did not take it amiss at all that he was dying, only that he was dying leaving such a son to survive him; for Commodus was already showing himself to be base and cruel.

Now his death came about like this: when he had begun to be ill, he called his son to him and first requested of him that he should not belittle what remained of the war, lest he appear to

76. December A.D.176.
77. The *senatus consultum de sumptibus gladiatoriis minuendis*, passed A.D.177.
78. *PIR*², B 165; the daughter was Bruttia Crispina (*ib.* 170).
79. A.D.178.

betray the republic. When his son replied that his first desire was good health, he allowed him to do as he wished, requesting however that he should wait a few days and not set off at once. Then he stopped eating and drinking, being eager to die, and made his illness worse. On the sixth day he summoned his friends and after deriding human affairs and scorning death he said to his friends: 'Why do you weep for me and do not rather think of the plague and of the death which is common to all?' When they wanted to withdraw, he said with a groan: 'If you give me leave now, I bid you farewell, while I go ahead of you.' When he was asked to whom he commended his son, he replied: 'To you if he prove worthy, and to the immortal gods.' The armies, when they learned of his ill-health, were greatly grieved, since they loved him to an extraordinary degree. On the seventh day he became worse and allowed only his son in to him, and he even sent him away at once, in case he caught the disease. When he had done so, he covered his head as though wanting to sleep, but during the night he breathed his last.[80] He is reported to have wanted his son to die when he saw that he would be what he became after his own death, so that – as he himself said – he might not be like Nero, Caligula and Domitian.

It is held against him that he promoted his wife's lovers, Tertullus and Tutilius and Orfitus and Moderatus, to various offices, although he caught Tertullus actually having breakfast with his wife. An actor spoke about this man on the stage when Antoninus was present: when the Fool asked the Slave the name of his wife's lover, and he replied three times 'Tullus', and the Fool still went on asking, he replied: 'I have told you thrice (ter), Tullus.' The people of course said a lot about this, and others said a lot as well, finding fault with Antoninus' complaisance.

Prior to the time of his death, indeed before he returned to

80. He died at Vindobona (Vienna) on 17 March A.D.180, just over a month before his fifty-ninth birthday.

the Marcomannic war, he swore on the Capitol that no senator
had been killed with his knowledge, while he said that he would
have saved the lives even of rebels if he had known. Certainly,
he both feared and deprecated nothing more than a reputation
for covetousness, on which count he cleared himself in many
letters. People have recorded as a fault on his part that he was
insincere and not so straightforward as he appeared or as either
Pius or Verus had been. They have also accused him of encouraging the arrogance of the court by keeping his friends
away from general society and from banquets. He decreed the
consecration of his parents. His parents' friends too, he honoured with statues on their death. He did not readily believe
those who canvassed his support, but always made a long search
for the truth. Fabia[81] strove to be united with him in marriage
when Faustina was dead, but he took as a concubine the
daughter of a procurator of his wife, so as not to put a stepmother over so many children.

81. Ceionia Fabia (sister of L. Verus), to whom he had once been
betrothed (p. 112 above): see stemma, p. 321.

VERUS*

BY JULIUS CAPITOLINUS

I KNOW that most have dedicated the lives of Marcus and
Verus to literature and history in such a way that they offer
Verus first to their readers, following the order not of their
rule as emperors but of their lives. But I, because Marcus began
to rule first and Verus afterwards – and he died while Marcus
survived – have thought it right to make Marcus known first
and then Verus.

Lucius Ceionius Aelius Commodus Verus Antoninus, then,
who was called Aelius by the wish of Hadrian and Verus
Antoninus from his connection with Antoninus,[1] is placed
neither among the good nor among the bad *principes*. It is
agreed that he did not bristle with vices and that he did not
abound in virtues; and further, that he lived not unrestricted in
his own principate but, with like and equal sovereignty, under
Marcus, from whose principles he differed in the looseness of
his morals and in the excesses of a somewhat licentious way of
life. For he was a person of open character and one who could
conceal nothing. His real father was Lucius Aelius Verus[2] who,

---

* For background, see Birley, *Marcus Aurelius*; and, further, the
analysis by T. D. Barnes, *JRS* 1967, pp. 68ff. Much of the material in
the *Life* is also found in the *Marcus*, but independent facts are also
supplied. I differ from Barnes in regarding this as the result of a single
original source having been chopped up, rather than of there having
been a separate *Life* of Verus in the source. Annotation is limited mainly
to items not dealt with in the notes to the *Marcus*.

1. On this error see p. 17f above.
2. See p. 17f above.

having been adopted by Hadrian, was the first to be called
Caesar and to die still in the same rank. His grandfathers and
great-grandfathers and likewise very many of his ancestors
were of consular rank. Lucius was born at Rome in his father's
praetorship on the eighteenth day before the Kalends of
January [15 December A.D. 130], the birthday of the emperor
Nero. His paternal ancestry was for the most part from Etruria,
his mother's from Faventia.

  Having been born a member of this stock, when his father
was adopted by Hadrian he passed into the Aelian family, and
on the death of his father, the Caesar, he remained in Hadrian's
family. By Hadrian he was given to Aurelius to be adopted
when Hadrian, making abundant provision for the succeeding
generations, wanted to make Pius his son and Marcus his grandson; and by the same enactment Verus was to marry the daughter of Pius. She was, however, given to Marcus because Verus
seemed ill-matched in age, as we have related in the *Life* of
Marcus – in fact Verus took Marcus' daughter Lucilla as his wife.
He was brought up in the Tiberian House, and attended
classes with Scaurinus the Latin grammarian, son of the Scaurus
who was Hadrian's grammarian, and the Greek grammarians
Telephus, Hephaestio and Harpocratio; with the rhetoricians
Apollonius, Celer Caninius and Herodes Atticus, and the Latin
orator Cornelius Fronto; and with the philosophers Apollonius
and Sextus. All of these he loved most particularly and was in turn
cherished by them, although not talented in literature. He did,
to be sure, in boyhood love to compose verses, and later on,
speeches. In fact he is said to have been a better orator than a
poet, or rather, to speak more truthfully, to be worse as a poet
than as a rhetorician. Nor are there lacking those who say that
he was assisted by the talent of his friends and that those very
things credited to him, such as they are, were written by others;
and in fact he is said to have always had with him many eloquent
and learned men. He had as his tutor Nicomedes.[3] He was a

3. L. Aurelius Nicomedes (*ILS*, no. 1140).

voluptuary and excessive in his pleasures, and very suited, within proper limits, to all sports, games and jesting. Having transferred after his seventh year into the Aurelian family he was moulded by the character and influence of Marcus. He loved hunting, wrestling and all the physical activities of youth, and he was a private citizen in the imperial household for twenty-three years.

On the day that Verus received the toga of manhood, Antoninus Pius, on that same occasion when he dedicated his father's temple, gave largess to the people; and Verus himself, when he put on a show for the people as quaestor sat between Pius and Marcus. After his quaestorship he was at once made consul, with Sextius Lateranus [A.D. 154], and some years later he was made consul a second time, with his brother Marcus [A.D. 161]. But for a long time he was a private citizen and lacked those marks of honour with which Marcus was decorated. For he did not sit in the Senate before his quaestorship, and on journeys he rode not with his father but with the prefect of the guard; and no other honorific title was bestowed on him except that he was called 'son of Augustus'. He was keen on the circus-games too, no less than on the gladiatorial show. Although his character suffered from such great faults, in his pleasures and luxurious living, he appeared to have been retained by Antoninus for the reason that Pius' father had ordered that Verus should be adopted by Pius so that Hadrian could call him his grandson. To Hadrian, as far as it appears, Verus showed loyalty, not love. Antoninus Pius, however, loved the openness of his nature and the cleanness of his way of living, and encouraged his brother, too, to imitate him.[4] On the death of Pius, Marcus conferred everything on Verus, even granting him a share of the imperial power, and made him his

4. The author may have misunderstood his source here: one might have expected that Lucius would have been encouraged to imitate Marcus, not vice versa.

colleague, although the Senate had bestowed the position of emperor on Marcus alone.

After giving him the imperial position, then, and granting the tribunician power, and after the honour of the consulship had been conferred on him too, Marcus ordered that he be called Verus, transferring his own name to him, whereas previously he had been called Commodus.[5] Lucius indeed, in return, obeyed Marcus whenever he undertook anything, as a legate obeys a proconsul or a governor the emperor. For at the outset he addressed the soldiers on behalf of both of them, and in consideration of their joint rule he conducted himself in serious fashion and in accordance with Marcus' character. But when he set out for Syria he acquired a bad reputation, not only for the looseness of his rather free living but for adulteries and love affairs with youths as well. In fact he is said to have displayed such great extravagance that after he returned from Syria he even set up a cookshop at home, to which he used to resort after Marcus' banquets, with all manner of base characters ministering to him.[6] He is also said to have played dice the whole night through, after he had taken up that vice in Syria; and to have been so much a rival of Gaius [Caligula], Nero and Vitellius in vices that he used to wander about at night through the taverns and brothels, with his head covered with a common travelling-cap, carouse with cheap-jacks, and engage in brawls, concealing his identity; and often, people say, he returned after being beaten with his face bruised, and was recognized in the taverns although he had hidden himself. He also used to throw the largest coins into cookshops and smash the cups with them. He loved the charioteers too, favouring the Green faction. Fairly frequently, as well, he held gladiatorial bouts at banquets,

5. For a change, the author has got the names right (though not all the details are supplied, see p. 17f above).

6. Much of what follows in this paragraph and the next bears a close resemblance to passages in Suetonius (*Caligula*, 11, 55; *Nero*, 26, 27, 30; *Vitellius*, 13), which must arouse suspicion.

prolonging the dinners late into the night and falling asleep on the banqueting-couch, so that he would be lifted up with the covers and carried to his bedroom. He took a moderate amount of sleep and had an excellent digestion.

But although Marcus knew well enough about all these things, he pretended not to know, with that well-known restraint of his, so as not to censure his brother. In fact Verus' most notorious banquet is said to have been one at which couches were set for twelve – for the first time, it is said – although there is a very well-known saying about numbers of diners that 'seven make a dinner, but nine make a din.' Moreover, the handsome boys who were serving were presented one each to the guests, and carving-servants and dishes were given, one to each as well, and live animals, either tame or wild, birds or quadrupeds, the same kind as the meats which had been served. Cups were presented too, one to each guest for each drink, of fluorspar or of Alexandrian crystal, as often as they drank; gold and silver and jewelled goblets were also given, and even garlands entwined with gold ribbons and flowers out of season; and gold vases were given with unguents, made in the shape of unguent-boxes. Even carriages were given, with mules and muleteers, and with silver mountings, so that the guests might return from the banquet in them. Now the whole banquet is said to have cost an estimated six million sesterces. When Marcus heard of it he is said to have groaned and to have lamented the ill fortune of the state. After the banquet they played at dice until dawn. These things of course were after the Parthian war, to which Marcus is said to have sent him either so that he would not transgress in the city before the eyes of all, or so that he might learn thriftiness by foreign travel, or so that he might return reformed by the fear which war inspires, or so that he might realize that he was an emperor.

He had such great interest in the circus-games that he frequently both sent and received letters from his province concerning the games. Finally, even when present at Rome and sitting with Marcus, he received many insults from the Blues because, they said, he shamefully took sides against them. For he had a golden statue made of the Green horse Volucer, which he used to carry around with him; indeed, he used to put grapes and nuts in his manger instead of barley, and to order that he should be brought to him in the Tiberian House covered in blankets dyed with purple; and he made a tomb for him when he was dead, on the Vatican.[7] It was because of this horse that gold pieces and prizes first began to be demanded for horses. Moreover, that horse was held in such great honour that often a peck of gold pieces was demanded for him by the supporters of the Greens.

When he set out for the Parthian war, Marcus accompanied him to Capua; from there on he gorged himself in everyone's villas, fell sick and was ill at Canusium. His brother hastened to see him there. Many weak and sordid aspects in his life were revealed even during the time of war. For although a legate had been slain, legions had been slaughtered, the Syrians were meditating rebellion and the east was being laid waste, he was hunting in Apulia and sailing about surrounded by orchestras and singers at Corinth and Athens, and was lingering at all the maritime cities of Asia, Pamphylia and Cilicia that were especially renowned for their pleasures. After he came to Antioch he gave himself over to luxurious living while his generals, Statius Priscus, Avidius Cassius and Martius Verus,[8] finished the Parthian war in the space of four years, reaching Babylon and Media and recovering Armenia. Verus himself gained the names Armeniacus, Parthicus and Medicus, which were conferred on Marcus too, who was at Rome. But for four years Verus spent the winter at Laodicea, the summer at Daphne[9] and

7. Perhaps a sly anti-Christian joke?

8. P. Martius Verus (*cos. II ord.* 179), known from several mentions in Dio (71.3.1, 23.3, 29.2) and from *ILS*, no. 2311.

9. i.e. Laodicea-on-Sea, a Syrian port (not to be confused with other towns of that name). Daphne was a fashionable resort close to Antioch.

the rest of the time at Antioch. He was an object of ridicule to all the Syrians, whose many jokes against him at the theatre are still preserved. He always admitted the house-born slaves to the dining-room at the Saturnalia and on holidays. However, he did on two occasions set out for the Euphrates at the urging of his staff-officers (*comites*).[10] He also returned to Ephesus to receive Lucilla, his bride, who had been sent by her father Marcus – and this was mainly in order that Marcus should not come to Syria with her and discover his shameful behaviour. For Marcus had told the Senate that he would conduct his daughter to Syria. When the war was finished he assigned kingdoms to kings and provinces to his own staff-officers to be governed. Then he returned to Rome to a triumph – unwillingly, because he was leaving behind in Syria what seemed like his own kingdom; and he held a triumph jointly with his brother, having accepted from the Senate the names which he had received from the army. Besides this, he is said to have shaved off his beard in Syria at the instance of a common mistress.[11] As a result many things were said against him by the Syrians.

It was his fate that he appeared to bring the plague with him into those provinces through which he made his return journey, as far as Rome. The pestilence is reported to have arisen in Babylonia, when a pestilential vapour escaped from a golden casket in the temple of Apollo, which a soldier had by chance cut open; and thence it filled the Parthians' land and the world. But this was not through the fault of Lucius Verus but of Cassius, by whom Seleucia, which had received our soldiers as friends, was stormed. Indeed, Quadratus, a writer on the Parthian war, excuses this charge, among others, blaming the

10. See p. 77, n. 66 above.
11. Panthea of Smyrna, whose beauty and charm were extravagantly praised by Lucian in the *Imagines* and the *Pro Imaginibus*.

Seleucenes who had broken faith first.[12] Such reverence for Marcus did Verus have that on the day of the triumph which they celebrated jointly he shared with his brother the names that had been conferred on himself. Having returned from the Parthian war Verus was less respectful towards him; for he both displayed indulgence towards freedmen in a rather shameful way and settled many things without reference to his brother. Added to these things is the fact that, as if he were leading some kings to the triumph, he brought actors out of Syria; the principal one was Maximinus, whom he called by the name of Paris. Furthermore, he built a most notorious villa on the *Via Clodia*. Here for many days he himself both held orgies with unbounded extravagance, with his own freedmen and the friends of Paris, in whose presence he felt no shame, and he even invited Marcus. Marcus came, so that he might show his brother the purity of his own morals, as worthy of respect and emulation; and for five days, staying at the same villa, Marcus gave attention to judicial examinations which went on uninterrupted, while his brother was either banqueting or preparing banquets. Verus also kept the actor Agrippus, surnamed Memphius; this same person he had also brought out of Syria like a trophy from Parthia, and he named him Apolaustus. He had brought with him both minstrels and pipers, actors, pantomime jesters and jugglers, and all kinds of slaves in which Syria and Alexandria take pleasure, to such an extent that he seemed to have finished not a Parthian war but an actors' war.

This difference in their way of life and many other things is said to have caused dissensions between Marcus and Verus though this was not proved but implied by dubious rumour. In particular there was a case when Marcus had sent one Libo,

12. *PIR*[2], A 1245: Asinius Quadratus, a third-century historian of Rome. The destruction of the Greek city on the River Tigris was certainly an atrocity, which dealt a death-blow to Hellenic culture in South Mesopotamia.

his father's brother's son,[13] as legate to Syria, and Libo bore himself more insolently than a respectful senator should, saying that he would write to his 'brother' if he should happen to be in doubt about anything. Verus, being there, could not endure this, and Libo expired in a sudden illness, with visible marks like those produced by poison. It seemed to some, but not to Marcus, that he might have been murdered by a plot on Verus' behalf. So that affair increased the rumour of dissensions. His freedmen had a lot of influence with Verus, as we have related in the *Life* of Marcus – namely Geminus and Agaclytus, to the latter of whom, against the wishes of Marcus, he gave Libo's widow in marriage; indeed, when the wedding was celebrated by Verus, Marcus did not attend the banquet. Verus had other freedmen too, bad ones, Coedes and Eclectus and the rest, all of whom Marcus dismissed after Verus' death with a show of honour, although Eclectus was retained – and he killed Marcus' son Commodus in the sequel.

They set off for the German war together, because Marcus was unwilling either to send Lucius to the war without himself or to leave him in the city, because of his extravagant living. They came to Aquileia, and, against Lucius' wishes, crossed the Alps, since Verus at Aquileia had only hunted and banqueted, but Marcus planned everything. Concerning this war a very full discussion has been given in the *Life* of Marcus, about what was done by envoys from the barbarians seeking peace, and what by our generals. But when the war in Pannonia had been settled, they returned to Aquileia, at Lucius' insistence; and, because Lucius was longing for the pleasures of the city, they hastened to Rome. But, not far from Altinum, Lucius was struck down in the carriage with the sudden illness which they call apoplexy. After being set down from the carriage and bled, he was taken to Altinum, and after living on speechless for three days he died there.

13. *PIR*², A 668: M. Annius Libo (now known to have been consul in A.D.161); see stemma, p. 319.

There was gossip that he had committed incest with his mother-in-law Faustina. He is said to have died through her treachery, after poison had been sprinkled on oysters, the reason being that he had betrayed to the daughter the relations he had had with the mother; although that other tale also arose which is set down in the *Life* of Marcus, which is inconsistent with the way of life of such a man; while many fasten the crime of his death on his wife as well, and for the reason that Verus had been too indulgent to Fabia, whose power his wife Lucilla could not tolerate. Certainly, there was such intimacy between Lucius and Fabia, his sister, that rumour spoke also of this: that they initiated a plot to remove Marcus, and when that had been betrayed to Marcus by the freedman Agaclytus, Lucius was forestalled by Faustina, lest he anticipate her.

He was physically handsome with a genial face. His beard was allowed to grow almost in barbarian style. He was a tall man, and his forehead projected somewhat above his eyebrows, so that he commanded respect. He is of course said to have taken so much care of his blond hair that he used to sprinkle gold dust on his head so that his hair might become brighter and blonder. In speech almost halting, he was very keen on gambling, and his way of life was always extravagant. In many respects he was a Nero, except for the cruelty and the acting. Among other luxury trappings he had a crystal goblet, named Volucer after his beloved horse, that surpassed the capacity of any human draught.

He lived forty-two years, and ruled as emperor, with his brother, for eleven.[14] His body was laid in Hadrian's tomb, where his real father, the Caesar, was also buried.

There is a well-known tale, which Marcus' life does not warrant, that Marcus handed Verus part of a sow's womb smeared with poison after he had cut it with a knife poisoned

14. This is mistaken: he was born in December A.D. 130 (p. 139 above), and died more or less exactly thirty-eight years later, after seven and a half years as emperor.

on one side. But it is sacrilege for this to be thought about Marcus, even if both Verus' thoughts and his deeds might have deserved it. We shall not leave it in the balance, but reject the whole story as disproved and refuted, since after Marcus not even flattery seems to have been able to fashion such an emperor – except for Your Clemency, Diocletian Augustus.

AVIDIUS CASSIUS*

BY THE RIGHT HONOURABLE VULCACIUS GALLICANUS

As some would have it, Avidius Cassius came from the
family of the Cassii on his mother's side, his father being
a new man, Avidius Severus, who had commanded centuries
and subsequently had attained to the highest rank.[1] Quadratus
refers to him in his history, and with respect, since he declares
that he was a leading man and indispensable to the republic, and
very influential with Marcus himself. For it was after Marcus
was already emperor that he is reported to have passed away,
in accordance with the decrees of fate.

This Cassius then, from the family, as we have said, of the
Cassii who conspired against C. Julius (Caesar), silently hated
the principate and could not endure the imperial name; and he
used to say that nothing was more burdensome than the name
of empire, because it could not be removed from the republic
except by another emperor. Indeed in boyhood he is said to
have tried to wrest the principate even from Pius, but on
account of his father, a just and influential man, he escaped
detection in this attempt at usurpation, although he was always
held suspect by the generals. But that he prepared a plot against
Verus is clear from a letter of Verus himself, which I append:

---

* Statements in this *Life* which appear to be factual are referred to in
the notes. The rest is fiction. For a brief account of his rebellion, see
Birley, *Marcus Aurelius*, pp. 252ff.
 1. False: Cassius' father was C. Avidius Heliodorus (*PIR²*, A 1405),
see p. 73 above.

Avidius Cassius is avid for imperial power, as it seems to me and as has already been shown under my grandfather, your father. I would like you to order that he be watched. Everything we do displeases him, he is getting ready resources that are not inconsiderable, he laughs at our letters. You he calls an old woman philosopher, me an extravagant moron. Consider what should be done. I do not hate the man, but consider whether you are consulting your own and your children's interests ill when you keep on among the men in uniform such a person – whom the soldiers are glad to listen to and glad to see.

Marcus' reply concerning Avidius Cassius:

I have read your letter, a worried letter rather than an imperial one and not in accordance with our times. For if the empire must be his by divine decree, we cannot slay him even if we wish. You know your great-grandfather's saying: 'No one kills his own successor.' And if this is not so, he himself of his own accord, without cruelty on our part, will fall into the toils of fate. Add that we cannot make guilty one whom no one has accused and whom, as you yourself say, the soldiers love. Moreover, in cases of treason it is natural that even those against whom it is proved seem to suffer rough justice. You yourself know what your grandfather Hadrian said: 'The lot of emperors is wretched, for they cannot be believed in cases of attempted usurpation – unless they have been killed!' I have preferred, moreover, to quote the example as his rather than as Domitian's (who is reported to have said this first); for in the case of tyrants even their good sayings do not have as much authority as they ought to have. Let him therefore keep his own ways, especially since he is a good general, and strict and brave and needed by the republic. As to what you say about taking heed for my children by his death; by all means let my children perish if Avidius Cassius should deserve to be loved more than they, and if it profit the republic that Cassius rather than the children of Marcus should live.

These are the things that Verus and Marcus wrote about Cassius.

But we shall briefly set forth the man's nature and character, and of course not much can be known about men whose lives no one dares to render famous because of those by whom they were overcome. We will add, further, the manner in which he attained to empire and in which he was killed, and where he was defeated. For I have undertaken, Diocletian Augustus, to commit to writing an account of all those who held the imperial title, whether with just cause or without, so that you, Augustus, may learn about all those who have worn the purple.

His character was such that not seldom he seemed truculent and rough, but sometimes placid and mild; often he was devout, but at other times scornful of sacred things; avid for wine, and again abstinent; eager for food but able to endure starvation; a devotee of Venus and a lover of chastity. Nor were there lacking those who called him a Catiline.[2] He himself also rejoiced in such a name, adding that he would be a Sergius if he killed the philosopher. By this name he meant Antoninus [i.e. Marcus], who was so brilliant in philosophy that when he was about to go to the Marcomannic war, and all were afraid that something fatal might happen, he was asked, not in flattery, but seriously, to publish his *Precepts of Philosophy*; and he did not fear to do so, but for three days expounded his *Exhortations* – that is, the *Precepts* – in order.[3] Besides this, Avidius Cassius adhered tenaciously to military discipline and was one who wished himself to be called Marius.[4]

Since we have begun to speak of his strictness, there are many indications of cruelty (rather than strictness) on his part. For, firstly, soldiers who had taken anything from provincials by force he crucified in the very places where they had committed their offence. He was also the first to devise this type of punishment: he set up a great post, 180 feet high, and tied condemned men to it from top to bottom, and placed a fire below it; and

2. L. Sergius Catilina, accused by Cicero of planning a *coup d'état* in 63 B.C.; driven into open rebellion and killed in battle the following year.

3. This is presumably intended as a reference to Marcus Aurelius' *Meditations,* in which case the story is clearly bogus.

4. C. Marius, famous for his victories against both Jugurtha and the Germans at the end of the second century B.C., and for his army reforms.

when some had been burnt, he killed the others by smoke, pain and even fright. He also ordered ten men at a time, chained together, to be plunged into a stream or into the sea. He also cut off the hands of many deserters, and broke the legs and knees of others, saying that a criminal living in misery was a greater example than one who had been executed. Once, when he was in command of an army, without his knowledge a band of auxiliaries on the authority of their centurions had killed three thousand Sarmatians who had been moving along the banks of the Danube without taking precautions. The auxiliaries returned to him with a vast quantity of booty, the centurions hoping for a reward because they had killed the enemy with a very small band, while the tribunes were behaving rather slackly and were in ignorance about it. He ordered them to be seized and crucified, and punished with the punishment of slaves, for which there was no precedent. He said that it could have turned out to be an ambush, and respect for the Roman empire might have perished. When a serious mutiny arose in the army, he came out naked, clad only in a loin-cloth, and said: 'Strike me, if you dare, and add crime to breach of discipline.' Then, as all grew quiet, he was deservedly feared, because he himself was not afraid. This affair so greatly added to Roman discipline and instilled such great terror into the barbarians, that they sought peace for a hundred years from the absent Antoninus, considering that they had seen condemned by the decision of a Roman general even those who had, contrary to what was lawful, defeated them.

Concerning this man many stern things that he did to combat the soldiers' indiscipline are found in Aemilius Parthenianus,[5] who has set down the history of those who have attempted usurpation, from the early examples onwards. For instance, when they had been beaten with rods in the forum, he both beheaded with the axe, in the middle of the camp, those who deserved this, and in many cases cut off their hands. Apart from

5. A bogus author: see p. 16 above.

bacon-fat and biscuit and vinegar, he prohibited soldiers from carrying anything on expedition; and if he found anything else he punished the excess with no light punishment. A letter of the Deified Marcus to his prefect about this man survives, somewhat as follows:

I have given the Syrian legions to Avidius Cassius. They are abandoned to luxury and behaving with the morals of Daphne;[6] and Caesonius Vectilianus has written that he found them all bathing in hot water. I think I have made no mistake, because in fact you too know Cassius, a man of Cassian strictness and discipline. Nor indeed can the soldiers be controlled except by old-fashioned discipline. For you know what the line of the good poet [Ennius], repeated by everyone, says:

'In ancient ways stands the Roman state, and in men.'[7]

You make sure only that abundant supplies are there for the legions – if I know Avidius well, they will not be wasted.

The prefect's letter to Marcus:

You have planned rightly, my lord, in putting Cassius in command of the Syrian legions. For nothing benefits Grecianized soldiers like a somewhat strict person. He will certainly get rid of all the bathing in hot water, all the flowers from the soldiers' heads, necks and breasts. The military food-supply has been prepared, and nothing is lacking under a good general; for not much is either asked for or spent.

Nor did he fail the judgement made of him. He at once ordered it to be proclaimed on parade, and fixed notices on the walls, to the effect that if anyone was found in uniform at Daphne, he would return without it. He always inspected the soldiers' weapons once a week, even their clothes and boots and greaves; he removed all their pleasures from the camp and ordered them to spend the winter in tents if they did not mend their ways – and they would have done so if they had not behaved in a more proper fashion. There was training for all soldiers once a week, at which they even shot arrows and

6. See p. 143, n. 9 above.
7. This line of Ennius' *Annales* is quoted by Cicero, *de republica*, 5.5.

practised with weapons. He used to say that it was lamentable that when athletes, wild-beast fighters and gladiators were trained, soldiers were not; for their future work would be less difficult if it became familiar.

So having set right the discipline he conducted campaigns in Armenia and Arabia and in Egypt most successfully, and he was loved by all the easterners, especially by the Antiochenes, who even acquiesced in his rule, as Marius Maximus relates in his *Life* of the Deified Marcus.[8] When the Bucoli soldiers, too, did many serious things in Egypt, they were given a hammering by him, as the same Marius Maximus reports in the second volume of his *Life* of Marcus Antoninus. When he was in the east, he proclaimed himself emperor,[9] some say at the wish of Faustina who was now in despair about Marcus' health, and feared that she alone could not protect her infant sons and that someone would arise who would seize the royal position and put the children out of the way. Others say that Cassius made use of this device with the soldiers and the provincials to counter their love for Marcus, so that they could join him, by saying that Marcus had met his end. He is said to have called him 'the Deified', too, so as to alleviate their longing for him. When he had proceeded with his plan to become emperor he at once made prefect of the guard the man who had made ready the royal insignia for him; but this man, against the wish of Antoninus, was killed by the army. The army, also, against the wishes and without the knowledge of Antoninus, slew, Maecianus as well, to whom Alexandria[10] had been entrusted, and who had joined Cassius in the hope of sharing his power.

However, Antoninus was not seriously angered on learning of the rebellion, and did not rage against his children or kins-

8. Most of the next three paragraphs seems to be based on authentic material, presumably the *Life* of Marcus by Marius Maximus, here utilized more copiously than in *Marcus*, 24.5ff. (p. 132f above).

9. Spring A.D.175.

10. Cassius' son and daughter: see p. 133, n. 69 above.

folk; but the Senate declared Cassius a public enemy and proscribed his property. Antoninus was unwilling for it to be collected into his privy purse and hence, on the instructions of the Senate, it was handed to the public treasury. There was panic at Rome; some were saying that Avidius Cassius would come there, in the absence of Antoninus – who was singularly loved by all, except by voluptuaries – and that he would ravage it like a tyrant, especially on account of the senators who had declared him a public enemy and had proscribed his property. The love felt for Antoninus was most clearly shown in the fact that Avidius was killed with the consent of everyone except for the people of Antioch. Indeed, Antoninus did not order him to be executed, but suffered it; it was clear to everyone that if it had been in his power he would have spared him. When Cassius' head was brought to Antoninus he did not exult and was not elated. He was even grieved that an opportunity for clemency had been snatched away from him – he used to say that he wanted to take him alive, so that he might reproach him with the kindnesses that he had done him, and spare him. Someone said that Antoninus deserved blame for being so lenient towards his enemy – and to his children and his kinsfolk, since he had discovered that they were implicated in the usurpation. The person who was reproaching him added: 'What if he had won?' Antoninus is said to have replied: 'We have not worshipped the gods in such a way, nor lived such a life, that he should defeat us.' Then he recounted how all the *principes* who had been killed had given cause for deserving death, and how no one that was unquestionably good had either been defeated by a usurper or killed, saying that Nero had merited it and Caligula deserved to die; and that Otho and Vitellius did not even wish to rule; while about Pertinax[11] and Galba his feelings were

11. This might be a scribe's insertion: Pertinax was of course murdered thirteen years after the death of Marcus himself. But as this and the next sentence are doubtless fiction, it may just be a revealing piece of carelessness by the author.

similar, for he said that avarice was the most painful defect in an emperor. Lastly, he said that not Augustus nor Trajan nor Hadrian nor his own father could be overcome by rebels, although there were many of them and they had been put out of the way either against the wishes or without the knowledge of the emperors. Moreover, Antoninus himself requested from the Senate that heavy punishment should not be taken against those implicated in the rising, at the very same time when he asked that no senator should be punished by the death penalty during his reign, something that won him the greatest affection. Finally, after a very small number of centurions had been punished, he ordered that those who had been exiled should be recalled.

The people of Antioch, who had sided with Cassius, he did not punish, but pardoned both them and the other communities that had helped Cassius, although at first he had been seriously angered with the Antiochenes and had deprived them of their shows and many other distinctions of the city, which he subsequently restored. To the sons of Avidius Cassius, Antoninus presented half their inheritance from their father, while he honoured the daughters with gold, silver and jewels. Indeed he allowed Alexandria, Cassius' daughter, and his son-in-law Dryantianus freedom of movement. They lived not as usurper's children but as members of the senatorial order in complete security, since he had prohibited the fortune of their own house from being cited against them even in a lawsuit. Some people who had been insulting towards them were convicted for damages. He did in fact entrust them to the husband of their aunt. If anyone wishes to know the whole of this story, let him read Marius Maximus' second book on the *Life* of Marcus, in which he tells the things which Marcus did when Verus was already dead.[12] For Cassius rebelled at that time, as a letter to Faustina proves, of which this is a copy:

12. The remainder of the *Life* seems to be fiction.

Verus wrote the truth to me about Avidius, that he wished to be emperor. For I suppose that you have heard what Verus' attendants reported about him. Come then to the Alban villa, so that we may deal with everything, if the gods are willing. Fear nothing.

From this, moreover, it appears that Faustina did not know about these matters, although Marius, wishing to defame her, says that Cassius had assumed the imperial position with her connivance. Indeed, a letter of hers to her husband survives, in which she urges Marcus to take heavy vengeance on him. A copy of Faustina's letter to Marcus:

I myself shall come directly to the Alban villa tomorrow, as you command. Yet I urge you now, if you love your children, to punish those rebels most severely. For both generals and soldiers, unless they are crushed, have a bad habit of crushing others.

Likewise another letter of the same Faustina to Marcus:

During the rebellion of Celsus my mother Faustina urged your father Pius to maintain loyalty first to his own people, and then to others. For an emperor is not loyal who does not consider his wife and children. Consider the age of our Commodus. Pompeianus our son-in-law is both too old and is a foreigner. Consider what to do about Avidius Cassius and his accomplices. Do not spare men who have not spared you and would not spare either me or our children if they won. I shall follow you on your journey presently; because our Fadilla was ill I could not come to the Formian villa. But if I cannot find you at Formiae, I shall follow to Capua, a city which can help both my illness and that of our children. I ask that you send the doctor Soteridas to the Formian villa – I do not in fact have any confidence in Pisitheus, who does not know how to cure an un-married girl. Calpurnius has given me a sealed letter. I shall reply to it, if I stay here, through Caecilius the old eunuch, a trustworthy person, as you know. And I shall entrust a verbal account to him of what the wife and children of Avidius Cassius are said to be repeating about you.

From these letters it can be seen that Faustina was not an accomplice of Cassius, but that she even earnestly demanded his punishment, since in fact she urged on Antoninus the necessity for vengeance, when he was taking no action, and contemplating more merciful measures.

The letter quoted below will give a complete account of what Antoninus wrote back to her:

You of course, my Faustina, are too anxious about your husband and our children. I re-read your letter, at the Formian villa, in which you urge me to take vengeance on Avidius' accomplices. However, I shall spare both his children and his son-in-law and wife, and shall write to the Senate that the confiscation should not be too severe nor the penalty too cruel. For there is nothing which better commends a Roman emperor to mankind than mercy. This is what made Caesar a god, this deified Augustus, this, in particular, honoured your father with the name of Pius. Indeed, if the verdict on the war had been in accordance with my sentiments, Avidius would not have been killed either. So keep calm:

'The gods protect me, the gods have my piety at heart.'[13]
I have appointed our Pompeianus consul for the coming year.[14]

Thus did Antoninus write to his wife.

It is relevant, further, to know what sort of address he sent to the Senate. An extract from the address of Marcus Antoninus:

You have, therefore, Conscript Fathers, in return for your congratulations on the victory, my son-in-law as consul; I mean Pompeianus, who is of an age that would long since have been rewarded with the consulship, had not brave men stood in the way, to whom it was right to give what was owed them by the republic. And now, as concerns Cassius' rebellion, I pray and beseech you, Conscript Fathers, that laying aside your stern judgement, you preserve my righteousness – and indeed your own – and mercy, and let the Senate not kill anyone. Let no senator be punished, let the blood of no nobleman be shed, let those who have been exiled return, let the proscribed recover their property. Would that I could summon back

13. Horace, *Odes*, 1.17.13f.
14. Ti. Claudius Pompeianus was actually consul (for the second time) in A.D. 173, two years before the rebellion of Cassius.

many even from the lower regions! For vengeance for personal affliction is never pleasing in an emperor; the juster it is the harsher it seems. Therefore you will grant pardon to the sons of Avidius Cassius and his son-in-law and wife. And why shall I say pardon? They have done nothing! Let them live free from anxiety therefore, knowing that they live under Marcus. Let them live in possession of their parents' property, on the share granted to each. Let them enjoy gold, silver, clothing, let them be rich, let them travel about freely and carry around before the eyes of peoples everywhere an example of my righteousness and of yours. Nor is this great mercifulness, Conscript Fathers, to grant pardon to the children and wives of the proscribed. I do indeed beg of you that you free the conspirators of the senatorial and equestrian orders from death, from proscription, from fear, from disgrace, from hatred, and in short from all harm, and that you grant this to my principate, that whoever, in the cause of the usurpation, has fallen in rebellion, may be esteemed even though he has been killed.

The Senate responded to this mercifulness on his part with these acclamations:

Righteous Antoninus, may the gods preserve you, merciful Antoninus may the gods preserve you! You have desired what was lawful, we have done what was fitting. For Commodus we ask imperial power. Strengthen your offspring! Make our children free from care! No violence harms good rule. For Commodus Antoninus we ask the tribunician power, we ask your presence. Praise to your philosophy, your patience, your principles, your nobility, your integrity! You conquer the foe, you overcome the enemy, the gods watch over you!

and so forth.

So the descendants of Avidius Cassius survived safely and were admitted to office. But Commodus Antoninus ordered that they should all be burnt alive, after his deified father's decease, as if they had been detected in conspiracy.

This is what we have learned about Avidius Cassius, whose own character, as we said above, was always changing, but was inclined more to severity and cruelty. If he had gained the imperial power, he would have been not only a merciful and good emperor, but a serviceable and excellent one. For a letter of his to his son-in-law survives, written when he was already emperor, which reads somewhat as follows:

Wretched is the republic which endures those men who are desirous of riches, and the rich. Wretched is Marcus, an excellent person to be sure, who, while he wishes to be called merciful, allows those men to live whose way of life he does not approve. Where is Lucius Cassius whose name we bear in vain? Where is that other Marcus, Cato and Censor? Where is all the discipline of our ancestors? It has of course long since perished, now indeed it is not even sought for. Marcus Antoninus philosophizes and investigates first principles and souls and what is honourable and just, and takes no thought for the republic. You see there is need for many swords, and many maxims, so that the form of the state may be restored to its ancient condition. Indeed, as far as those governors of provinces are concerned – am I to regard as proconsuls, am I to regard as governors, men who believe that provinces were given them by the Senate and by Antoninus so that they might be extravagant, so that they might become rich? You have heard that our philosopher's prefect of the guard was a beggar and a pauper three days before being made prefect, but suddenly became rich. How so, I ask, except from the vitals of the republic and the personal fortune of provincials? Let them be rich, to be sure, let them be wealthy – they will stuff the public treasury. Only let the gods favour the good side. Let the Cassians restore the principate to the republic.

This letter of his shows how severe and strict an emperor he would have been.

COMMODUS ANTONINUS*

BY AELIUS LAMPRIDIUS

CONCERNING Commodus Antoninus' parents there has been sufficient discussion in the *Life* of Marcus Antoninus. Now he himself was born at Lanuvium with his twin brother Antoninus on the day before the Kalends of September, his father and uncle being the consuls [31 August A.D. 161], in the place where his maternal grandfather is also said to have been born. Faustina, when pregnant with Commodus and his brother, dreamed that she was giving birth to snakes, one of which however was fiercer than the other. But when she had given birth to Commodus and to Antoninus, the latter, for whom the astrologers promised a horoscope equal to Commodus, was carried off at the age of four.[1] So when his brother was dead, Marcus tried to educate Commodus both by his own precepts and by those of great and excellent men. He had as teacher of Greek letters Onesicrates, and for Latin Capella Antistius; his oratory teacher was T. Aius Sanctus.[2] But teachers in so many disciplines profited him nothing. So great is the power either of innate qualities or of those kept as tutors at court. For straight from his earliest boyhood he was base, shameless, cruel, lecherous, defiled of mouth too and debauched, already adept at those arts which do not accord with

---

* For a brief sketch of the reign of Commodus, see Birley, *Severus*, pp. 97ff. It is impossible to annotate all the individuals mentioned in this *Life*.

1. Commodus' twin was T. Aurelius Fulvus Antoninus: see stemma, p. 320.

2. The MSS. give the name as Ateius Sanctus: the correct form is supplied by a recently published inscription.

the position of emperor, in that he could mould cups, dance, sing, whistle, even play the buffoon and the gladiator to perfection. He gave advance warning of his future cruelty in his twelfth year, at Centumcellae. For when he happened to have taken a bath in rather tepid water, he ordered the bath-keeper to be cast into the furnace. Whereupon a sheepskin was burned in the furnace by the slave-tutor to whom this order had been given, to make him believe from the smell of the fumes that the penalty had been paid.

He was called Caesar as a boy with his brother Verus,[3] and in the fourteenth year of his age he was enrolled in the college of priests. He was co-opted among the . . .[4] as Leader of the Youth (*princeps iuventutis*) when he assumed the toga. While still wearing the bordered tunic of a boy he gave largess and presided in Trajan's basilica. He was in fact robed in the toga on the Nones of July [7 July A.D. 175], the day on which Romulus disappeared from the earth, and at the time when Cassius revolted from Marcus. Having been commended to the soldiers he set out with his father for Syria and Egypt, and returned with him to Rome. After this, when exemption from the law of the appointed year had been granted, he was made consul, and with his father he was hailed *imperator* on the fifth day before the Kalends of December, when Pollio and Aper were the consuls [27 November A.D. 176], and he celebrated a triumph with his father. Then he accompanied his father to the German war.

Of those appointed to supervise his life he could not endure the more honourable, but retained all the most evil men and those that were dismissed he yearned for to the point of falling ill. When they were reinstated through his father's soft-heartedness, he always kept cookshops and low dives for them in the

3. In A.D.166, see p. 121 above. His younger brother, M. Annius Verus, died in A.D.169, see p. 129 above.
4. The MSS. are defective here.

palace, and never spared either decency or expense. He played at dice in his house. Women of particular beauty of appearance he gathered together like bought harlots, creating a brothel to make sport of their chastity. He purchased chariot-horses for himself and drove chariots in the dress of a charioteer. He conducted himself like a procurer's attendant, so that you would have believed him born rather for shameful things than for that station to which fortune had advanced him. His father's older ministers he dismissed, and aged friends he cast away. The son of Salvius Julianus, who was in command of armies, he vainly tempted to immodest conduct, and then plotted against Julianus. All the most honourable men he cast aside either by insult or by an unworthy office. He was named by actors as a defiled person and he exiled them so quickly that they did not appear again. The war, also, which his father had almost completed, he abandoned, having accepted the enemy's conditions, and then returned to Rome.

When he came back to Rome he celebrated a triumph,[5] with Saoterus his debaucher placed behind him in the chariot. In the course of the triumphal procession Commodus several times turned his head and kissed him, quite openly. He even did this in the orchestra. He would drink till dawn and squander the resources of the Roman empire. In the evening he even flitted through the taverns to the brothels. He sent to rule the provinces persons who were either his allies in crime or had been recommended by criminals. He became so hated by the Senate that he was filled with a savage passion to destroy that great order; and from having been despised, he became cruel.

Commodus' way of life compelled Quadratus[6] and Lucilla to initiate plans to murder him, with the advice of the prefect of

5. October A.D.180.
6. Ummidius Quadratus, adopted son of M. Aurelius' nephew: see stemma, p. 319.

the guard Tarrutienus Paternus.[7] But the business of carrying out the murder was given to Claudius Pompeianus,[8] a kinsman. He approached Commodus with drawn sword, when he had the chance of action, bursting out with these words: 'This dagger the Senate sends,' gave away what he was doing, the fool, and did not carry it out; and there were many who had a share in the business with him. After this, Pompeianus first, and Quadratus, then Norbana and Norbanus and Paralius were put to death; and the latter's mother and Lucilla were sent into exile.

Then the prefects of the guard, having seen that Commodus had become so detested on account of Saoterus, whose power the Roman people could not endure, had the man courteously led out of the palace on the pretext of a sacrifice, and murdered him, as he was returning to his own mansion, by means of commissary agents. But that was more offensive to Commodus than the plot against himself. At any rate, at the instigation of Tigidius,[9] by the expedient of giving the honour of the broad stripe,[10] he removed Paternus from the administration of the prefecture. Paternus not only appeared to be the instigator of this murder but had also, as far as could be seen, been involved in the attempt to kill Commodus himself – and had stood in the way of further punishment of the conspiracy. A few days afterwards he accused him of conspiracy, saying that the reason why the daughter of Paternus had been betrothed to the son of Julianus was so that the empire could be handed over to Julianus. Hence he put to death both Paternus and Julianus and

7. The correct form of the name is supplied by a recently published inscription.

8. The conspiracy took place in A.D.182. Pompeianus was nephew of Lucilla's second husband (*PIR*², C 975).

9. i.e. Sex. Tigidius Perennis, soon to be mentioned under the latter name.

10. i.e. by making him a senator and thus ineligible to be prefect of the guard.

Vitruvius Secundus, a very close intimate of Paternus, who had charge of the imperial correspondence. Besides this, the whole house of the Quintilii was wiped out, because Sextus the son of Condianus, by pretending death, was said to have escaped for the purpose of rebellion. Vitrasia Faustina[11] was also put to death, and Velius Rufus and Egnatius Capito, an ex-consul. The consuls Aemilius Juncus and Atilius Severus were also exiled, and savage treatment was meted out in various ways against many others.

After this, Commodus never readily appeared in public, and never permitted anything to be announced to him unless Perennis had previously dealt with it. Perennis in fact, knowing Commodus very well, discovered how to gain power for himself. He persuaded Commodus to free himself for a life of pleasure while he, Perennis, would devote himself to the administration; and this Commodus gladly accepted. Under this agreement, therefore, Commodus began a life of orgiastic abandonment in the palace, amid banquets and baths: he had three hundred concubines, whom he assembled together for the beauty of their person, recruiting both married women and whores, together with youths of ripe age, also three hundred in number, whom he had collected, with beauty as the criterion, equally from the commons and the nobility, by force and by payment.

In the meanwhile, in the dress of a victim-slayer, he slaughtered sacrificial victims, and he fought in the arena with foils and as a gladiator, among the chamberlains, with the swords' points uncovered. By this time, Perennis had arrogated everything to himself: he made away with anyone he wanted, robbed a great many, subverted all the laws, and put all the booty into his own purse. Commodus himself, indeed, killed his sister Lucilla after he had sent her to Capreae [Capri]. Then, having debauched his other sisters, as it is said, and being joined in

11. Daughter of M. Aurelius' cousin, see stemma, p. 319.

embraces with a cousin of his father,[12] he even gave one of the concubines the name of his mother. His wife, whom he had caught in adultery, he drove out, then banished her, and subsequently killed her. He used to order the concubines themselves to be debauched before his own eyes, and he was not free from the disgrace of submitting sexually to young men, being defiled in every part of his body, even his mouth, with both sexes.

At this time also Claudius, whose son had once approached Commodus with a dagger, was killed, ostensibly by brigands; and many other senators were made away with, without trial, and rich women as well. In the provinces not a few, having been falsely accused by Perennis on account of their riches, were robbed or even made away with. Those who could not be prosecuted even on a trumped-up charge were accused of being unwilling to name Commodus as their heir.

At that time Perennis gave his own son the credit for successes in Sarmatia won by other generals. Yet in spite of his great power, because he had dismissed senators and put men of equestrian status in command of the troops in the British war, when the matter was made known by the legates of the army this same Perennis was suddenly declared a public enemy and given to the soldiers to be lynched.[13] Commodus appointed Cleander, one of the chamberlains, to his position of power. Of course, after the execution of Perennis and his son Commodus rescinded many measures, as though they had not been carried out with his authority, on the pretext that he was restoring things back to normal. In fact, he could not keep up this repentance for his crimes for longer than thirty days – what he was to do through the agency of Cleander was more serious

12. Annia Fundania Faustina, mother of Vitrasia Faustina (p. 165 above).

13. The British war lasted from soon after Commodus' accession (A.D.180) until A.D.184. Perennis' death was in A.D.185.

than what he had done through the aforementioned Perennis. In influence at any rate, Cleander was the successor of Perennis, although Niger,[14] succeeded him in the prefecture – he is said to have been prefect of the guard for only six hours. In fact the prefects of the guard were changed hourly and daily: everything Commodus did was worse than what he had done before. Marcius Quartus was prefect for five days. The successors of these men were either retained in office or killed at the whim of Cleander, at whose nod even freedmen were enrolled into the Senate and among the patricians. Then, for the first time, there were twenty-five consuls in a single year.[15] All the provinces were sold – Cleander sold everything for cash. He rewarded with office men recalled from exile, and rescinded legal decisions. Through Commodus' stupidity he had such power that he brought the husband of Commodus' sister, Burrus[16] – who was denouncing and reporting to Commodus everything that was being done – under suspicion of an attempt on the throne, and killed him; and he made away with many others who tried to defend Burrus. Among these the prefect Aebutianus was also put to death. In his place Cleander himself, with two others whom he himself had chosen, was made prefect, and then for the first time there were three prefects of the guard – one of them a freedman, with the title 'Bearer of the Dagger'.

Eventually, however, Cleander's life too had a fitting end. When Arrius Antoninus[17] was killed on charges that were trumped up as a favour to Attalus, whom Arrius had convicted during his proconsulship of Asia, Commodus was unable to endure the ill-feeling that ensued at that time, for the populace

14. Hardly Pescennius Niger – the name was fairly common.

15. This was evidently A.D.190. Severus, the future emperor, was one of the twenty-five (p. 204 below).

16. *PIR*[2], A 757: L. Antistius Burrus (*cos. ord.* 181), husband of Commodus' youngest sister Vibia Aurelia Sabina: see stemma, p. 320.

17. *PIR*[2], A 1088: so far as is known this man was no relative of the imperial family, in spite of the names.

were in a fury. So Cleander was presented to the common people to pay the penalty. At the same time, Apolaustus and other court freedmen were put to death in like manner. Cleander, among other things, had debauched some of Commodus' concubines, on whom he begot sons. They were put to death after his removal, together with their mothers. Julianus[18] and Regillus were appointed to his post. Subsequently Commodus condemned them as well.

When these men had been killed, Commodus put to death Servilius Silanus and Duilius Silanus, with their families, then Antius Lupus and the Petronii, Mamertinus and Sura, Mamertinus' son Antoninus, Commodus' own sister's son,[19] and after them six ex-consuls at the same time, Allius Fuscus, Caelius Felix, Lucceius Torquatus, Larcius Eurupianus, Valerius Bassianus and Pactumeius Magnus, with their families; in Asia, Sulpicius Crassus the proconsul and Julius Proculus, with their families, and Claudius Lucanus an ex-consul; and in Achaia, his father's cousin Faustina Annia; and countless others. He had intended to kill another fourteen also, when the resources of the Roman empire could not sustain his expenditure.[20]

In the meantime, as an act of mockery on the part of the Senate, Commodus was named Pius after he had designated his mother's lover to the consulship, and Felix after he had killed Perennis – amidst a great many murders of many citizens, as if he were some new Sulla. This same Commodus, the 'Dutiful' (*pius*), the 'Fortunate' (*felix*), is said to have invented a plot against his own life as well, to justify the killing of a great many people. Yet there was no other rebellion apart from the one by Alexander, who subsequently took his own life, and those of

18. *PIR*², J 615: L. Julius Vehilius Gratus Julianus.

19. Cornificia, married to M. Petronius Sura Mamertinus (*cos. ord.* 182): see stemma, p. 320.

20. This statement seems to refer to his plans at the time just before his murder.

his family, and by Commodus' sister Lucilla. Commodus was named Britannicus[21] by flatterers, although the Britons even wanted to choose an emperor in opposition to him. He was called 'the Roman Hercules' too, because he had killed wild animals at Lanuvium in the amphitheatre; for it was his practice to kill wild beasts at home. Besides this, he was insane enough to want the city of Rome to be called the 'Commodian Colony': this crazy idea is said to have been instilled into him in the midst of Marcia's blandishments. He also wanted to drive four-horse chariots in the circus. He appeared in public in the Dalmatian tunic and in this garb gave the signal for starting the chariots. Indeed, at that time, when he proposed to the Senate his motion to make Rome *Commodiana*, not only did the Senate gladly accept this, in mockery as far as can be understood, but it even called itself 'Commodian', naming Commodus 'Hercules' and 'god'.

He pretended that he was going to go to Africa too, so that he could exact travelling expenses; and he did exact them and spent them on banquets and gambling instead. He put to death Motilenus, the prefect of the guard, by means of poisoned figs. He accepted statues in the dress of Hercules, and sacrifices were made to him as to a god. He had intended to put many others to death in addition, as was revealed by a little boy who tossed out of his bedroom a tablet on which were written the names of those who were to be killed.[22]

He practised the rites of Isis, even to the extent of shaving his head and carrying the figure of Anubis. He ordered the votaries of Bellona actually to cut off an arm, in his zeal for cruelty. The Isis worshippers, indeed, he forced to beat their breasts with pine-cones, to the point of death. When he was carrying the Anubis figure he used to strike the head of the Isis worshippers

21. A.D.184.
22. This story seems to derive from Herodian (1.17.1ff.), who may well have invented it.

hard with the face of the statue. Clad in woman's dress and a lionskin he struck with his club not only lions but many humans as well. Men who were lame in the feet and those who could not walk he dressed up like giants, in such a way that they were covered from their knees downwards with bandages and cloths, to look like serpents, and he dispatched them with arrows. He polluted the Mithraic rites with real murder, although the custom was merely for something to be said, or pretended, to create an impression of fear.

As a boy he was already both gluttonous and lewd. As a youth he disgraced every kind of person that was with him and was disgraced by all of them. Those who mocked him he cast to the wild beasts. One man who had read Tranquillus'[23] book containing the *Life* of Caligula he even ordered to be cast to the beasts, because his own birthday was the same as Caligula's. Of course, if anyone expressed a wish to die, he ordered him to be cast headlong, although reluctant. In his jokes, too, he was destructive. For example, he put a starling on the head of a man who, he had seen, had some hairs that were going white among the black ones, like worms; the bird thought it was chasing worms and made the man's head fester with the striking of its beak. He cut open a fat man in the middle of the stomach so that his innards suddenly poured out. He used to name men 'one-footed', or 'one-eyed' when he had removed one of their eyes or snapped off one of their feet. Besides this, he murdered many others in different places, some because they had met him when they were wearing barbarian dress, others because they were noble and rather handsome. He had among his minions men called after the private parts of either sex, and on them he used to bestow his kisses with particular pleasure. He had, too, a man whose penis projected further than does that of animals; he called him Onos and was very fond of him – he even enriched him, and appointed him to the priesthood of the

23. i.e. Suetonius.

Rural Hercules. He is said often to have mixed human excrement with the most expensive foods, and did not refrain from tasting it, making a fool of other people, as he thought. He displayed on a silver dish two misshapen hunchbacks covered with mustard; and straight away he gave them advancement and riches. He pushed into a swimming-pool his prefect of the guard Julianus, clad in a toga, in the presence of his staff; and he ordered him to dance – naked, as well – before his concubines, shaking cymbals and with his face contorted. It was seldom that he did not call for every kind of cooked vegetable for a banquet, to provide continuous luxury. He used to bathe seven or eight times a day and eat actually in the baths. He used to enter the temples of the gods polluted with adulteries and with human blood. He even posed as a surgeon, to the extent of letting blood, using scalpels that were deadly in their effect.

The months, too, flatterers renamed in his honour: Commodus instead of August, Hercules instead of September, Invictus instead of October, Exsuperatorius instead of November, and Amazonius, after his own surname, instead of December.[24] He was called Amazonius because of his passion for his concubine Marcia, whom he loved to have depicted as an Amazon, and for whose sake he even wished to enter the Roman arena in Amazon's dress. He also engaged in gladiatorial combat and accepted a gladiator's name, with pleasure, as if he were accepting triumphal honours. He always entered the public shows and as often as he did so, he ordered it to be inscribed in the public records. He is in fact said to have fought seven hundred and thirty-five times.

He was nominated a Caesar on the fourth day before the Ides of October (which he afterwards called Hercules), when Pudens and Pollio were the consuls [12 October A.D. 166]. He was called Germanicus on the Ides of 'Hercules' when Maximus and Orfitus were the consuls [15 October A.D. 172]. He was received into all the priestly colleges on the thirteenth day

24. According to Dio (72.15.3) all the months were renamed.

before the Kalends of 'Invictus', when Piso and Julianus were
the consuls [20 January A.D. 175]. He set out for Germany on
the fourteenth day before the Kalends of 'Aelius', as he afterwards called it, in the same year [19 May A.D. 175], and took the
toga of manhood when the same men were consuls. Together
with his father he was called *imperator* on the fifth day before
the Kalends of 'Exsuperatorius', when the consuls were Pollio
for the second time and Aper for the second time [28 November
A.D. 176]. He celebrated a triumph on the tenth day before the
Kalends of January when the same men were the consuls [23
December A.D. 176]. He set out on expedition a second time on
the third day before the Nones of 'Commodus', when Orfitus
and Rufus were the consuls [3 August A.D. 178]. He was presented to be maintained in perpetuity by the army and the Senate
in the Commodian Palace on the eleventh day before the
Kalends of 'Romanus', when Praesens was consul for the
second time [22 October A.D. 180]. When contemplating
departure on expedition for a third time he was dissuaded by
his Senate and people. Vows were taken for his sake on the
Nones of 'Pius', when Fuscianus was consul for the second
time [5 April A.D. 188]. In the meantime, it is recorded, he
fought three hundred and sixty-five times under his father and
further, he subsequently achieved so many gladiatorial crowns
by defeating or killing net-fighters that he reached a thousand.
Moreover, he killed with his own hand many thousands of wild
animals, even elephants. Frequently it was before the eyes of
the Roman people that he did these things.

For such things as these, to be sure, he was strong enough, but
otherwise he was weak and feeble, even having something
wrong with him in the groin, which stuck out so much that the
Roman people could detect the swelling through his silk
clothing. Many verses were written on this subject, and Marius
Maximus prides himself on recording them in his work. Such
was his strength in slaying wild animals that he transfixed an
elephant with a pole, pierced a wild goat's horn with a spear,

and dispatched many thousands of huge beasts, each with a single blow. Such was his lack of propriety that he very often drank in public, sitting in the amphitheatre or theatre, in women's clothing.

The Moors were conquered during his reign, but, since he himself lived in this way, it was by means of legates; the Dacians were conquered too, and the Pannonian provinces were set in order; while in Britain, Germany and Dacia the provincials rejected his rule. All these troubles were settled by generals. Commodus himself was tardy and careless in signing documents; he used to answer many petitions with a single formula, while in very many letters he used to write merely 'Farewell'. All business was carried out by others, and they are said to have used even condemnations for the benefit of their purses. In fact, through this carelessness, when the men who were administering the republic had been plundering the grain-supply, a tremendous famine arose at Rome,[25] although there was no shortage of crops. As for those who were plundering everything, Commodus subsequently killed and proscribed them. But he himself, pretending that there was a golden age, 'Commodian' by name, declared that prices were to be cheap, as a result of which he caused a greater shortage.

In his reign many persons obtained for cash both punishment for others and acquittal for themselves. He also sold alternative punishments and the right of burial and alleviation of wrongs; and he killed different people in place of others. Provinces and administrative posts he sold also, and in these instances the men through whose agency he made the sale received one share and Commodus the other. To some he even sold the murder of their enemies. In his reign the freedmen sold even the results of lawsuits. He did not long put up with Paternus and Perennis as prefects; even in the case of those prefects whom he had appointed himself, none of them completed three years' tenure, and many of them he put to death either with poison or the

25. A.D. 190.

sword. Prefects of the city he changed with the same readiness. He took pleasure in killing his chamberlains, even though he had always done everything at their behest. The chamberlain Eclectus, when he saw how readily Commodus put his chamberlains to death, forestalled him and took part in the conspiracy which caused his death.

Commodus would take up the weapons of a gladiator as a 'pursuer', covering his bare shoulders with a purple cloth. Besides this he had the practice of ordering that everything he did that was base, impure, cruel, gladiatorial or pimp-like, should be included in the *Records of the City* – as the writings of Marius Maximus bear witness. He called the people of Rome the 'Commodian people', since he had very often fought as a gladiator in their presence. But although the people had applauded him as if he were a god at his frequent bouts, in the belief that he was being mocked he had instructed the marines who spread the awnings to slaughter the Roman people in the amphitheatre. He had ordered the city to be burned, seeing that it was his own colony; and this would have been done if Laetus the prefect of the guard had not deterred him. At any rate, among his other triumphal titles he was called 'First stake of the Pursuers'[26] six hundred and twenty times.

There were the following prodigies in his reign of both a public and a private kind. A comet appeared. Footprints of gods were seen in the Forum, going out of it. And before the deserters' war the sky blazed. A sudden mist and darkness arose in the circus on the Kalends of January; and before dawn there had been fire-birds too and Furies. He himself moved from the palace to the Vectilian House on the Caelian Hill, saying that he could not sleep in the palace. The twin gates of Janus opened of their own accord, and the marble image of Anubis was seen to move. In the Minucian Portico a bronze statue of Hercules

26. The *palus* (stake) was the wooden pike with which gladiators practised. The leading gladiator was entitled *primus palus* by analogy with the title of the chief centurion in a legion, *primus pilus*.

sweated for several days. A horned owl was caught above his
bedroom, both at Rome and at Lanuvium. He himself moreover created a not insignificant omen: after thrusting his hand
into the wound of a gladiator who had been killed, he wiped
it on his head and, contrary to custom, ordered the spectators
to come to the show in cloaks, which was usual at funerals, instead of togas, while he presided in dark clothes. Further, his
helmet was twice carried out through the Gate of Libitina[27].
He gave largess to the people, seven hundred and twenty-five
denarii apiece. Towards everyone else he was very mean, because
he had been draining the treasury by his expenditure on luxury.
He held many circus races, but for pleasure rather than for
religion, and also in order to enrich the faction leaders.

Stirred up by these things, but all too late, Quintus Aemilius
Laetus the prefect and Marcia the concubine entered into a
conspiracy to kill him. First they gave him poison; and when
that was less than effective, they had him strangled by an athlete
with whom he used to train.

Physically, at least, he was well proportioned. His expression
was vacant as is usual with drunkards, and his speech disordered.
His hair was always dyed and made to shine with gold dust. He
used to singe his hair and beard from fear of the barber.

Senate and people demanded that his body be dragged with
the hook and thrown into the Tiber. But subsequently, by
order of Pertinax, it was transferred to Hadrian's tomb. No
public works of his still exist except the baths which Cleander
had built in his name. Where his name was inscribed on public
works of others, the Senate deleted it. Indeed, he did not even
complete his father's public works. He did organize the African
fleet, which was to be in reserve if the Alexandrian grain-supply
happened to fail. He even gave Carthage the name Alexandria
Commodiana Togata, after naming the African fleet Commodiana Herculea as well. He made certain embellishments to the

27. The goddess of funerals; the gate through which the bodies of
gladiators were carried was named after her.

Colossus, of course, all of which were subsequently removed. In fact he took off the head of the Colossus, which was that of Nero, and put his own on it, inscribing beneath it an inscription in the usual style, not even omitting those gladiatorial and effeminate titles. Yet Severus, a stern emperor and a man like his own name, from hatred of the Senate, as it seems, enrolled this man among the gods, with the grant of a Herculean-Commodian *flamen* (which Commodus had planned to have for himself while still alive). Three sisters survived him. Severus ordained that his birthday should be celebrated.

There were great acclamations by the Senate after Commodus' death. In fact, so that the Senate's verdict on Commodus may be known, I have included the acclamations verbatim, from Marius Maximus, and the content of the decree of the Senate:

From the enemy of the fatherland let the marks of honour be dragged away! Let the parricide's honours be dragged away! Let the parricide be dragged along! Let the enemy of the fatherland, the parricide, the gladiator, be mangled in the charnel-house! The executioner of the Senate is the enemy of the gods, the murderer of the Senate is the enemy of the gods! The gladiator to the charnel-house, he that killed the Senate, let him be put in the charnel-house! He that killed the Senate, let him be dragged with the hook, he that killed the innocent, let him be dragged with the hook! Enemy! Parricide! Truly! Truly! He that did not spare his own blood, let him be dragged with the hook! He that was about to kill you, let him be dragged with the hook! You were afraid with us, you were in danger with us. That we may be safe, Jupiter Best and Greatest, preserve Pertinax for us! Good fortune to the trustiness of the praetorians, good fortune to the loyalty of the Senate! Let the parricide be dragged along! We ask, Augustus, that the parricide be dragged along! This we ask, that the parricide be dragged along! Give heed, Caesar! Informers to the lion! Give heed, Caesar! Speratus to the lion! Good fortune to the victory of the Roman people, good fortune to the trustiness of the soldiers, good fortune to the trustiness of the praetorians, good fortune to the praetorian cohorts! The enemy's statues are everywhere, the parricide's statues are everywhere, the gladiator's statues are everywhere – let the statues of the gladiator and parricide be dragged away! Let the slayer of citizens be dragged along, let the murderer of citizens be dragged along! Let the statues of the gladiator be dragged away! While you are safe, we are safe and free from care, truly, truly, if truly then with honour, if truly then in freedom! Now we are free from care – let the informers tremble! That we may be free from care, let the informers tremble! That we may be safe, out with informers from the Senate, the club for informers! While you are safe, informers to the lion! With you as emperor, the club for informers! Let the remembrance of the parricide, the gladiator, be wiped out, let the statues of the parricide, the gladiator, be dragged down, let the remembrance of the foul gladiator be wiped out! The gladiator to the charnel-house! Give heed, Caesar! Let the executioner be dragged with the hook, let the executioner of the Senate be dragged with the hook, in the ancient fashion! More savage than Domitian, more foul than Nero, as he did to others, let it be done to him! Let the remembrance of the innocent be preserved, restore the honours of the innocent, we ask! Let the parricide's corpse be dragged with the hook, let the gladiator's corpse be dragged with the hook, let the gladiator's corpse be placed in the charnel-house! Call for the vote, call for the vote! We all vote that he be dragged with the hook! He that killed all, let him be dragged with the hook, he that killed persons of all ages, let him be dragged with the hook, he that killed both sexes, let him be dragged with the hook, he that did not spare his own blood, let him be dragged with the hook, he that plundered temples, let him be dragged with the hook, he that destroyed testaments, let him be dragged with the hook, he that plundered the living, let him be dragged with the hook! We have been slaves to slaves! He that exacted payment for a life, let him be dragged with the hook, he that exacted payment for a life and did not keep faith, let him be dragged with the hook, he that sold the Senate, let him be dragged with the hook, he that took sons from their inheritance, let him be dragged with the hook! Spies out of the Senate, informers out of the Senate, suborners of slaves out of the Senate! You too were afraid with us, you know everything, you know both good men and bad, you know everything, set everything to rights! We have been afraid for your sake! Happy are we with you emperor in truth! Put the question on the parricide, put the question, put it to the vote! We ask your presence! The innocent have not been buried – let the parricide's corpse be dragged along! The parricide dug up the buried – let the parricide's corpse be dragged along!

When, by Pertinax's order, Livius Larensis, procurator of the patrimony, had given Commodus' corpse to Fabius Cilo,[28] consul designate, it was buried during the night. The Senate cried out: 'On whose authority did you bury him? Let the buried murderer be dug up, let him be dragged along!' Cincius Severus said:

Wrongly was he buried. I speak as pontifex; the college of pontiffs says this. Since I have recounted glad tidings, now I turn to what is needful: I give it as my opinion that those things which that man, who lived only for the destruction of citizens and for his own shame, compelled to be decreed in his own honour, must be wiped out; that his statues, which are everywhere, should be destroyed; that his name be erased from all public and private monuments; and that the months be called by the names by which they were called when that evil first fell upon the republic.

28. Larensis is portrayed as the host in Athenaeus' *Deipnosophistae*. L. Fabius Cilo (*cos. II ord.* 204) was to be a prominent supporter of Severus (*PIR*², F 27).

PERTINAX*

BY JULIUS CAPITOLINUS

Publius Helvius Pertinax had a freedman father, Helvius Successus, who declared that he had given the name to his son on account of his unbroken connection with the wool trade,[1] because he had carried on that business pertinaciously. Pertinax was born[2] in the Apennines, at his mother's villa. At the hour when he was born a dark horse climbed onto the roof tiles, and after staying there for a short time fell down and expired. Moved by this event his father approached a Chaldaean, who predicted future greatness for the child, then said that he had lost his progeny. The boy was taught his elementary letters and arithmetic, and given over to a Greek grammar-teacher as well, and then to Sulpicius Apollinaris. After being taught by him, Pertinax in turn took up the profession of teaching grammar.

But since there was little profit in this, through the mediation of Lollianus Avitus,[3] a man of consular rank and his father's patron, he sought an appointment to command in the ranks.[4] Then, as prefect of a cohort,[5] he set out for Syria, Titus Aurelius[6]

* For a sketch of Pertinax's career, see Birley, *Severus*, pp. 106ff.

1. I read *lanariae* in preference to the MSS,' *lignariae*.

2. 1 August A.D.126.

3. *PIR²*, H 40.

4. i.e. a commission as a centurion. The implication is that he failed to obtain one.

5. The career as given here has been confirmed, as far as the first appointment in Dacia, by an inscription discovered at Brühl, near Cologne, published by H. G. Kolbe, *Bonner Jahrbücher*, 1962, pp. 407ff.

6. i.e. Antoninus Pius.

being emperor, and was compelled by the governor of Syria to make the journey to his command on foot, because he had used the posting service without official passes. Having been promoted for his hard work in the Parthian war, he was transferred to Britain, and was kept on there. After this he commanded a cavalry regiment in Moesia. Then he was procurator in charge of distributing the state child-welfare payments along the *Via Aemilia*. Next he commanded the German fleet. His mother followed him as far as Germany and died there, and her tomb is actually said to be still standing. From there he was transferred to Dacia at a salary of 200,000 sesterces, and having come under Marcus' suspicion through certain people's contriving, he was sacked; and subsequently, through Claudius Pompeianus, Marcus' son-in-law, he was appointed to command detachments, to be a kind of assistant to Pompeianus. In this post he won approval and was enrolled in the Senate. Subsequently, after a second success, the plot which had been concocted against him was revealed and the emperor Marcus, in order to compensate him for the wrong, gave him praetorian rank and placed him in command of the First legion. He then immediately liberated Raetia and Noricum from the enemy. For this outstanding assiduity he was designated to the consulship on the recommendation of Marcus. The speech is extant in Marius Maximus, containing a eulogy of him and everything that he had done and suffered; and, apart from that speech, which would be too lengthy to be included here, Marcus very frequently praised Pertinax, both at military assemblies and in the Senate, and publicly lamented that because Pertinax was a senator he could not be created prefect of the guard. When the Cassian disturbance had been settled, he set out from Syria to protect the bank of the Danube, and then received the command of both Moesias, and presently of Dacia. After successfully administering these provinces he obtained Syria.

Up to the Syrian command Pertinax preserved his honesty. After Marcus' death he became eager for money, and for this he was attacked in remarks from the people. He entered the Roman Senate House only after governing four consular provinces – because he had held the consulship in his absence[7] – already a rich man, although he had not seen it previously as a senator. Immediately thereafter he was ordered by Perennis to withdraw to Liguria, to his father's villa; for his father had kept a cloth-maker's shop in Liguria. After coming there he bought up a lot of land, and surrounded his father's shop – which remained in its original form – with countless buildings. He was there for three years and traded through his slaves. When Perennis had been killed, Commodus made amends to Pertinax and asked him by letter to set out for Britain. On his arrival, he deterred the soldiers from any mutiny, although they wanted to make some other man emperor, preferably Pertinax himself. At this time Pertinax incurred the reproach of spitefulness, because he is said to have insinuated to Commodus that Antistius Burrus and Arrius Antoninus were making an attempt on the empire. He did in fact suppress the mutinies against Commodus in Britain, but came into immense danger, being almost killed in a mutiny of a legion – at any rate, he was left among the dead. This affair, of course, Pertinax punished very severely. As a result of this he sought to be excused from his legateship, saying that the legions were hostile to him because of his maintenance of discipline.

When he had been given a successor, the supervision of the state child-welfare scheme was entrusted to him. Then he was made proconsul of Africa. In this proconsulship he is said to have endured many riots provoked by prophetic verses of the *canes*,[8] which issue from the temple of Caelestis. After this he was made prefect of the city. In this prefecture, as successor to Fuscianus, a severe person, Pertinax was very mild and humane,

7. A.D.175.

8. The MSS. may be defective here, but G. C. Picard interprets *canum* as a Latinized rendering of a Punic word for priests of the goddess Caelestis-Tanit: see *Revue de l' histoire des religions*, 1959, pp. 41ff.

and pleased Commodus himself a great deal, since when Commodus took his seventh consulship Pertinax was made consul for the second time [A.D. 192]. At this time, Pertinax did not shrink from a share in the plot to put Commodus to death, when it was offered him by others.

When Commodus had in fact been done to death, Laetus the prefect of the guard and Eclectus the chamberlain came to Pertinax to instil courage into him, and led him to the camp. There he addressed the soldiers, promised a donative, and said that the empire had been thrust on him by Laetus and Eclectus. Moreover, it was pretended that Commodus had expired from an illness, because the soldiers were afraid that their loyalty was being tested. Finally, Pertinax was hailed as emperor, by a few only at first. He actually became emperor on the day before the Kalends of January [31st December A.D. 192], being more than sixty years old.

He came to the Senate from the camp by night and ordered the hall of the Senate House to be opened, but when the door-keeper could not be found, he seated himself in the Temple of Concord. Then Claudius Pompeianus, Marcus' son-in-law, came to him and wept at the fate of Commodus, and Pertinax urged him to take the imperial power. But he refused, seeing Pertinax to be emperor already. Then straightaway all the magistrates, with the consul, came to the Senate House and, when Pertinax entered, hailed him as emperor. It was still night. Pertinax, for his part, after his praises had been spoken by the consuls, and after Commodus had been execrated in the Senate's outcries, rendered thanks to Laetus, the prefect of the guard, on whose initiative Commodus had been put to death and he himself had been made emperor. But when he had thanked Laetus, Falco[9] the consul said: 'We can tell what sort of emperor you are going to be from this – that we see behind you Laetus and Marcia, Commodus' agents in crime.' 'You are young, consul,' Pertinax replied, 'and do not know the

9. Q. Pompeius Sosius Falco.

necessity of obedience. They obeyed Commodus against their will, but as soon as they had the opportunity they showed what they had always wanted.'

On the same day that he was named Augustus, Flavia Titiana his wife was also named Augusta, at the very hour that he was fulfilling the vows on the Capitol. He was the first of all emperors to receive the title 'Father of the Fatherland' as well, on the same day that he was named Augustus. At the same time he also received proconsular power, likewise the right of making a fourth proposal in the Senate; and this was like an omen to Pertinax.

Then he set out for the palace, which was unoccupied, because Commodus had been killed in the Vectilian House. On the first day he gave the tribune who asked for it the watch-word 'Let us be soldiers', as if reproving the slackness of the previous reign. It was in fact the watchword that he had given in all his commands as general. But the soldiers did not tolerate the supposed reproof and at once took thought about changing the emperor. On that day also he invited the magistrates and the leading men to a banquet, a custom which Commodus had discontinued. At any rate, when the statues of Commodus were pulled down on the day after the Kalends [2 January A.D. 193], the soldiers groaned, for the emperor had given the same watchword a second time, and, moreover, military service under an old emperor was dreaded. Finally, on the third day before the Nones [3 January A.D. 193], at the actual vow-taking, the soldiers tried to lead Triarius Maternus Lascivius, a noble senator, into the camp, to place him at the head of the Roman state. But he fled, naked, and came to Pertinax in the palace, and afterwards left the city.

Induced by fear, then, Pertinax ratified everything that Commodus had granted to the soldiers and the veterans. He also said that he had received from the Senate the imperial power which he had already entered into on his own initiative. He totally abolished the treason court, binding himself by oath, and he recalled those who had been exiled on the charge of treason, while the good name of those who had been killed was restored. The Senate named his son Caesar, but Pertinax did not even accept the name Augusta for his wife, and as regards his son said: 'When he has earned it.' Since Commodus had added to the ranks of ex-praetors by countless special enrolments, Pertinax framed a senatorial decree and ordered that those who had not held the praetorship but had gained the rank by special enrolment should be junior to those who had actually been praetors. But from this he also stirred up abundant hatred against himself on the part of many. He ordered that property-ratings should be reassessed. He also ordered all informers to be severely punished, and yet with more leniency than previous emperors, ordaining a separate penalty for each rank if a member of it should commit this crime. Moreover, he brought in a law that previous wills should not be invalidated before the new ones were completed, to prevent the imperial treasury from ever succeeding to an inheritance for this reason. He declared that he personally would not accept from anyone a legacy which was left him either through flattery or because there was a complex lawsuit, which would deprive legitimate heirs and kinsmen. To the senatorial decree he added these words: 'It is better, Conscript Fathers, to keep the republic in poverty than to arrive at the pinnacle of riches through paths of peril and dishonour.' He paid out the donatives and largesses which Commodus had promised, and he provided most carefully for the grain-supply. But he was so short of cash in the treasury that he admitted he had not found more than a million sesterces in it, and hence he was forced to make certain exactions that Commodus had imposed, contrary to what he had promised. In the end, Lollianus Gentianus,[10] an ex-consul, who had attacked him for acting contrary to his promises, accepted the explanation that it was necessary.

10. *PIR²*, H 42: evidently the son of his father's patron Avitus (p. 179 above).

He held an auction of Commodus' possessions, even ordering
both the youths and the concubines to be sold, except for those
who appeared to have been introduced into the palace by force.
Many of those whom he ordered to be sold were subsequently
brought back to service and ministered to the old man's[11]
pleasures. Some of them even reached senatorial rank through
other *principes*. The buffoons that bore the disgrace of shameful
names he proscribed and sold. The immense sums he obtained
from this trafficking he gave to the soldiers as a donative. At any
rate, at the auction of Commodus' property the following items
were of particular interest: clothing of silk thread with gold
embroidery, in addition to tunics and cloaks, coats and long-
sleeved tunics in Dalmatian style, and fringed military cloaks,
and purple cloaks, Greek style, for use in camp. There were, too,
Bardaean hooded cloaks[12] and gladiators' mantles and weapons,
adorned with jewels and gold. He also sold both Herculean
swords and gladiatorial torcs, vases made of amber, gold, ivory,
silver and glass, phallus-shaped cups of the same material, and
Samnite pots for heating resin and pitch, for depilating people
and making their skin smooth. There were also carriages of a
new type of construction with intricate, separately mounted
wheels, and seats carefully designed at one moment to avoid the
sun and at another to catch the breeze, by turning around;
others that measured the distance travelled and showed the
time; and the remainder adapted for his vices. Besides this, he
restored to their masters those slaves that had gone to court
from private households. He reduced imperial banquets from
an unlimited state to a fixed standard; in fact he cut back on all
the expenditure of Commodus. Through the example of the

11. I prefer to retain the MSS.' reading *senem*, 'old man', rather than
amend to *Severum* with Hohl: the author is not wholly sympathetic to
Pertinax and the text makes good sense as it stands.

12. Evidently a type of cloak originating among the Bardaei, an
Illyrian tribe.

emperor, since he lived fairly economically, there resulted a general abstemiousness which brought about a reduction in prices; for by getting rid of non-essential items he reduced imperial expenditure to half the usual amount.

He established bounties for the soldiers; paid off the debt which he had contracted at the beginning of the reign; restored the treasury to its proper condition; set aside a fixed sum for public works; provided money for repairing the roads; made good arrears in pay which were owing to a great many persons; and, finally, made the fisc equal to sustaining all its tasks. Also, resisting his sense of shame, he cancelled the state child-welfare payments which were owing for nine years, in accordance with Trajan's ordinance.[13] As a private citizen he was not free from suspicion of avarice, since he extended his own boundaries at Vada Sabatia by foreclosing mortgages – in fact he was called a 'land-cormorant' (from the line of Lucilius).[14] Indeed, many have set it down in writing that even in the provinces which he governed as an ex-consul he conducted himself in a mean fashion, for he is said to have sold both exemptions from service and military appointments. Finally, although what he inherited from his parents was very little, and no legacies came his way, he suddenly became rich. He did at any rate restore to everyone their own possessions which Commodus had taken away – but not without payment.

He always attended regular Senate meetings and always made some proposal. And he always conducted himself like an ordinary citizen towards those who came to greet him or importuned him. He set free those who had been accused on false charges by slaves, the accusers being condemned and all

13. For the *alimenta* system see p. 47, n. 84 above. The meaning of this sentence is not completely clear. Magie (vol. 1, p. 333) renders it as follows: 'and with rigorous honesty he even assumed responsibility for nine years arrears of money for the poor which was owed through a statute of Trajan's.'

14. The well-known satirical poet of the second century B.C.

such slaves being crucified. He also rehabilitated the memory of some who were dead.

Falco planned a conspiracy against him . . . he complained in the Senate . . . wishing to be emperor. In fact, when this . . . believed . . . when a certain slave posing as the son of Fabia and Plautius Quintillus, from the family of Ceionius Commodus, had in an absurd fashion laid claim to the palace for himself . . . and having been recognized was sentenced to be beaten with the lash and restored to his master.[15] It was in the punishment given to this person that those who hated Pertinax are said to have found an opportunity for rebellion. However, he spared Falco and requested the Senate not to punish him. Indeed, Falco lived on in security with his own property, and when he died his son inherited. Nonetheless, many said that Falco did not know that a plan was afoot to make him emperor, and others that he had been attacked on trumped-up charges made by slaves who had falsified his accounts.

But a conspiracy was prepared against Pertinax by Laetus the prefect of the guard, and by those who had been displeased by Pertinax's virtuousness. Certainly Laetus had regretted making Pertinax emperor because Pertinax used to reprimand him for being foolish as a supplier of information on several matters. Besides this, it seemed harsh to the soldiers that in the case of Falco he had given orders for many soldiers to be executed on the testimony of one slave. And so three hundred soldiers formed a wedge and came to the imperial residence. On the same day, however, when Pertinax was sacrificing, it is said that no heart was found in the victim, and although he wanted to avert this omen, he found that the innards had no top to them. At this time in fact all the other soldiers stayed in the camp – they had come out of the camp to escort the *princeps*, and Pertinax, because of the omen from the sacrifice, had postponed for that day a visit he had planned to the Athenaeum, where he was to hear a poet. So the men who had come to escort him began to

15. The MSS. are defective here.

187

return to the camp. But suddenly the other group reached the palace, and neither could be kept out nor could they be announced to the emperor. In any case, there was such loathing of Pertinax among all the court personnel that they urged the soldiers on to do the deed. They caught up with Pertinax as he was inspecting the slave household of the court, and went into the palace porticoes as far as the place called Sicilia, and Jupiter's Dining-Room. When he learned this, Pertinax sent Laetus the prefect of the guard to them; but he avoided the soldiers, went through the porticoes with his head covered, and took himself home. Still, when they had burst into the interior, Pertinax came to meet them and calmed them with a long and serious speech. But then a certain Tausius, one of the Tungrians,[16] after inciting the soldiers to rage and fear by his words, hurled a spear at Pertinax's breast. Then, after a prayer to Jupiter the Avenger, Pertinax covered his head with his toga and was stabbed by the rest. Eclectus, at least, after stabbing two men, perished with him, whereas the other palace chamberlains – for he had given his own chamberlains to his emancipated children[17] as soon as he had become emperor – fled in all directions. Many of course say that the soldiers actually burst into his bedroom and killed Pertinax there, near his bed, as he tried to flee.

Pertinax was an old man, of an appearance that commanded respect, with long beard and hair brushed back. In figure he was rather stout and his stomach projected somewhat, but his stature was that of an emperor. As an orator he was mediocre. He possessed charm rather than kindliness, and he was never

16. The fact that this soldier was a Tungrian (from the area of Tongres in Belgium), from a people that did not normally supply recruits to the praetorians, suggests that he was in the *equites singulares*, or horse guards.

17. His son and daughter had had Pertinax's private property transferred to them and were thus freed from the paternal authority (*patria potestas*).

regarded as straightforward. While he was affable in conversation, in reality he was ungenerous and almost mean – to the extent of serving half-portions of lettuce and artichoke at banquets while a private citizen. Unless he had been sent something to eat, however many friends were present he used to serve nine pounds of meat in three courses. Moreover, if anything extra had been sent he would keep it over for the next day, although he always invited a great number of people to his banquets. Even as emperor, if he had no guests he used to dine in the same fashion. If he ever wanted to send friends something from his meal, he would send a couple of scraps or a piece of tripe, occasionally chicken legs. He never ate pheasant at his private banquets or sent them to anyone else. When he dined without guests he used to invite his wife and Valerianus, who had been a teacher with him, so that he might have literary conversation.

He did not in fact replace any of those that Commodus had placed in administrative posts; he was waiting until the anniversary of the city's foundation,[18] for he intended that that day should mark the commencement of state business. This is a further reason why Commodus' servants are said to have planned to murder him, in his bath. The position of emperor and everything imperial Pertinax abhorred to the extent of always showing that it was distasteful to him. In short, he did not wish to seem different from what he had been. In the Senate House he displayed very great respect, revering the Senate when it applauded him and joining in conversation with everyone as though he were still the prefect of the city. He even wished to lay down the empire and return to private life, and he was unwilling to have his children brought up in the palace. On the other hand, he was so thrifty and so eager for profit that as emperor he carried on trade at Vada Sabatia through his agents, just as he used to when a private citizen. Nevertheless he was

18. 21 April.

not greatly loved: all who talked freely together used to speak ill of Pertinax, calling him 'the smooth-tongued', a man who talks well and acts badly. Even his fellow-townsmen, who had flocked to him when he became emperor, and had gained nothing from him, used to call him this. He readily accepted presents too, in his lust for profit. A son and daughter survived him, and also his wife, the daughter of Flavius Sulpicianus, whom he had made prefect of the city in place of himself. About his wife's chastity he cared little, although she was openly in love with a lyre-player. He himself, besides, is said to have had a love affair with Cornificia,[19] in a most disgraceful fashion. He put very vigorous restraints on the court freedmen, and for this too he won great hatred.

The signs of his death were these. He himself, three days before he was killed, thought he saw in a swimming-pool a man with a sword attacking him. On the day he was killed they say that no pupils were visible in his eyes to those who looked at him, nor the reflections which they give. When he was sacrificing to the Lares, the living coals died, although usually they flare up. As was said above, the heart and upper part of the entrails were not found in the victims. Very bright stars, also, were seen next to the sun in the daytime, on the day before he died. He is said to have provided an omen himself about Julianus his successor. When Didius Julianus had presented his nephew, to whom he was betrothing his daughter, Pertinax exhorted the young man to show deference to his uncle and added: 'Honour my colleague and successor.' (Julianus had previously been his colleague in the consulship and had succeeded him in the proconsulship.)

The soldiers and court-retainers regarded him with hatred, but the people reacted to his death with great indignation, for they saw that all the ancient ways could be restored through him. The soldiers who had killed him carried his head, fixed on

19. One of Marcus Aurelius' daughters, now aged about 33. See p. 121, n. 40, and stemma, p. 320.

a pole, through the city to the camp. His remains were placed in the tomb of his wife's grandfather, when the head had been recovered. Julianus, his successor, buried the body with as much honour as he could, when he had found it in the palace. He never made any mention of Pertinax, either before the people or in the Senate. But when Julianus, too, had already been deserted by the soldiers, Pertinax was enrolled among the gods by the Senate and people. Moreover, under the emperor Severus, when Pertinax had received a fulsome tribute from the Senate, a funeral was provided for him, an honorific one of the kind reserved for censors, and he was honoured by Severus himself with a funeral oration. Furthermore, Severus himself, out of love for a good *princeps*, accepted the name of Pertinax from the Senate. The son of Pertinax was made *flamen* for his father. The Marcian *sodales*[20] who used to take charge of the rites of the Deified Marcus were called Helvian in honour of Helvius Pertinax. Circus-games were added, both for the anniversary of his accession – these were subsequently cancelled by Severus – and for his birthday, which still remain.

In conclusion, he was born on the Kalends of August when Verus and Ambibulus were the consuls [1 August A.D. 126], and he was murdered on the fifth day before the Kalends of April when Falco and Clarus were the consuls [28 March A.D. 193]. He lived sixty years, seven months and twenty-six days, and was emperor for two months and twenty-five days.[21] He gave the people largess of one hundred denarii each. To the praetorian guard he promised twelve thousand sesterces a man, but gave six thousand. What he promised to the armies was not given, because death forestalled him. Moreover, a letter which was appended to his *Life* by Marius Maximus shows that he shrank from being emperor. I did not wish to include it because of its excessive length.

20. See p. 87, n. 93, above.
21. An error: it should be sixty-six years, seven months and twenty-seven days; and the reign lasted two months and twenty-eight days.

DIDIUS JULIANUS*

BY AELIUS SPARTIANUS

DIDIUS JULIANUS, who gained the empire after Pertinax, had for great-grandfather Salvius Julianus, twice consul, prefect of the city and jurisconsult, a fact which increased his fame. His mother was Aemilia Clara, his father Petronius Didius Severus, his brothers Didius Proculus and Nummius Albinus, and his maternal uncle Salvius Julianus. His paternal grandfather came from Mediolanium [Milan] in the Insubrian territory and his maternal grandfather from the colony of Hadrumetum [Sousse].[1]

He was brought up in the household of Domitia Lucilla, mother of the emperor Marcus, and was selected for a post on the Board of Twenty (*vigintiviri*) with her support.[2] He was designated quaestor a year before attaining the legal minimum age, and he gained the aedileship with the support of Marcus, which he likewise received when becoming praetor. After the praetorship he commanded the legion XXII Primigenia in Germany and then governed Belgica, with probity and for a long term. In this post he resisted a sudden invasion by the Chauci, a German people who inhabited the valley of the

---

* For a brief account, see Birley, *Severus*, pp. 152ff. F. Kolb, *Literarische Beziehungen zwischen Cassius Dio, Herodian und der Historia Augusta* (1972), pp. 54ff., argues that much of this *Life* is based on excerpts from Dio and Herodian, deliberately distorted. I am not totally convinced and the biography seems to be mainly factual.

1. In Tunisia.

2. The career as supplied here is largely confirmed by an inscription from Rome: *ILS*, no. 412, cf. *PIR²*, D 77.

Alba,[3] using auxiliary troops which he levied in his province – for this action he was appointed to the consulship, on the emperor's recommendation; and he also defeated the Chatti. Then he received the governorship of Dalmatia and freed that province from enemies on its borders. Next he governed Lower Germany, and after that served as curator of the state child-welfare system in Italy. At this time he was accused by a marine named Severus of conspiring against Commodus, together with Salvius. But Didius was set free by Commodus; the emperor had already put many senators to death on charges of treason (men who were noble and powerful) and did not wish to deal too harshly with Didius – whose accuser was condemned. After his acquittal he was sent out to a provincial governorship again. Then he governed Bithynia, but not with the same good reputation as he had gained in other provinces. He was consul with Pertinax and was his successor in the proconsulship of Africa; Pertinax always called him his 'colleague and successor'. In particular, on the day when Julianus was betrothing his daughter to one of his own kinsmen, and had approached Pertinax and informed him of this, Pertinax said: 'And regard him with due respect, for he is my colleague and successor.' In fact, the death of Pertinax followed immediately after this.

After Pertinax's murder, at the moment when Sulpicianus was aiming to be named as emperor in the camp, Julianus, with his son-in-law, came to the Senate, having been informed that it had been summoned, but found the doors were closed. He came upon two tribunes there, Publicius Florianus and Vectius Aper, who began to urge him to seize the opportunity. While he was telling them that another man had already been hailed as emperor, they took hold of him and led him to the camp of the praetorian guard. When they reached the camp, Sulpicianus

3. Not the Elbe, as in Magie 1, p. 351, but the Aube, a tributary of the Seine.

the prefect of the city, father-in-law of Pertinax, was making a speech and claiming the empire for himself, and no one would allow entrance to Julianus, in spite of the enormous promises he made from outside the wall. First Julianus warned the praetorians not to make a man emperor who would avenge Pertinax, and then he wrote on tablets a statement that he would restore the good name of Commodus. As a result he was not only let in but was named emperor, the praetorians making the request that he should do no harm to Sulpicianus for having wanted to be emperor.

Then Julianus made Flavius Genialis and Tullius Crispinus prefects of the guard, on the recommendation of the praetorians, and he was attended by the imperial bodyguard through the agency of Maurentius, who had previously allied himself with Sulpicianus. Although he had promised the soldiers twenty-five thousand sesterces each, in fact he gave them thirty thousand. After holding a military assembly, in the evening he came to the Senate and entrusted himself to it completely. On the passing of a decree of the Senate, he was named emperor and acquired the tribunician power and proconsular *imperium*; and he was enrolled among the patrician families. In addition, his wife Manlia Scantilla and his daughter Didia Clara were named Augusta. Then he repaired to the palace, and his wife and daughter were summoned there. They moved into it nervously and unwillingly, as though they already foresaw imminent catastrophe. He made his son-in-law Cornelius Repentinus prefect of the city in place of Sulpicianus.

In the meantime Didius Julianus was held in loathing by the people, because it had been their belief that through the agency of Pertinax the abuses of the Commodan era were to have been reformed; and thus it was felt that Pertinax had been made away with at the prompting of Julianus. Those who had begun to hate Julianus were now the first to spread it abroad that on his very first day, despising Pertinax's dinner, he had prepared a luxurious banquet embellished with oysters and fattened birds and fish. This is agreed to have been untrue, for Julianus is said to have been so frugal that he shared out a sucking-pig over a three day period, likewise a hare, if anyone happened to send him one. Often, moreover, even if there was no religious reason, he dined happily on green vegetables and beans, without meat. Finally, he did not even dine until Pertinax had been buried, and he took food in a very sad state on account of his murder, and spent the whole of the first night awake, disturbed by such a fate.

But when it was first light, he admitted the Senate and equestrian order when they came to the palace, and spoke most affably to each member, according to his age, either as a brother or son or father. But the people, at the rostra and in front of the Senate House, began assailing him with violent abuse, hoping for the possibility that he might lay down the imperial power which the soldiers had given him. They cursed him as he was coming down with the soldiers and the Senate into the Senate House, and as he was making sacrifice they expressed the wish that he might not have favourable omens. They threw stones at him, too, while Julianus was all the time wanting to calm them by gestures. At any rate, when he entered the Senate House, he made an address calmly and with discretion. He gave thanks that he had been chosen and that both he himself and his wife and daughter had received the Augustan name. He also accepted the title of 'Father of the Fatherland'; a silver statue he rejected.

As he proceeded out of the Senate to the Capitol the people obstructed him, but by the sword, by wounds and by promises of gold pieces, the number of which Julianus himself, to inspire trust, kept showing them with his fingers, they were moved away and driven back. Then a move was made to the circus-show. But when all the seats had been taken indiscriminately, the people redoubled their insults against Julianus; they called on Pescennius Niger, who was said to be already emperor, to protect the city. All this Julianus bore calmly – and during his whole time as emperor he was extremely lenient. The people also violently accused the soldiers of killing Pertinax for money. Therefore, many things which Commodus had established and Pertinax had done away with Julianus restored, to win the people's favour. As concerns Pertinax himself, he did nothing, either bad or good; and this seemed disagreeable to many. It is in fact certain that it was through fear of the soldiers that he was silent about honouring Pertinax.

To be sure, Julianus was not in awe of either the British or the Illyrican armies, but he had given instructions for Niger to be killed, and a former chief centurion (*primipilaris*) was sent out for the purpose, as he feared the Syrian armies in particular. Accordingly, Pescennius Niger in Syria and Septimius Severus in Illyricum, together with the armies which they commanded, revolted from Julianus. But when it was announced to him that Severus, whom he had not suspected, had revolted, he was troubled; he came to the Senate and prevailed upon them to declare Severus a public enemy. For the soldiers, also, who had followed Severus, a day was set after which, if they were still with him, they would be regarded as public enemies. Furthermore, ex-consuls were sent to the soldiers by the Senate as envoys, to persuade them that Severus should be repudiated and that the man that the Senate had chosen should be the emperor. Among others Vespronius Candidus was appointed an envoy, an old ex-consul, long since hated by the soldiers on account of his strictness and meanness as a Commander. As successor to Severus, Valerius Catullinus was sent – as if a successor could be appointed for a man who already had the soldiers under his control! Besides this, Aquilius,[4] a centurion well known for murders of senators, was dispatched to kill Severus. Moreover, Julianus himself ordered the praetorian guard to be led out onto the parade-ground and towers to be fortified. But he led out soldiers who were idle and made slack by urban extravagance, and who were most reluctant for mili-

4. *PIR*², A 988: M. Aquilius Felix.

tary training, to the extent that they hired paid substitutes to do the work appointed for each one.

Severus meanwhile was approaching the city with a hostile column, but Didius Julianus accomplished nothing with his praetorian army, and every day the people both hated him and laughed at him the more. Julianus, expecting that Laetus would be a supporter of Severus, although it was through his help that he had escaped the grasp of Commodus, ordered him to be killed, ungrateful for such a great service. He ordered that Marcia be put to death at the same time as well.

But while Julianus was thus engaged, Severus seized the fleet at Ravenna, and the envoys of the Senate, who had promised their services to Julianus, crossed over to Severus. Tullius Crispinus, the prefect of the guard, having been sent against Severus to lead out the fleet, was driven back and returned to Rome. When Julianus learned what had happened, he asked the Senate that the Vestal Virgins and the other priests, together with the Senate, should go out to meet Severus' army and entreat them with outstretched fillets – a vain task for him to plan against barbarian soldiers. However, Plautius Quintillus[5] the ex-consul, an augur, spoke against Julianus as he urged these measures, declaring that the man who could not resist an adversary with arms ought not to be emperor; and many senators agreed with him. Didius, angered by this, called for soldiers from the camp who were either to compel the Senate to obedience or to slaughter it. But that plan was unacceptable. For it was not right that when the Senate had adjudged Severus a public enemy for the sake of Julianus, it should have to put up with the same Julianus as its foe. So he came to the Senate with a better plan, and asked that a senatorial decree be passed regarding a division of the empire; and this was done at once.

Then an omen which Julianus had created for himself when

5. M. Peducaeus Plautius Quintillus (cos. ord. 177), son of L. Verus' sister Ceionia Fabia and husband of M. Aurelius' daughter Fadilla, and hence a person of immensely great authority: see stemma, p. 320.

he accepted the imperial position came to everyone's mind. When the consul designate, giving his vote on him, had spoken thus: 'I vote that Didius Julianus be named emperor', Julianus put in the words: 'Add "Severus" too' – this surname of his grandfather and great-grandfather Julianus had added to his own. There are, however, those who say that there was never any plan by Julianus to slaughter the Senate, because the Senate had passed such great decrees for him. After the decree of the Senate, Didius Julianus at once dispatched one of the prefects, Tullius Crispinus. He himself, moreover, created a third prefect, Veturius Macrinus, to whom Severus had sent a letter appointing him as prefect. But the people for its part openly declared, and Severus suspected, that the peace was a pretence, and that the mandate of Tullius Crispinus, the prefect of the guard, was the murder of Severus. In the end, Severus preferred, in accordance with the soldiers' wishes, to be Julianus' enemy rather than his colleague. Moreover Severus immediately wrote to a great many persons at Rome and secretly dispatched edicts which were posted up.

Julianus also had the insane idea of performing a great many acts through magicians, by means of which he thought either that the people's hatred might be alleviated, or the arms of the soldiers might be restrained. For they both immolated certain victims not in accordance with Roman rites, and they chanted impious incantations, and Julianus performed those rites which they think are done at a mirror, at which boys are said to gaze with their eyes bandaged after their heads have been consecrated with spells. One boy is said at this time to have seen both the arrival of Severus and the departure of Julianus.

As for Tullius Crispinus, when he had actually met Severus' vanguard he was put to death by Severus on the instigation of Julius Laetus.[6] Moreover, the decrees of the Senate were torn

---

6. Not to be confused with Commodus' prefect Q. Aemilius Laetus (pp. 174f, 182f, etc. above).

down, and when Julianus summoned the Senate and sought opinions he learned nothing definite from it. But afterwards, of his own accord, he ordered that the gladiators at Capua should be armed by Lollianus Titianus[7]; and he summoned Claudius Pompeianus from his villa at Tarracina to be his colleague in the empire, because he had been son-in-law of an emperor and had for a long time commanded soldiers. But Pompeianus refused this, replying that he was an old man and that his eyes were weak. The soldiers from Umbria had also crossed over to Severus, and Severus had in fact sent ahead a letter in which he ordered that the murderers of Pertinax should be kept in custody. In a short time, indeed, Julianus was deserted by everyone, and remained in the palace with one of his prefects and his son-in-law Repentinus. Finally, it was proposed that Julianus' imperial power should be revoked; and revoked it was, and Severus was at once named emperor, while it was pretended that Julianus had taken his own life by poison. Nevertheless, some people were sent from the Senate, by whose efforts he was killed in the palace by a common soldier, imploring the protection of Caesar, that is, of Severus. He had emancipated his daughter when he gained the empire, and she had been given her inheritance; and this was at once taken from her, as well as the name Augusta. His body was given back by Severus to his wife Manlia Scantilla and his daughter, and was moved to the tomb of his great-grandfather at the fifth milestone on the *Via Labicana*.

These charges, certainly, were brought against Julianus: that he had been a glutton and a gambler; that he had trained with gladiatorial weapons; and that he had done all these things as an old man, whereas previously in his youth he had never been disgraced by these vices. The charge of pride was also levelled at him, although he had been very humble even as emperor – moreover he was, on the contrary, very polite at banquets, very

7. Unknown, but perhaps to be identified with Lollianus Gentianus (p. 184 above); otherwise a kinsman.

liberal with signing petitions, and very reasonable over cases of personal freedom. He lived for fifty-six years and four months and reigned for two months and five days.[8] It was held against him in particular that those whom he ought to have controlled with his own authority he himself had made into officials to control the republic for him.

8. He was born either 30 January A.D.133 or 2 February 137 (Dio, 73.17.5 gives differing figures) and was killed on 1 June 193.

SEVERUS*

BY AELIUS SPARTIANUS

A FTER the murder of Didius Julianus, Severus, a native of
Africa, gained the empire. His home town was Lepti-
magna,[1] his father was Geta and his ancestors had been Roman
knights before citizenship had been given to all.[2] His mother was
Fulvia Pia, his uncles were Aper and Severus,[3] ex-consuls, his
paternal grandfather was Macer[4] and his maternal grandfather
was Fulvius Pius. He himself was born on the third day before
the Ides of April, when Erucius Clarus, for the second time, and
Severus were the consuls [11 April A.D. 146].[5] In his earliest
boyhood, before he became steeped in Latin and Greek literature, in which he was highly educated, the only game he played
with other boys was 'Judges'. In this game the *fasces* and axes
would be carried before him and, with a council of boys standing around him, he would sit and give judgement. In his eighteenth year he gave a formal speech in public, after which he

* For further details, see Birley, *Severus*.

1. This is the late Roman name: the normal earlier form is Lepcis
Magna.

2. i.e. to all the people of Lepcis: this took place under Trajan when
the town was given the status of *colonia* (Birley, *Severus*, pp. 42f.).

3. P. Septimius Aper (*cos.* 153) and C. Septimius Severus (*cos.* 160?).
They were cousins of his father, rather than uncles, see stemma, p. 322.

4. An error: the emperor's grandfather had the same names as himself, Lucius Septimius Severus (Birley, *Severus*, pp. 35ff.). Macer may
have been a more remote ancestor.

5. Dio (76.17.4) gives figures which make A.D.145 the year and J.
Guey, *Bulletin de la société nationale des antiquaires de France*, 1956, p. 33,
has shown that this should be preferred.

came to Rome to pursue his studies, and applied for and received the broad stripe from the deified Marcus, with the backing of his kinsman Septimius Severus, who had already been consul twice.[6]

On his arrival at Rome he chanced upon an innkeeper who was reading the *Life* of the emperor Hadrian at that very time. This he seized upon as an omen of future good fortune. He also had another omen that he was to be emperor. When invited to an imperial banquet he had come wearing a Greek mantle instead of the toga he should have worn, and he was given the emperor's own official toga to put on. The same night he dreamed he was sucking the teats of a she-wolf, like Remus or Romulus. Further, he sat in the imperial chair, which had been put in the wrong place by an attendant, being unaware that it was not permitted. Another time, when he was sleeping in a tavern, a snake wound itself round his head, and when his friends were alarmed and shouted out, the creature went away without harming him.

He did a lot of wild things in his youth, not all of them innocent. He was sued for adultery and spoke in his own defence, being acquitted by the proconsul Julianus.[7] (He succeeded Julianus in the proconsulship, was his colleague in the consulship and also succeeded him as emperor.)[8] His quaestorship he held with diligence, having omitted the military tribunate. After his quaestorship he received Baetica by lot and then set out for Africa to settle affairs at home, as his father had died. But while he was in Africa he was assigned to Sardinia

6. C. Septimius Severus was probably consul in A.D.160, but it is unlikely that he ever received a second consulship, let alone by this date (*c.* A.D.162). The text may be wrong here.

7. The jurist P. Salvius Julianus (*cos. ord* 148) was proconsul of Africa A.D.168–9.

8. A confusion, no doubt caused by the story about Pertinax and Didius Julianus (pp. 190, 193 above). Didius Julianus was evidently on the staff of his kinsman Salvius (see note 7), which probably aided the confusion.

instead of Baetica, because the Moors were ravaging Baetica.[9]
After completing his Sardinian quaestorship, then, he took the
post of legate to the proconsul of Africa.[10] During this legateship, when he was walking along preceded by the *fasces*, one of
his fellow-townsmen, a man of Lepcis and a plebeian, embraced
him as an old comrade. Severus gave the man a beating with
cudgels, while his herald proclaimed: 'Let no plebeian embrace
a legate of the Roman people with impunity.' The result of this
incident was that legates too rode in a carriage, whereas
previously they used to go on foot.

At that time, in a certain African town, he had anxiously
consulted an astrologer. When his horoscope had been cast, he
saw a tremendous future ahead of him, and the astrologer said
to him: 'Give me your own horoscope not another man's.'
Severus swore that it was his, and the man foretold everything
that afterwards came to pass. He gained the tribunate of the
plebs on the recommendation of the emperor Marcus, and
carried it out with great strictness and energy. At that time he
married Marciana,[11] about whom he was silent in his own account of his life as a private citizen. Subsequently, during his
reign, he set up statues to her. He was designated praetor by
Marcus, not as a candidate of the emperor but as one of a crowd
of competitors, in his thirty-second year. Then, after he had
been sent to Spain, he dreamed first that he was told to restore
the temple of Augustus at Tarraco, which was by then in a state
of decay. After this he dreamed that from the peak of a very
high mountain he was looking down on the whole world, and
on Rome, and the provinces were singing together to the
accompaniment of the lyre or flute. After his departure for

9. A.D.171 (cf. p. 129 above).

10. This is now confirmed by a recently discovered inscription from
Lepcis showing Severus as legate to the proconsul in A.D.174 – and the
proconsul was his kinsman C. Septimius Severus.

11. Paccia Marciana, evidently a native of Lepcis: see stemma, p. 322.

Spain he put on public games *in absentia*. Then he was placed in command of the legion IV Scythica, near Massias.[12] After this post he made for Athens, both to pursue his studies and for religious reasons, and in order to see the public buildings and antiquities. While there, he was offended in various ways by the Athenians, as a result of which he became hostile to them and took his revenge, after becoming emperor, by reducing their privileges. Next he was appointed legate of Lugdunensis. When he wished to marry a second time, after losing his wife, he investigated the horoscopes of potential brides, being very skilled in astrology himself, and since he had heard that there was a certain woman in Syria whose horoscope forecast that she would marry a king, he sought her hand. It was of course Julia, and he gained her as his bride through the mediation of friends. She at once made him a father.[13] He was loved as no other by the Gauls for his strictness, honourable conduct and restraint. Next he ruled the Pannonias with proconsular power.[14] After this he gained the proconsular province of Sicily in the lot; and he was given another son, at Rome.[15]

In Sicily he was placed on trial on a charge of consulting soothsayers or astrologers about the imperial position. The prefects of the guard who were assigned to hear his case acquitted him – Commodus was already becoming hated – and the false accuser was crucified. He held his first consulship with Apuleius Rufinus, as one of a very large number that Commodus designated.[16] After this consulship he was without official

12. The MSS. have *Massiliam* = Marseille, but the legion was based in Syria, and R. Thomsen's emendation *Massiam* (a place in Syria) is to be preferred.

13. With a son, Bassianus, i.e. Caracalla, born 4 April, A.D.188.

14. An error: he became governor of *Upper* Pannonia (not both Pannonias) after his consulship.

15. Geta, born in A.D.189, probably on 7 March.

16. A.D.190, the year when there were twenty-five consuls (p. 167 above).

duties for about a year and then, on the recommendation of Laetus, he was put in command of the German army.[17] On his departure to the German armies he purchased spacious pleasure-grounds, whereas previously he had owned only a very small house at Rome and one farm in the territory of Veii.[18] He was eating a modest dinner lying on the ground in these gardens, with his sons, and his elder son, then aged five, was dividing out with a rather lavish hand among his childish playmates the fruit that was placed nearby; his father said, reproving him: 'Share it out more sparingly, for you do not possess royal wealth,' and the boy replied: 'But I will possess it.' After his departure to Germany he conducted himself in such a way in his governorship as to increase his reputation, which had already become noteworthy.

Up to this point his military activity was as a private citizen. But then, after it had been learned that Commodus had been murdered and, moreover, that Julianus held the empire amid universal hatred, he was proclaimed emperor by the German legions at Carnuntum, on the Ides of August,[19] although he did put up some resistance to the many who urged him on. He gave the soldiers . . .[20] sesterces each. Then, after strengthening the provinces which he was leaving in his rear, he marched on Rome. All yielded to him wherever he went, while the armies of Illyricum and Gaul, under the pressure of their generals, had already sworn allegiance to him – for he was received by every-one as the avenger of Pertinax. At the same time, on the instiga-tion of Julianus, Septimius Severus was declared a public

17. An error: it was the army of Upper Pannonia.

18. I follow M. Hammond's emendation of the text to *Veientem*: his grandfather had had property at Veii, near Rome.

19. An error: the actual date is now known to have been 9 April (from the evidence of the *Feriale Duranum*), so even the emendation *Idibus Aprilibus* is unsatisfactory; and the legions were of course those of Pannonia, not the German provinces.

20. The MSS. are defective here.

enemy, and envoys were sent to the army who were to order
the soldiers to desert him, on the instructions of the Senate. At
first, when Severus heard that the envoys had been sent by
authority of a senatorial decree, he was very frightened. Afterwards, by bribing the envoys, he ensured that they spoke in his
favour before the army and crossed to his side. Having learned
this, Julianus caused a decree of the Senate to be passed regarding
his sharing of the empire with Severus. It is uncertain whether
or not he did this as a trick, since he had already, before this,
dispatched certain men, well known for their assassinations of
generals, who were to kill Severus. Similarly he had sent men to
assassinate Pescennius Niger, who had also assumed the position
of emperor in opposition to him, on the instigation of the
Syrian armies. But Severus escaped the hands of those that
Julianus had sent to murder him and sent a letter to the praetorian guard, giving them the signal either to desert Julianus or to
kill him. He was obeyed at once; Julianus was killed in the
palace and Severus was invited to Rome. Thus Severus became
the victor merely at will – something that had never happened
to anyone – and hastened to Rome under arms.

After Julianus had been killed, Severus still remained in camp
and under canvas, as if moving through enemy territory, and
the Senate sent a deputation to him of a hundred senators, to
congratulate him and to beg his favour. They met him at
Interamna [Terni], and after their clothes had been shaken in
case they were carrying any weapons, they greeted him, armed
as he was, with armed men standing around. On the following
day, when all the palace household had presented itself, he gave
the members of the senatorial deputation seven hundred and
twenty gold pieces each, and sent them ahead of him, having
given any who wished the opportunity of remaining and
returning to Rome with him. He also appointed as prefect of
the guard Flavius Juvenalis, whom Julianus had taken as his
own third prefect.

Meanwhile at Rome there was immense trepidation among

soldiers and civilians, for they knew that Severus, in arms, was now coming against them – and they had declared him a public enemy. Added to this, Severus learned that Pescennius Niger had been proclaimed emperor by the Syrian legions, but he intercepted Niger's edicts and letters to the people and the Senate, through the messengers, to prevent them from being put before the people or read in the Senate House. At the same time he also thought of making Clodius Albinus his deputy, to whom the power of a Caesar had already been decreed by Commodus.[21] But being very nervous of these same men, about whom his opinion was correct, he sent Heraclitus to take control of the British provinces and Plautianus[22] to seize Niger's children. When Severus reached Rome, he ordered the guard to meet him unarmed, clad only in the clothes that are worn under the armour. He summoned them thus to his tribunal, with armed men placed around on all sides.

Then, entering Rome under arms, with armed soldiers, he ascended the Capitol. From there, in the same attire, he proceeded to the Palatine, with the standards which he had taken from the guard carried before him, held downwards not on high. Then, all over the city, soldiers took up their station, in the temples, in the porticoes and in the palace, treating them as their quarters; and the entry of Severus aroused hatred and terror, for the soldiers snatched goods without payment, threatening to plunder the city. On the next day, tightly surrounded by armed men – not only soldiers but his friends as well – he came to the Senate. In the Senate House he rendered an explanation of his assumption of the imperial position and gave it as his pretext that Julianus had sent men known for their assassinations of generals to murder him. He also compelled the

21. The second half of this sentence is a piece of fiction which is given elaborate treatment in the *Clodius Albinus*, pp. 241f, 248f below.

22. C. Fulvius Plautianus, a kinsman of Severus, soon to become prefect of the guard and then father-in-law of Caracalla: see stemma, p. 322.

passage of a senatorial decree that it should not be lawful for the emperor to kill a senator without the consent of the Senate. But while he was in the Senate, the soldiers, in a state of mutiny, demanded ten thousand sesterces a man, on the precedent of those who had conducted Octavianus Augustus[23] to Rome and had received such a great sum. Severus wanted to restrain them and was unable to, but he sent them away mollified by an additional bounty.

He then held a state funeral, with an effigy of Pertinax, and consecrated him as one of the deified emperors, adding a Helvian *flamen* and *sodales*, who had previously been Marcian. He also ordered that he himself should take the name of Pertinax, although later he wanted that name to be abolished as if it were an omen. Then he paid off his friends' debts. He gave his daughters, with dowries, in marriage to Probus and Aëtius. He offered his son-in-law Probus the prefecture of the city, but he refused, saying that to be prefect seemed a lesser thing than to be the emperor's son-in-law. Moreover he straightaway made each of his sons-in-law consul, and each of them he enriched.[24] On the next day he came to the Senate, and after making accusations against them, proscribed and executed the friends of Julianus. He heard a great many lawsuits, and punished severely magistrates who had been accused by provincials, when the charges against them were proved. He took such care over the grain-supply, which he had found to be very low, that when he died he was to leave the Roman people a surplus amounting to seven years' tribute.

He left Rome to settle the eastern situation, saying nothing publicly about Niger as yet. However, he sent legions to Africa to prevent Niger from moving through Egypt and

23. 43 B.C.
24. This seems to be fiction: there is no other evidence for his having had any daughters, and the names of the alleged sons-in-law evoke the fourth century.

Libya[25] to occupy it, and causing hardship to the Roman people
by cutting off the grain-supply. He left Domitius Dexter as
prefect of the city in place of Bassus, and departed within thirty
days of his arrival at Rome. Having moved out from the city to
Saxa Rubra he had to endure a serious outbreak of mutiny on
the part of the army, on account of the place chosen for pitch-
ing camp. His brother Geta came to meet him at once, and was
instructed to govern the province entrusted to him,[26] although
he was hoping for something else. The children of Niger, who
were brought to him, he treated with the same respect as his
own. He had indeed sent ahead a legion to take possession of
Greece and Thrace, to prevent Pescennius from occupying
them; but Niger was already holding Byzantium and, wishing
to seize Perinthus as well, killed a great many men from this
force. He was therefore declared a public enemy, together with
Aemilianus.[27] Niger invited Severus to share the empire, but he
was treated with contempt. Severus did, to be sure, promise him
a safe exile, if he wanted it, but he did not pardon Aemilianus.
Then Aemilianus was defeated in the Hellespont by the generals
of Severus, and fled first to Cyzicus and then to another city,
where he was killed on their orders. Niger's own forces were
also put to flight by the same generals. When he had heard
these things, Severus sent a letter to the Senate, as if everything
had been dealt with. Then he fought with Niger and killed
him at Cyzicus,[28] and carried his head round on a spear. After
this he sent Niger's children, whom he had treated on an equal
basis to his own, into exile with their mother. He sent a letter to

25. i.e. Cyrenaica.

26. P. Septimius Geta is known to have been governing Dacia in A.D.
195 and, prior to that, Lower Moesia.

27. Asellius Aemilianus, proconsul of Asia A.D.192–3, Niger's predecessor as governor of Syria, and his principal lieutenant: *PIR*[2], A 1211.

28. An error, also found in Victor, *de Caes.*, 20.8 and Eutropius
8.18.4: Niger was actually defeated at Issus.

the Senate concerning the victory and he did not inflict punishment on any of the senators who had belonged to Niger's party, except for one.

He was more angry with the people of Antioch, for two reasons: they had made fun of him when he was serving in the east and they had helped Niger even when he had been defeated. Eventually he took away many of their privileges from them. He also deprived the people of Neapolis [Nablus] in Palestine of their citizenship, because they were in arms on behalf of Niger for a long time. He took savage reprisals against many who had followed Niger, other than members of the senatorial order. He inflicted penalties and indemnities on many cities of the same party too. He put to death those senators who had served in Niger's army with the rank of general or tribune. Then he undertook a great deal in the region of Arabia, bringing the Parthians back under Roman authority, and the Adiabenians too, all of whom, indeed, had taken the side of Pescennius. On account of this, when he returned, a triumph was offered him, and he was named Arabicus Adiabenicus Parthicus. But he rejected the triumph, so as not to seem to be triumphing for a victory in civil war. He also declined the name of Parthicus, so as not to provoke the Parthians. While he was actually on his way back to Rome, after the civil war with Niger, another civil war, with Clodius Albinus who rebelled in Gaul, was announced to him. For this reason his sons were later put to death, together with their mother. He therefore at once declared Albinus a public enemy, together with those who had written to Albinus, or had replied to his letters, in favourable terms. At Viminacium, on his march against Albinus, he nominated his elder son Bassianus,[29] who had been given the name Aurelius Antoninus, as Caesar. This was in order to destroy the hopes which Severus' brother Geta had conceived of gaining the imperial position. The reason why he gave his son the

29. i.e. Caracalla.

name Antoninus was that he had dreamed that an Antoninus would succeed him. Hence some think that Geta [his younger son] was also called Antoninus, so that he too might succeed him as emperor.[30] Some think that Bassianus was called Antoninus because Severus himself wanted to pass over into the family of Marcus.[31]

At first, indeed, the generals of Severus were defeated by those of Albinus. Severus, in his anxiety, then consulted Pannonian augurs, from whom he learned that he would be the victor, but that his adversary would neither fall into his power nor escape, but would perish beside the water. Many friends of Albinus at once deserted and came to Severus, and many of Albinus' generals were captured, and punished by Severus. Meanwhile, after many varying encounters, Severus fought against Albinus successfully in Gaul for the first time at Tinurtium. It was then that he came into extreme peril by a fall from his horse; he was believed to have died from a lead ball, and the army was on the point of choosing another man as emperor.[32] At that time, Severus read in the senatorial minutes a motion congratulating Clodius Celsinus, a Hadrumetine and a kinsman of Albinus.[33] Severus was enraged with the Senate, as though it had recognized Albinus by this act. He therefore decreed that Commodus should be enrolled among the deified emperors, as though in this way he would be able to revenge himself on the Senate. He proclaimed the deification of Commodus before the soldiers first, and then announced the fact in a letter to the Senate, with the addition of a victory speech. Next, he ordered that the bodies of the senators who had been killed

30. False: see p. 18.

31. Severus named himself 'son of the deified Marcus' in A.D.195.

32. The final battle of the civil war, at Lugdunum, is not named here directly although the author knew about it (see *Clodius Albinus*, 12.3, p. 246 below). The omission illustrates the haste and carelessness of the author.

33. This statement is somewhat suspect.

in the war should be torn limb from limb. Then he ordered that
the head of Albinus, whose body had been brought to him half
alive, should be cut off and sent to Rome, and he accompanied
it with a letter. Albinus was defeated on the eleventh day before
the Kalends of March [19 February A.D. 197]. Moreover,
Severus ordered that the remains of Albinus' corpse should be
exposed before his own house and should lie there for a long
time. Besides this, he himself rode on horseback over the corpse
of Albinus, and admonished his horse when it took fright and
even loosened its reins so that it might trample boldly. Others
add that he ordered the man's corpse to be thrown into the
Rhône – and the bodies of his wife and children at the same time.
Countless members of Albinus' party were put to death, including many leading men in the state and many distinguished
women; the property of all of them was confiscated and swelled
the state treasury. Many of the Spanish and Gallic notables were
also killed at this time. Finally, he gave the soldiers a rate of pay
that none of the emperors had reached. To his sons, too, he left
an inheritance from this proscription greater than any of the
emperors had left, since he had made a large part of the gold
throughout Gaul, Spain and Italy. This was the time when
the procuratorship of the Privy Purse was first established.[34]
Of course, many who remained loyal to Albinus after his
death were defeated in battle by Severus. At that time, moreover, the legion of Arabia was reported to have defected to
Albinus.

Therefore, having taken a heavy vengeance on the desertion
of the Albinians by putting a great many of them to death, and
also wiping out Albinus' family, he came to Rome, angry with
both the people and the Senate. He praised Commodus in the

34. An error: the Privy Purse or *res privata* is now known to have
existed at least twenty years before when Aius Sanctus (*Commodus*, 1.6,
p. 161 above) was in charge of it; but Severus evidently expanded its
operations and some statement to this effect in his source may have been
misunderstood by the author in his haste.

Senate and at an assembly of the people, declared him to be a god and said that it was the depraved with whom he had been unpopular. It was apparent that Severus was quite openly in a rage. After this he dealt with the subject of his own clemency, although he was exceedingly cruel and killed the senators listed below. He did in fact kill, without any hearing of their case, these nobles:

Mummius Secundinus, Asellius Claudianus, Claudius Rufus, Vitalius Victor, Papius Faustus, Aelius Celsus, Julius Rufus, Lollius Professus, Aurunculeius Cornelianus, Antonius Balbus, Postumius Severus, Sergius Lustralis, Fabius Paulinus, Nonius Gracchus, Masticius Fabianus, Casperius Agrippinus, Ceionius Albinus, Claudius Sulpicianus, Memmius Rufinus, Casperius Aemilianus, Cocceius Verus, Erucius Clarus, Julius Solon, Clodius Rufinus, Egnatuleius Honoratus, Petronius Junior, the Pescennii (Festus and Veratianus and Aurelianus and Materianus and Julianus and Albinus), the Cerellii (Macrinus and Faustinianus and Julianus), Herennius Nepos, Sulpius Canus, Valerius Catullinus, Novius Rufus, Claudius Arabianus, Marcius Asellio.[35]

Yet the murderer of these men, so many and so distinguished – for many among them were consulars, many praetorian in rank, all certainly of high degree – is regarded by the Africans as a god! He falsely accused Cincius Severus of making an attempt on his life with poison, and for this reason put him to death. Then he cast to the lions Narcissus, the man who strangled Commodus. Besides this, he put to death many persons of lowly status, not counting those whom the fury of battle had consumed.

After this, since he wanted to make himself popular with people, he transferred the posting service from private individuals to the imperial treasury. Then he caused his son Bassianus

---

35. Some of these names are evidently bogus, but most are genuine: see G. Alföldy, HAC, 1968/9, pp. 1ff.

Antoninus to be named Caesar by the Senate, and the imperial insignia were granted him by decree. A rumour then arose of a Parthian war.

*

He set up statues to his father, mother, grandfather and first wife.[36] Plautianus had been a very close friend, but when Severus learned of his way of life he held him in such hatred that he declared him a public enemy, had his statues throughout the world overthrown, and made him famous for the severity of his punishment. Severus was particularly angered that Plautianus had set up his own statue among the likenesses of Severus' relatives and kinsmen. He revoked the penalty imposed on the Palestinians for supporting Niger.[37] Afterwards Severus returned to his friendship with Plautianus, and after entering the city as though celebrating an ovation, he came to the Capitol. However, he killed him eventually. He gave his younger son Geta the toga of manhood and joined the daughter of Plautianus in marriage with his elder son.[38] Those who had called Plautianus a public enemy were deported. Thus there is always change in everything, as if by a law of nature. Then he designated his sons to the consulship.[39] He buried his brother Geta.[40]

*

Then he set out for the Parthian war,[41] having put on a gladiatorial show and given largess to the people. In the meantime he killed many people on charges that were either genuine or

36. What follows is muddled and out of order. The author has tried to lump together what he could find on 'the rise and fall of Plautianus', but in his carelessness has failed to eliminate extraneous items.

37. This sentence is clearly out of place and presumably belongs at the beginning of 17 (p. 216, below).

38. The marriage took place in A.D.204.

39. They were consuls in A.D.205.

40. A.D.204.

41. A.D.197.

faked. A great many were condemned for making jokes, others because they kept silent, others for making a lot of contrived remarks, such as: 'Behold an emperor true to his name, a true Pertinax, a true Severus!' It was certainly commonly said that Septimius Severus' motive for the Parthian war was a desire for glory, and that it was not launched out of any necessity. At any rate, having taken the army across from Brundisium he came to Syria without breaking his journey and drove off the Parthians. After this he returned to Syria so as to prepare himself and take the offensive against the Parthians. In the meantime on the instigation of Plautianus he hunted down the remnants of Pescennius' following, to the extent that he even laid hold on some of his own friends as conspirators against his life. He also killed many for allegedly consulting astrologers or seers about his health, especially each and every person suitable for the imperial office, since he himself had sons who were still small boys, and he either believed, or heard, that this was being said by those who were predicting the position of emperor for themselves. In the end, when not a few had been killed, Severus made excuses for himself, and after their death denied that he had ordered what had been done. This applied particularly to Laetus,[42] according to Marius Maximus. When his sister,[43] a woman of Lepcis, had come to him, scarcely able to speak Latin, and the emperor was very embarrassed about her, he gave the broad stripe to her son and many gifts to her, and told the woman to return to her home town – with her son as well, who died shortly afterwards.

When the summer was already ending, therefore, he invaded Parthia, defeated the king, came to Ctesiphon, and took it. It

42. Probably the Julius Laetus mentioned briefly above (*Didius*, 8.1, p. 198); see Birley, *Severus*, p. 345. He was almost certainly the man nearly chosen as emperor at Lugdunum (*Severus*, 11.2, p. 211 above, where the name is not given).

43. Septimia Octavilla: see stemma, p. 322.

was almost winter – for in those regions wars are better carried out in winter, although the soldiers live on the roots of grasses and contract diseases and sickness as a result. Therefore, when he was unable to proceed farther, because the Parthians were making a stand, and the soldiers' bowels were loosened on account of the unfamiliar diet, he nonetheless persisted and took the town, put the king to flight, killed a great number of men and earned the title Parthicus. Because of these things, also, the soldiers hailed his son Bassianus Antoninus, then in his thirteenth year[44] and already with the title Caesar,[45] as co-emperor. They called Geta his younger son Caesar also, naming him Antoninus as well, according to most writers.[46] He gave the soldiers a very generous donative on account of these titles, and all the booty of the Parthian town was handed over to them. Then he returned into Syria, as a conqueror and as Parthicus. The senators offered him a triumph, but he refused, the reason being that his arthritis made it impossible for him to stand up in the chariot. He did, to be sure, allow his son to triumph – the Senate had decreed him a triumph over the Jews,[47] because of successes achieved in Syria by Severus. Then, when he had crossed to Antioch, he bestowed the toga of manhood on his elder son and designated him as consul, as colleague to himself; and they at once entered on their consulship, while still in Syria.[48]

After this, he gave the soldiers an increase in their pay and then set out for Alexandria.[49] On the journey he established many laws for the Palestinians. He prohibited conversion to Judaism under heavy penalties, and laid down the same penalty

44. An error: Caracalla was in his tenth or eleventh year.
45. These titles were evidently granted on 28 January A.D.198.
46. An error: see p. 18 above.
47. Presumably fictional: there is no other evidence.
48. A.D.202.
49. The order has gone astray here: the visit to Egypt was in A.D. 199–200.

in the case of Christians too[50]. Then he gave the Alexandrians the right to have town-councillors – up till that time they used to live without a public authority just as they had under their kings, content with the single magistrate whom Caesar had appointed. Besides this he changed many of their laws. This tour was pleasant for him – as Severus himself subsequently always made clear – because of his devotion to the god Sarapis, because he became acquainted with the antiquities and because he saw rare animals and strange places. For he diligently inspected Memphis and Memnon, the pyramids and the labyrinth.

*

But since it is tedious to follow up minor details, this man's great deeds were the following:[51] when Julianus had been conquered and killed, he dismissed the praetorian cohorts, enrolled Pertinax among the gods contrary to the will of the soldiers, and ordered that the decrees of Salvius Julianus should be abolished; here, however, he was unsuccessful. Then he appears to have had the surname of Pertinax not so much at his own wish as on account of his parsimonious character. In fact, through the unlimited slaughter of many he was regarded as somewhat cruel. When a certain man from the enemy had surrendered to him as a suppliant and had asked, what would Severus have done in his place, he was not softened by the good sense of such a question, and ordered the man to be put to death. Besides this, his fervent aim was to liquidate opposing factions, and there was almost no encounter from which he did not emerge the victor. He subdued Abgarus, king of the Persians.

50. This is highly dubious.

51. The section from 'when Julianus . . .' to '. . . that he even deified Commodus' on p. 219 closely resembles Aurelius Victor, de Caes., 20, and most would agree that it derives from there. Note that the author avoids Victor's mistake of confusing Didius Julianus with his kinsman the jurist, but nonetheless has failed to delete the reference to 'abolishing the decrees of Salvius Julianus'.

He received the submission of the Arabs. He compelled the Adiabeni to pay tribute. He fortified Britain – and this was the greatest glory of his reign – with a wall led across the island to the Ocean at each end;[52] in recognition of this he also received the title Britannicus. He rendered Tripolitania, from whence he sprang, completely safe, having battered the most warlike tribes; and he donated to the Roman people in perpetuity a free and lavish daily supply of olive oil.

The same emperor, although implacable towards offences, likewise displayed singular judiciousness in encouraging all hard-working persons. He was quite interested in philosophy and the practice of rhetoric, and enthusiastic about learning in general. He took stern measures against brigands everywhere. He composed a convincing autobiography dealing with both his private and his public life, making excuses only for the vice of cruelty. With regard to this, the Senate pronounced that either he ought not to have been born or that he ought not to die, since he appeared to be both excessively cruel and excessively useful to the republic. However, as concerns his family he was less careful, retaining his wife Julia who was notorious for her adulteries and was also guilty of conspiracy.

Once, this emperor, when crippled in his feet, was delaying a war, and the soldiers in their anxiety made his son Bassianus, who was there with him, Augustus. Severus had himself lifted up and was carried to the tribunal, and then summoned all the tribunes, centurions, generals and cohorts responsible for the deed. Finally, he ordered that his son, who had accepted the name of Augustus, should appear before him. He ordered that all those responsible for the deed should be punished except for his son, and all of them, prostrate before the tribunal, begged for pardon. Then he touched his head with his hand and said: 'At last you realize that it is the head that rules and not the feet.' It was he that said, when fortune had led him from a humble status

52. Although some rebuilding work was carried out on the line of Hadrian's Wall in his reign, Severus was not its builder.

through pursuits of study and military posts to the imperial power, through many stages: 'I have been everything – and gained nothing.'

He died at Eboracum [York] in Britain, having subdued the tribes which appeared hostile to Britain, in the eighteenth year of his reign, stricken by a very grave illness, now an old man.

★

He left two sons, Antoninus Bassianus, and Geta, to whom he had given the same name, in honour of Marcus Antoninus. He was laid in the sepulchre of Marcus Antoninus, whom of all the emperors he so greatly revered that he even deified Commodus, and thought it right that the name of Antoninus should be added to the name of all future emperors just like the name Augustus. He himself was enrolled among the deified emperors by the Senate, on the motion of his sons, who gave him a splendid funeral.

His outstanding public buildings now extant are the Septizodium[53] and the Severan Baths[54]; and his too are the doors in the Transtiberine region, next to the gate that bears his name. Their frame collapsed at once, interfering with their use by the public.

The universal judgement on him after his death was that he was great, especially because for a long while no benefit came to the republic from his sons, while subsequently, with many usurpations, the Roman state was a prey to plunderers.

This emperor wore such meagre clothing that even his tunic scarcely had any purple, while he covered his shoulders with a shaggy cloak. He ate sparingly, being very addicted to his

53. A three-storied building nearly 100 feet high and over 300 feet long, erected in A.D.203 at the south-eastern corner of the Palatine Hill. See Birley, Severus, p. 236.

54. The precise location of these baths is unknown and they were perhaps incorporated in the Baths of Caracalla (p. 258 below).

native vegetable[55], sometimes fond of wine, often abstaining from meat. His person was handsome, he was of huge size,[56] with a long beard and curly white hair. His face inspired reverence, his voice was resonant but with a trace of an African accent right up to his old age. He was equally beloved after his death, when envy, or the fear of his cruelty, had disappeared.

I recall that I have read in Aelius Maurus[57], a freedman of Hadrian's Phlegon, that when he was dying Septimius Severus rejoiced quite unrestrainedly because he was leaving the republic two Antonines with equal power, after the example of Pius, who left the republic Verus and Marcus Antoninus, his sons by adoption. He was doing better than this because Pius left sons by adoption and he was giving the Roman republic rulers begotten by himself; Antoninus – Bassianus that is – was of course born to him from his first marriage and he had Geta by Julia. But his hope greatly deceived him, for fratricide made the one hateful to the republic and his own character the other, and the name of Antoninus did not long remain sanctified in any instance. Indeed, when I reflect on the matter, Diocletian Augustus, it is sufficiently clear that no great man has left a son who is excellent and useful. For such men either die without children or for the most part have children of such a kind that it would have been better for the human race if they had died without descendants. To begin from Romulus: he left no children, and Numa Pompilius left none that could be of use to the republic. What of Camillus? He surely did not have children

55. The identity of this vegetable is uncertain: Magie, I, p. 419, translates 'beans' without comment. But Syme, *AHA*, p. 201, after speculating on the possibilities of garlic, leeks and chick-pea, rightly concludes that the story is an invention, like the description of Severus' size in the next sentence.

56. Dio, who knew Severus personally, describes him as 'physically small but strong' (76.16.1); the statement here must therefore be regarded as fiction.

57. A bogus author; and what follows is padding.

like himself? What of Scipio? What of the Catos, who were such great men? And then, what shall I say about Homer, Demosthenes, Virgil, Crispus [Sallust and Terence, Plautus and all the rest? What about Caesar? What about Tullius [Cicero], for whom especially it would have been better not to have had children? What about Augustus, who did not even have a good son by adoption, although he had the power of choosing from all men? Trajan himself, also, made a mistake in choosing his fellow-townsman and nephew. But to omit adoptive sons, lest the Antonines, Pius and Marcus, divine spirits of the republic, occur to us, let us turn to real sons. What would have been more fortunate for Marcus, than not to have Commodus as his heir? What more fortunate for Severus Septimius, than not to have Bassianus? – who straightaway destroyed his brother, supposed to have designed a conspiracy against himself, a fratricidal contrivance; who took his stepmother – and what stepmother? rather she was his mother! – to wife,[58] in whose bosom he had killed her son Geta; who killed Papinian, sanctuary of the law and treasury of legal learning, and who was prefect (so that a man great in himself and through his knowledge might not be lacking in rank)[59]. Finally, to omit other things, I think it was because of Bassianus' character that Severus, a somewhat harsh man in every way, indeed somewhat cruel also, was held to be righteous and worthy of the altars of the gods. He at any rate, labouring under his disease, is said to have sent his elder son the god-like speech of Sallust, in which Micipsa urged his sons to peace.[60] But that was in vain . . . and so great a man, in ill

58. The story that Caracalla 'married' Julia Domna, who is incorrectly called his stepmother, is also found in Victor, *de Caes.*, 21.2–3, Eutropius, 8.20.1, *epitome*, 21.5 and Orosius, 7.18.2; cf. also *Caracallus*, 10.1–4 (p. 259 below). The author usually seems to be aware that Julia was Caracalla's real mother and not his stepmother (but see p. 266).

59. Aemilius Papinianus, a kinsman of Severus by marriage, was made prefect of the guard in A.D.205 after the murder of Plautianus.

60. Sallust, *Jugurtha*, 106. Dio (77.15.2) has a quite different account.

health . . .[61] Antoninus lived on then, hated by the people for a long time, and that hallowed name was for a long time less beloved, although he both gave clothes to the people, whence he was called Caracallus, and built most magnificent baths. There survives of course at Rome a portico of Severus portraying his deeds, set up by his son, according to most accounts.

The signs of his death were these: he himself dreamed that he was dragged up into the sky by four eagles and a jewelled chariot, while some kind of huge creature of human shape flew in front; and while he was being carried away, he counted out numbers up to eighty-nine, beyond which number of years he did not live even a single one,[62] for he came to the imperial position as an old man; and when he had been placed in a huge bronze circle, for a long while he stood solitary and set apart; then when he began to be afraid that he might fall headlong, he saw himself being called by Jupiter and placed among the Antonines. On the day of the circus games, three little plaster Victories had been set up, in the usual fashion, holding palms. The middle one, which carried a globe inscribed with his own name, was struck by the wind and fell down upright from the podium, and stayed on the ground; the one which was inscribed with the name of Geta collapsed and shattered completely; but the one which carried the inscription of Bassianus, though it lost its palm in the gust of wind, managed to remain standing, although only just. After giving a Moor his discharge from the army, on the Wall, he was returning to the nearest halting-place (*mansio*), not merely as victor but having established eternal peace. He was turning over in his mind what sort of man should meet him, when a certain 'Ethiopian' [black man] from the military unit (*numerus*), with a famous reputation among the jesters and whose jokes were always much quoted, met him with a wreath made of cypress. Enraged,

61. The MSS. are defective here.
62. An error (repeated below, p. 229): he died at the age of 65.

Severus instructed that the man should be removed from his sight, being nettled by the ominous colour and wreath; and the man is recorded to have said, as a joke: 'You have overthrown all things, you have conquered all things, now be a conquering god!' Coming to the town, he wanted to make sacrifice; but first he was led to the temple of Bellona by a mistake on the part of the rustic soothsayer, and then the sacrificial victims provided were black. He rejected them and was on his way back to the palace, when through the attendants' carelessness the black sacrificial victims followed the emperor, right up to the threshold of the imperial residence.

There are in many cities outstanding building works of his. There was indeed magnanimity in his graciousness, in that he restored all the public buildings at Rome that were falling into disrepair from the effects of time, and virtually nowhere had his own name inscribed on them, the inscriptions of the original builders being preserved. On his death he left enough grain for seven years supply to be weighed out at a daily rate of 75,000 pecks; and so much olive oil, in fact, that for five years there was sufficient not only for the use of the city but also for the whole of Italy which needed oil.

His last words are said to have been the following: 'I took over the republic in a disturbed condition everywhere, and I leave it pacified even among the Britons. Now an old man crippled in the feet, I bequeath to my Antonines, a stable empire if they will be good, a weak one if bad.' Then he ordered the watchword 'Let us work' to be given to the tribune, because Pertinax when he was admitted to the imperial position had given the watchword 'Let us be soldiers'. He had intended next that the royal image of Fortune, who customarily accompanies the emperors and is placed in their bed-chambers, should be duplicated, so that he might leave that most sacred figure to each of his sons; but when he saw that the hour of death was pressing strongly upon him, he is supposed to have ordered that Fortune should be placed on alternate days in the bed-chambers of his sons the emperors. Bassianus ignored this – and then committed fratricide.

His body was carried from Britain as far as Rome, greatly revered by the provincials; although some say that it was only a golden urn containing the remains of Severus, and that this was laid in the sepulchre of the Antonines, since Septimius had been cremated in the place where he died.

When he was building the Septizodium he had no other thought but that his building might present itself to those approaching from Africa; and it is said that if a statue of himself had not been placed in the centre of it by the prefect of the city, during his absence, he wanted to make an entrance into the Palatine House, i.e. into the royal entrance-hall, from that side. Subsequently, Alexander too wanted to do this, but he is said to have been forbidden by the soothsayers, since his consultations had not met with a favourable response.

PESCENNIUS NIGER*

BY AELIUS SPARTIANUS

IT IS unusual and difficult to set down a proper written
account of those whom the victory of others made into
usurpers. For this reason not all the facts about these men are
fully recorded in the chronicles and annals. For, firstly, great
deeds which redound to their honour are distorted by the
writers; other events are suppressed; and, finally, not much care
is spent in research on their ancestry and life, since it suffices to
mention their presumption, the war in which they were defeated, and their punishment.

Pescennius Niger, then, had humble parents, as some relate,
although others say that they were noble. His father was Annius
Fuscus and his mother Lampridia. His grandfather was super-
intendent of Aquinum, whence the family took its origin –
although this point is even now regarded as doubtful. He was
moderately well educated in literature, of ferocious character,
immeasurably wealthy and thrifty in his way of life, of un-
restrained licentiousness in every variety of desire. For a long
while he held a centurion's commission, and by way of
many generalships he reached the position of commanding the Syrian armies by order of Commodus, mainly –
as happened with everything at that time – through the

---

* Most of this *Life* is fiction, except where material from the *Lives* of
Didius Julianus and Severus (or their source) is re-used. For the background, see Birley, *Severus*, pp. 172ff.

recommendation of the athlete who was to strangle
Commodus.[1]

After he learned that Commodus had been killed, that
Julianus had been named emperor, and then, by order of
Severus and of the Senate, had been killed, and that Albinus,
too, in Gaul had assumed the title of emperor, he was named
emperor by the Syrian armies which he was commanding –
more on account of hatred for Julianus, as some say, than out of
rivalry with Severus.[2] Because of the detestation of Julianus in
his first days as emperor, there was such support for Pescennius
at Rome, as far as the senators were concerned – who loathed
Severus as well – that there were prayers for his success amid the
stone-throwing and general execration, with the people shouting, 'May the gods give him to us as *princeps*, him as Augustus!'
The mob hated Julianus, moreover, because the soldiers had
killed Pertinax and named him emperor contrary to the wish of
the people. Eventually there were violent riots on account of
this. Furthermore, Julianus had sent a former chief centurion
(*primipilaris*) to kill Niger, a foolish action against one who had
an army and could protect himself – as if any sort of emperor
could be killed by an ex-chief centurion! With the same sense-
lessness, moreover, Julianus had sent a successor for Severus
when the latter was already *princeps*. In the end he had also sent
Aquilius, a centurion well known for murdering generals – as if
so great an emperor could be killed by a centurion! It was a
like act of insanity to try to deal with Severus – or so it is
reported – by issuing a proclamation prohibiting him from
taking the imperial power, so that he himself might appear
to have a prior claim to the principate by law.

1. Niger was certainly appointed governor of Syria by Commodus;
but no other source confirms that it was through the recommendation
of the athlete Narcissus. The rest of the paragraph is pure fiction.

2. This paragraph and the first two sentences of the next are based on
the same source as *Didius Julianus*, 4–5 (p. 195f above), only rearranged; hence the material is largely authentic.

The people's verdict on Pescennius Niger is clear from this fact. When Julianus was giving circus-games at Rome, and the seats in the Circus Maximus had been filled up without distinction of rank, and the people were moved by a powerful sense of injury, Pescennius Niger was called upon by all with one accord to protect the city, out of hatred for Julianus, as we have said, and love for the murdered Pertinax. At this time, indeed, Julianus is reported to have said that neither he himself nor Pescennius ought to have a long rule, but rather Severus, who was more deserving of hatred by senators, soldiers, provincials and people. Events proved this to be so.

Pescennius was in fact very friendly with Severus at the time when the latter was governing the province of Lugdunensis, for he had been sent himself to arrest the deserters, countless numbers of whom were then ravaging Gaul. In this post he pleased Severus a great deal because he conducted himself honourably, so much so that Septimius reported back to Commodus about him, stating that he was a man indispensable to the republic. Certainly he was vigorous in military affairs. Under him no soldier ever extorted wood, oil, or service from a provincial, and he himself never accepted anything from a soldier. When he was serving his tribunates he allowed nothing to be accepted. Indeed, as emperor, too, he ordered two tribunes, who were proved to have permitted deductions to be made from soldiers' rations, to be stoned by the auxiliaries. There is extant a letter of Severus, in which he writes to Ragonus Clarus, who was governing Gaul:

It is unfortunate that we cannot imitate the military discipline of the man that we have defeated in war. Your soldiers straggle about, the tribunes bathe in the middle of the day, they have cook-shops instead of mess-rooms, brothels instead of bedrooms. They dance, drink, sing – and they call drinking without limit a proper limit to banquets! Could these things come about if the innate quality of our ancestral discipline was still alive? So – reform the tribunes first, then the soldiers. As long as they fear you, you will hold them in check. But you should learn from Niger too, that soldiers cannot be made to fear unless the soldiers' tribunes and generals are above reproach.

This is what Severus Augustus wrote about Pescennius.

When he was still a common soldier, Marcus Antoninus wrote about him to Cornelius Balbus:

You praise Pescennius to me. I recognize the man, for your predecessor too said that he was strenuous in action, serious-minded in behaviour and already at that time more than just a soldier. I have therefore sent a letter, to be read out on parade, in which I have ordered him to take command of three hundred Armenians, a hundred Sarmatians, and a thousand of our men. It is your task to point out that the man has attained – not by canvassing support, which does not accord with our character, but by merit – to a post which my grandfather Hadrian and my great-grandfather Trajan did not give to any except the most tested men.

Commodus wrote about this same man:

I have known Pescennius to be a brave man and I have given him two tribunates. Soon I shall give him a general's command, when Aelius Corduenus has retired from public service on account of old age.

These were the verdicts of everyone about him. But Severus himself often said that he would have pardoned Pescennius if he had not persisted.

In the end, having been appointed consul by Commodus, Pescennius was placed ahead of Severus, who, in fact, was angry, on the grounds that Niger had gained the consulship on the recommendation of former chief centurions (*primipilares*). In his autobiography Severus says that before his sons were old enough to be emperor, he had it in mind that if anything should happen to him Niger Pescennius and Clodius Albinus should succeed him – both of whom became Severus' worst enemies. From this it is clear what even Severus thought of Pescennius.

If we believe Severus, Niger was eager for glory, hypocritical

in his way of life, of low character and of advanced age when he
seized the imperial power, for which reason Severus criticizes
his ambitions – as if Severus was younger when he attained the
power! He understated his years, for he reigned for eighteen
years and died in his eighty-ninth year.[3]

At any rate, Severus sent Heraclitus to take control of
Bithynia, and Fulvius to seize Niger's grown-up children.[4]
Yet, in the Senate, Severus said nothing about Niger, although
he had already heard about his becoming emperor. He himself
moreover set out on an expedition merely 'to set eastern
affairs in order'. In fact, when setting off, he took steps to send
legions to Africa, in case Niger occupied it and caused the
Roman people trouble by a food-shortage. He did actually seem
to be capable of doing that, through Libya and Egypt, which
are adjacent to Africa, even if the land-route and the sea-voyage
are difficult. Pescennius for his part, while Severus was on his
way to the east, was holding Greece, Thrace and Macedonia,
having killed many illustrious men; and he invited Severus to
share the empire. He was named a public enemy by the latter,
together with Aemilianus, on account of the men he had killed.
Then, with his army fighting under the command of Aemilianus, he was defeated by Severus' generals. Although Severus
promised him safe exile if he laid down his arms, he went on
and fought again, was defeated and, while taking flight near a
marsh at Cyzicus, was wounded and brought to Severus in this
state, and immediately died. His head was carried round on a
spear, and sent to Rome; his children were killed, his wife
slaughtered, his property proscribed and his entire family wiped
out. But all these things were done after the news of Albinus'

3. False: Severus died at the age of 65.
4. This sentence is repeated almost *verbatim* from *Severus*, 6.10,
except that *Bithyniam* has been substituted for *Brittannias* (which is
probably correct). The rest of this paragraph is based largely on the
same material as *Severus*, 8–9, rearranged.

rebellion, for before this Severus had sent both Niger's children and their mother into exile. But Severus became incensed by the second – or, rather, the third – civil war and became harder, at that time when he put countless senators to death and got from some people the name 'the Punic Sulla', from others 'the Punic Marius'.[5]

Niger was tall in stature and handsome in his person, his hair being brushed back gracefully towards the crown. His voice was raucous but resonant, so that when he spoke on the parade-ground he could be heard a mile away if the wind was not against him. His face was dignified and always ruddy, his neck was so black that according to what many say he got the name of Niger from that, the rest of his body being white and rather fat. He was very fond of wine, a sparing eater, and absolutely unacquainted with sex other than for begetting children. Indeed, he even performed certain rites in Gaul which they vote by common consent to the most chaste to celebrate. We see this man depicted in the mosaic in the curved portico in the gardens of Commodus, carrying the sacred objects of Isis, amongst Commodus' closest friends. Commodus was so devoted to these rites that he used to shave his head and to carry the image of Anubis and make all the ritual pauses.[6]

He was, then, an excellent soldier, an exceptional tribune, an outstanding general, a very strict legate, a distinguished consul, a man of distinction at home and abroad – and an unfortunate emperor. He could in fact have been of use to the republic under Severus, a sombre man, if he had wanted to be on his side. But he was deceived by the sinister advice of Aurelianus, who

5. A reference to the severe proscriptions of their political enemies in the 80s B.C. by Marius and Sulla. Dio (75.8.1) says that Severus 'praised the severity and cruelty of Sulla, Marius and Augustus' in a speech to the Senate (presumably the one also described in *Severus*, 12, p. 212f above).

6. This sentence is repeated from *Commodus*, 9.4 (p. 169 above). The remainder of the *Life* from this point onwards seems to be fiction.

betrothed his daughters to Niger's sons and made him persist in his attempt on the imperial power.

He had such great influence that he wrote first to Marcus and then to Commodus when he saw the provinces being turned upside down by the rapid changing of administrations. He advocated firstly that no governor, legate or proconsul should receive a successor before a term of five years, because they were laying down their power before they knew how to administer. Then, too, he argued that men should not take part in running the republic without experience, apart from military posts, and he recommended that men should have administrative posts in the provinces in which they had served as assessors. This practice, in the sequel, Severus and many after him maintained, as is proved by the prefectures of Paulus and Ulpian, who were on Papinian's council; after that, when one had served as secretary of the records and the other as secretary for petitions, they straightaway become prefects.[7] It was also his plan that no one should be an assistant to the governor in his own province and that no one should govern a province who was not a Roman of Rome, that is, born in the city. He added, further, that there should be salaries for counsellors, so that they should not be a burden on those whose assistants they were, saying that a judge ought neither to give nor to receive.

Towards his soldiers he showed such great strictness that when, in Egypt, the frontier-troops asked him for wine, he replied: 'You have the Nile and you ask for wine?' – seeing that the waters of that river are so sweet that those who dwell beside it do not ask for wine. Likewise when the men, who had been defeated by the Saracens, were in uproar and were saying: 'We haven't had wine, we cannot fight', he replied: 'Blush for shame, for the men who are defeating you drink water.'

7. This statement is only partially correct: there is no evidence that Paulus ever became prefect, and some of the other details are dubious: see Syme, *EB*, pp. 148f., *HAC*, 1968/9, pp. 309ff. For Ulpian, see p. 302 below: for Papinian, p. 221 above.

Again, when the Palestinians were asking that their tribute-assessment should be reduced, on the grounds that it had been burdensome, he replied: 'You want me to reduce your tax-assessment – but I would like to tax your air as well.'

In the end, while the republic was in the greatest upheaval, when it was announced that there were three emperors, Severus Septimius, Pescennius Niger and Clodius Albinus, the seer of the Delphic Apollo was consulted as to which one it would profit the republic to have as emperor. He is said to have produced a Greek verse somewhat as follows:

Best is the Dark one, good is the African, worst is the White one.

From this priestly utterance it was understood that Niger was called 'the Dark one', Severus 'the African' and Albinus was meant by 'the White one'. There was no lack of further in-quiry, and it was asked who would gain control of the republic. To this he replied with further verses, to this effect:

While they still live, from White and Black shall blood be pour'd:
He that from Punic city starts shall rule as Lord.

Again, when it was asked who would succeed that man, he is said to have replied with another Greek line:

He that the heav'nly ones have giv'n Pius for name.

This was not understood at all, until the time when Bassianus received the name of Antoninus, which was the true surname of Pius. Then, when asked how long the man would be emperor, he is said to have replied:

If but one bark shall cross the wat'ry plain,
With twice ten ships he'll sail th' Italic main.

From this it was understood that Severus would complete twenty years.

These are the things, Diocletian Augustus, greatest of Augusti, that we have learned from many books concerning

Pescennius. For it is not easy, as we said at the beginning of the book, for anyone to commit to books the lives of those who were not *principes* in the republic nor were declared emperor by the Senate, or who, having been killed fairly quickly, could not attain to fame. It is for this reason that Vindex[8] is obscure, that Piso[9] is unknown, and all those who were merely adopted or who were hailed as emperors by the soldiers – such as Antonius[10] under Domitian – or who, having been put to death quickly, laid down their life at the same time as their usurpation of the empire. It follows that I now speak of Clodius Albinus,[11] who is regarded as a kind of ally of this man, both because they rebelled against Severus in similar fashion and because they were defeated and killed by the same man. No adequate information about that person survives either, since his fate was the same as that of Pescennius, even if his life was quite different.

But lest we seem to have overlooked any of the facts that are relevant to Pescennius, even if they can be learnt from other books, the seers told Severus Septimius, regarding this man, that he would come into Severus' power neither dead nor alive, but that he would perish near water. Some say that Severus himself made this statement, based on astrology, in which he was skilled. Nor was the prophecy lacking in truth, since Pescennius was found next to a marsh, half-alive.

He was so strict that when he had seen some soldiers drinking from a silver cup at the time of an expedition, he ordered all the silver to be taken out of use on campaign, adding the command that they should use wooden vessels. This of course stirred up

8. C. Julius Vindex began the rebellion which caused the downfall of Nero in A.D.68.

9. C. Calpurnius Piso, unsuccessful conspirator against Nero in A.D.65.

10. L. Antonius Saturninus, who attempted a *coup* against Domitian in A.D.89.

11. But the Augustan History biography of Albinus is actually assigned to 'Julius Capitolinus'.

the soldiers' hatred against him. For he used to say that it could happen that the soldiers' packs might come into the hands of the enemy, and barbarian nations were not to be given cause for boasting on account of our silver when other things would seem less likely to bring glory to the enemy. He likewise ordered that no one should drink wine on campaign, but that all should be content with vinegar. Again, he prohibited pastry-cooks from following expeditions, ordering soldiers, and everyone, to be content with hard tack. Further, he ordered ten comrades in the same maniple to be beheaded with the axe for the theft of a single cock which they had all eaten after it had been taken by one of them; and he would have carried it out, if he had not been begged by the whole army to such an extent that there was almost fear of mutiny. When he had spared them, he ordered that the ten who had feasted together on what they had stolen should each give back to the provincials the price of ten cocks; and he added the order that throughout the duration of the campaign no one should make a hearth in his maniple-quarters, that they should never take any freshly cooked food, but should live on bread and water – posting scouts to see that it was done. Again, he ordered that soldiers about to go to war should not carry gold or silver coins in their belt, but should deposit them with an official, to get back what they had handed in after the battles, adding that the man who took it would see it was paid back to surviving wives and children if anything happened to them. This was so that no booty should come to the enemy if fortune should bring some disaster. But all these things counted against him, the laxness of the Commodan era being what it was. In short, even if there was no one who seemed to his own times a sterner general, these things damaged him more: after his death, when envy and hatred were laid aside, exemplary conduct like this had its value.

On every expedition, also, he took a military meal in front of his tent before all the men, and never sought the aid of a covering against sun or against rain if the soldiers did not have one.

Indeed, in time of war, he assigned to himself and his slaves or aides burdens as heavy as those of the soldiers, having shown the soldiers the list, for he used to load his slaves with grain so that they should not walk free of burdens while the soldiers were weighed down – and that might have been regarded by the army as something to complain about. He also swore, at an assembly, that as long as he had been campaigning and would be in the future, he had not in the past and would not in future act otherwise than as a soldier, having before his eyes Marius and generals like him. His conversation was never about anyone except Hannibal and other such men. Indeed, when someone wanted to recite a panegyric to him when he had become emperor, he told him: 'Write the praises of Marius or Hannibal or any excellent general you wish who has departed this life, and tell what he did, so that we may imitate him. For it is a mockery to praise the living, especially emperors, who raise expectations, who are feared, who can advance men in public life, who can proscribe, who can put to death.' He said that he wanted to please while he lived and when he died to be praised as well.

Of the *principes* he loved Augustus, Vespasian, Titus, Trajan, Pius and Marcus, calling the rest either men of straw or poisonous. Of the historical figures on the other hand, he was particularly fond of Marius and Camillus and Quinctius [Cincinnatus] and Marcius Coriolanus. But when he was asked what he thought of the Scipios, he is reported to have remarked that they were fortunate rather than stout-hearted; and that their domestic life and their youth proved this, which in both cases had been unattractive at home. All are agreed that if he had gained power, he would have put right all those things which Severus either could not or would not reform – and, of course, without cruelty, indeed even with mercifulness, but that of a soldier, not lax or inappropriate or ridiculous.

His house is still to be seen at Rome today, on the Field of Jupiter. It is called the Pescennian House and in it a statue of him is set up, in a tripartite room; it is of Theban marble[12] and he had received it, made in his likeness, from the king of the Thebans. A Greek epigram survives too, the sense of which in Latin is as follows:

> Terror of Egypt's soldiers stands Niger the great,
> Thebaid's ally, desiring an age of gold.
> Him kings and nations and golden Rome venerate,
> Him the Antonines and the empire dear do hold.
> Black is the name he has and we have shaped him black,
> So that you, the metal, your right form may not lack.

These verses, actually, Severus was unwilling to have erased, although this was suggested both by the prefects and by the heads of the secretariat (*magistri officiorum*).[13] 'If he was like this,' he added, 'let everyone know what kind of man we have defeated; if he was not, let everyone think that we have defeated such a man. In fact, let it be – for such a man he was!'

---

12. Black basalt, imported from Upper Egypt by the Romans.

13. The *magister officiorum* is an official first attested in the early fourth century – this may therefore be regarded as a tell-tale anachronism (cf. p. 12 above.)

CLODIUS ALBINUS*

BY JULIUS CAPITOLINUS

At one and the same time, in succession to Pertinax, who was killed on the instigation of Albinus, Julianus was named emperor by the Senate, Septimius Severus by the army in Syria,[1] Pescennius Niger in the east and Clodius Albinus in Gaul. Herodian says that Clodius at any rate was Severus' Caesar.[2] But since each considered the other unworthy to be emperor, nor could the Gauls or the German armies[3] endure that they should not have a *princeps* of their very own, everything was thrown into confusion on all sides.

Now Clodius Albinus was from a family that was noble, although he was a native of Hadrumetum in Africa,[4] on account of which he used to apply to himself that oracle in praise of Severus which we related in the *Life* of Pescennius, not wanting to be thought of as 'the worst, the White one', words contained in the same line in which Severus is praised and Niger Pescennius is commended. But before I discourse on his life or death, I must tell what made him noble. Commodus had once written

---

* Almost wholly fiction, except where otherwise indicated (mainly where Herodian is used). For the background, see Birley, *Severus*, pp. 189ff.

1. An error: Severus was proclaimed in Pannonia, Niger in Syria.

2. Herodian, 2.15.3.

3. In fact, the German armies remained loyal to Severus and resisted Albinus.

4. This seems to be correct (although it has been vigorously rejected): see G. Alföldy, *HAC* 1966/7, pp. 19ff.

a letter to Albinus, when appointing his successor, in which he ordered that he should be Caesar. I append a copy:

Emperor Commodus to Clodius Albinus.

On another occasion I sent you a public letter about your successor and about your own rank. But this I have sent as a private and confidential letter, all written with my own hand, as you see, by which I give you the power, should the necessity arise, of presenting yourself to the soldiers and assuming the name of Caesar. For I hear that both Septimius Severus and Nonius Murcus are speaking ill of me before the soldiers, in order to make ready for themselves their seizure of the position of Augustus. You shall have, besides, when you have done this, full power to give out soldiers' pay, up to three gold pieces, since I have sent a letter on this matter also to the procurators, which you yourself will receive, signed with my signet of an Amazon, and, when the need arises, you will give it to the finance officers, so that they will not refuse to listen to you when you wish to put in an order to the treasury. So that you may receive some symbol of the imperial majesty, you shall also have the right to wear a scarlet cloak, either when I am present or when you have been admitted to my presence, and when you are with me. You shall have the purple too, but without the gold trimmings, since my great-grandfather Verus, who died in boyhood, received this from Hadrian who adopted him.

Having received the letter, Albinus was unwilling to carry out this order, for he saw that Commodus, on account of his character, through which he had destroyed the republic and disgraced himself, must in due course be struck down; and he feared that he himself would likewise be killed. Indeed, a speech of his is still extant in which, when he accepted the imperial power – and it was in fact confirmed by the wish of Severus, as some say – he makes mention of this affair. This is a copy of it:

It is against my will, fellow-soldiers, that I am brought to the imperial power, as is also proved by the fact that when Commodus gave me the name of Caesar I scorned it. But your wishes and those of Severus Augustus I must obey, since I believe that under an upright man and a brave one the republic can be well ruled.

Now it cannot be denied – and even Marius Maximus says this – that Severus had it in mind at first that if anything happened to him Pescennius Niger and Clodius Albinus should take his place.[5] But he is said to have changed his mind subsequently, being zealous for the interests of his sons, who were by then older, and envious of the affection in which Albinus was held – above all, being persuaded by his wife's entreaties. Severus did in fact designate him as consul too, which he would not have done except for an excellent man, being painstaking over the choice of magistrates.

But to return to Albinus, he was, as I have said, Hadrumetine by origin, but was noble among his own people and traced his descent from families of Rome, namely the Postumii and Albini and Ceionii. The latter family is still one of the noblest today, greatest Constantine: by you it has been exalted and deserves to be exalted, although it gained its greatest prestige through Gallienus and Gordian. Albinus was however born in a modest home, with very little family property, of upright parents, his father being Ceionius Postumus and his mother Aurelia Messallina, and he was his parents' first child. Because, unlike normal children who are red when they are born, he was very white when taken from the womb, he was named Albinus. A letter of his father written to Aelius Bassianus the proconsul of Africa, a kinsman, as it seems, of these people, proves that this is true.

Letter of Ceionius Postumus to Aelius Bassianus:

A son was born to me on the seventh day before the Kalends of December [25 November], his whole body being straightaway of such whiteness as to outdo the cloth in which he was wrapped. And so I have acknowledged him as one of the family of the Albini – membership of which I share with you – having bestowed the name

---

5. It is difficult to believe that Severus ever thought of Niger as his successor, even for a matter of days; but Albinus was something like Severus' deputy from A.D. 193–5.

Albinus on him. See that you esteem the republic and yourself and us, as you do.

All his boyhood, then, he passed in Africa, being educated in Greek and Latin literature, not above average standard, for he was at that time already of a martial and haughty nature. At school, indeed, he is reported to have recited very frequently among the little boys:

Madly my arms I take up, and in arms there is not enough reason,[6]

repeating the words 'Madly my arms I take up'. Many signs of his future imperial rule are said to have occurred when he was born. For instance, a white bull was born with horns completely purple in colour. He himself, when he had already been a tribune for a long while, is said to have placed them in the temple of Apollo at Cumae; and when he took up the oracular response concerning his fate there, the reply is said to have been in these verses:

> He, when his country (threaten'd with alarms)
> Requires his courage, and his conqu'ring arms,
> Shall more than once the Punic bands affright:
> Shall kill the Gaulish king in single fight.[7]

It is well known that he did in fact conquer many tribes in Gaul. He used to suspect that 'Punic bands affright' was a prophecy made to him about Severus, because Septimius was an African. There was another sign of his future imperial power as well. The family of the Caesars had this special custom that the infants of that family were washed in tortoiseshell bath-tubs, and when he was a new-born infant a huge tortoise was brought to his father as a present by a fisherman. He, being an educated man, took it as an omen and accepted the tortoise gladly, ordering it to be prepared and set aside for the infant for

6. Virgil, *Aeneid*, 2.314.
7. Virgil, *Aeneid*, 6.857ff. (Dryden's translation).

the hot baths that children have, hoping that in this way he was to be ennobled. Whereas it is uncommon for eagles to be seen in the area where Albinus was born, on the seventh day after his birth, at the hour of the banquet allotted as a celebration for the boy, seven little eagles were taken from a nest and set round the boy's cradle, as though by way of a joke. His father did not reject this omen either, and ordered the eagles to be fed and looked after carefully. There was another omen, too. Boys in his family used to be wrapped in red swaddling clothes, but because the red cloths that his mother had prepared when she was pregnant had been washed, and were wet, he was wrapped in a purple bandage of his mother's. For this reason, as a joke by his nurse, the name Porphyrius was given to him. These and other signs indicated his future imperial power. Anyone wishing to learn about them should read Aelius Cordus, who relates all the trivial details concerning omens of this kind.[8]

As soon as he came of age, he enrolled for military service and gained the notice of the Antonines, thanks to Lollius Serenus, Baebius Maecianus and Ceionius Postumianus, his kinsmen. As tribune he commanded Dalmatian cavalry. He also commanded a legion, drawn from the Fourth and First. At the time when Avidius was in rebellion, he loyally kept the Bithynian armies under control. Then, having been transferred to Gaul by Commodus and having there routed tribes from across the Rhine, he made his name famous among both Romans and barbarians.[9] Impressed by these achievements, Commodus offered him the name of Caesar and the right to give out soldiers' pay and to wear a scarlet cloak. But sensibly he did not accept all this, saying that Commodus was either looking for a man who would perish with him or men that he himself could

8. See p. 16 above.
9. This sentence might contain a basis of fact: see G. Alföldy, *HAC*, 1966/7, pp. 19ff., who produces possible evidence for him having governed Lower Germany (after his first consulship) before going to Britain. But the rest of the career given in this paragraph is spurious.

with justification kill. He was excused the quaestorship. After
this concession he was aedile no longer than ten days, because
he was sent in haste to the army. Then he served his praetorship
under Commodus, a very famous one, for at his games Commodus is said to have put on gladiatorial bouts both in the
Forum and in the theatre. Severus declared him consul[10] at the
time when he was planning to make him his successor,
together with Pescennius.

He attained to the imperial power when already at quite an
advanced age, being older than Pescennius Niger, as Severus
himself says in his autobiography. But when Severus had
defeated Pescennius, he wanted to keep the empire for his sons.
He could see that there was immense love for Clodius Albinus
in the Senate – because he was a man of ancient family[11] – and so
sent him, by the hand of certain men, a letter, couched in the
most loving and affectionate terms, in which he urged that,
since Pescennius Niger had been killed, they should govern the
republic jointly. Cordus declares that this is a text of the
letter:

Emperor Severus Augustus to Clodius Albinus Caesar, his most
loving and most fond brother, greeting. When Pescennius was
defeated, we sent a letter to Rome, which the Senate, being most
devoted to you, has received with gladness. I entreat you that in the
same spirit in which you were chosen as brother of my heart you
will govern the republic as brother in imperial power. Bassianus and
Geta salute you. Our Julia salutes both you and your sister. To your
little child Princus we shall send presents worthy of his station and of
yours. I would that you keep the armies loyal to the republic and to
us, my loyal, my most dear, my most loving friend.

This letter he handed to trustworthy attendants, who were
sent with instructions that they should deliver the letter in

10. He was *cos. II ord.* in A.D.194 – his first consulship must have been
held under Commodus.
11. This is derived from Herodian, 3.5.2.

public, but after that should say that they wanted to add various things in private, concerning military affairs, secrets of the camp and the loyalty of the court; but when they had come to a private place as if to tell their orders, the five strongest were to put him to death with daggers concealed in their clothing. They did not in fact lack fidelity, for when they had come to Albinus and had handed over the letter, and he had read it, they then said that there were certain things to be added more privately and asked for a place away from all witnesses. When they would not let anyone at all go with Albinus to this distant portico, on the grounds that their orders must not be made known, Albinus realized that it was a plot. In the end, giving way to his suspicions, he handed them over to be tortured. At first, for a long time they utterly denied it, but then, yielding to necessity, they confessed what Severus had instructed them to do. Then Albinus, now that things had been revealed and the plots made plain, realizing that what he had been suspecting was manifestly the case, collected an enormous army and advanced against Severus and his generals.[12]

In the first clash, against Severus' generals, he actually had the advantage. But then Severus himself, after taking steps in the Senate to have Albinus adjudged a public enemy, set out against him and fought in Gaul, very bitterly and boldly, not without vicissitudes of fortune. In the end, when he consulted augurs in his anxiety, the reply was given him, as Marius Maximus says, that Albinus would indeed come into his power, but neither alive nor dead. And so it fell out. For when the final battle had been fought, and countless numbers of his own men had been killed, and a great many put to flight, and many had surrendered too, Albinus fled and, as many say, stabbed himself, or according to others, after being stabbed by his slave was brought to Severus half alive. Thus the augury which had been made before the battle was fulfilled. Many moreover say that he was

12. This paragraph is based on Herodian, 3.5.3–8 (embroidered).

killed by soldiers, who asked Severus for a reward for his death.[13]

Albinus had one son according to some versions; according to Maximus he had two. Severus pardoned them at first, but afterwards beheaded them, together with their mother, and ordered them to be thrown into the stream. Albinus' head was cut off, and Severus carried it round on a spear, then sent it to Rome; with it he sent a letter to the Senate, taunting them because they had loved Albinus so much and had heaped such honour on his kinsmen, particularly on his brother. Albinus' body is said to have lain for a great many days in front of Severus' headquarters, until it stank and was thrown into the stream after being torn by dogs.[14]

About his character there are differing versions. Severus, for his part, says this about him: he calls him base, crafty, shameless, dishonourable, greedy and extravagant. But this was during the war or after the war, and what he said at that time cannot be believed, considering that it was about someone who was already an enemy. Yet he had sent him very frequent letters as though to a very close friend, and many thought well of Albinus, while Severus himself wanted him to be called Caesar; and when he was thinking about a successor Albinus was the first man he had in view. In addition, letters of Marcus about this man survive, which bear witness to his virtues and his character. It would not be out of place to include one of them, addressed to his prefects and carrying his name:

Marcus Aurelius Antoninus to his prefects, greeting. I have given the command of two mounted cohorts to Albinus, from the family of the Ceionii, a native of Africa, to be sure, but not having much of the Africans' qualities – he is the son-in-law of Plautillus. He is a person of experience, strict in his way of life and of serious character.

13. This paragraph is a reworking of part of *Severus*, 10–11 (p. 211 above).

14. This paragraph is based on *Severus*, 11 (p. 212 above).

I think that he will be an asset in camp matters, certainly I am sure that he will not be a hindrance. I have allotted him a double rate of ration money, a uniform allowance at single rate (but appropriate to his rank), and fourfold pay. You should encourage him to make himself known to the republic, and he will have the reward that he deserves.

There is another letter too, which the same Marcus wrote about him at the time of Avidius Cassius. This is the text:

Albinus' firmness deserves praise: he kept under control armies that were in a serious state of disaffection, when they were going to take flight to Avidius Cassius. And they would have all done it, if it had not been for him. We have therefore a man worthy of the consulship, and I shall appoint him in place of Cassius Papirius, who, it has just been reported to me, is at the point of death. But in the meantime I do not want you to make this public, in case it gets to Papirius himself or his relatives, and we seem to have appointed a substitute consul to replace one who is still alive.

Thus these letters prove that Albinus was a man of constancy, as does, in particular, the fact that he sent money to restore the cities that Niger had laid waste, with the aim of more easily winning over their inhabitants.

Cordus, who recounts such things in his books, says that he was a glutton, so much so indeed that he used to consume a greater quantity of fruit than human capacities permit. For he says that Albinus, when hungry, ate five hundred dried figs (called *callistruthiae* by the Greeks), a hundred Campanian peaches, ten Ostian melons, twenty pounds of Labican grapes, a hundred fig-peckers and four hundred oysters. He does however say that he was moderate with wine – which Severus denies, claiming that he was drunk even during the war. With his own people he was never in agreement, either because of drunkenness, as Severus says, or because of his acrimonious character. To his wife he was most hateful, to his slaves unjust, and he was brutal towards the soldiers. Frequently he crucified

even centurions on active service, when the nature of the charge
did not require it. Certainly he very often beat them with rods,
and he never pardoned offences. In his dress he was very elegant, over banquets very niggardly, being interested only in
quantity. He was among the leading lovers as a womanizer,
but he remained innocent of unnatural sex and persecuted such
practices. He was very skilled in agriculture, and even wrote
Georgics. Some say that he was also the author of Milesian tales,
the reputation of which is not undistinguished, although they
are written in an indifferent style.

By the Senate he was loved to an extent that none of the
principes had been, especially because of the hatred for Severus,
whom the senators hated violently because of his cruelty. In
fact, when Albinus had been defeated, a great many senators
were put to death by Severus; those who had either been in his
party or who appeared to have belonged to it. Indeed, when
Severus had put him to death at Lugdunum, he at once ordered
his correspondence to be searched, in order to find out whom
he had written to and who had written to him. All those whose
letters he found, he caused to be declared public enemies by the
Senate. He did not spare these men, but put them to death and
also put their property on sale and deposited the proceeds in
the public treasury.[15]

There survives a letter of Severus, sent to the Senate, in
which he shows what his feelings were. This is a text of it:

Nothing could be more disagreeable to me, Conscript Fathers, than
that Albinus rather than Severus should have your verdict. It was I
who supplied grain for the republic; I have waged many wars for the
republic; I supplied the Roman people with a quantity of oil
such as nature scarcely possessed. I put Pescennius Niger to death and
liberated you from the evils of tyranny. You have rendered me a
great requital, to be sure, great gratitude! One of the Africans, a
Hadrumetine in fact, who has invented descent from the blood of

15. See Herodian, 3.8.6.

the Ceionii, you have exalted to such a degree that you have even wanted him as *princeps*, although I am the *princeps* and my children are living. Was there no one, I ask, in so great a Senate, whom you should love, and who might love you? You exalted his brother with honours, while from him you hope for consulships, for the praetorship, for the insignia of any office whatsoever. You have not rendered to me the thanks which your ancestors rendered in the face of the Pisonian conspiracy, which they offered for Trajan, which they offered recently in the face of Avidius Cassius. You have preferred to me that man, a deceiver and one ready for lies of every kind, who has even fabricated his noble lineage. Nay more, Statilius Corfulenus had to be heard in the Senate, proposing that honours be decreed to Albinus and his brother – this was all he lacked, that this noble person should decree him a triumph over me as well! It caused considerable resentment that most of you thought he should be praised as a man of learning, when in fact he is busy with old women's incantations and growing old amidst the Milesian tales – from Carthage – of his own Apuleius,[16] and literary trivia such as that.

From this it can be seen with what severity he took vengeance on the followers of both Pescennius and Clodius. All these matters are of course set down in Severus' biography. Anyone who wishes to know further details about them should read Marius Maximus of the Latin writers, and Herodian among the Greeks, who have related many things, with fidelity.

He was tall of stature, his hair was loose and curly, and his brow was broad. He was remarkably white, so much so that many think he got his name from that. His voice was womanish and sounded almost like that of a eunuch. He was easily roused, harsh when angered and very stern in rage. In his pleasures he was changeable, for often he was eager for wine and frequently he abstained from it. He was expert in arms. In short, he was called not inappropriately the Catiline of his age.

We believe that it is not irrelevant to set forth the reasons why Clodius Albinus earned the affection of the Senate. When by

16. The author of the *Golden Ass*, a native of Madauros in Numidia.

order of Commodus he was commanding the British armies,[17] and, after the title of Caesar had been offered him by Commodus himself, he had heard that Commodus had been put to death (at that stage this was not true), he went to meet the soldiers and delivered the following address:

If the Senate of the Roman people had its ancient power and so great a state were not under the sway of one man, the destinies of the commonwealth would never have devolved upon men like Vitellius or Nero or Domitian. Those families of ours, Ceionii, Albini and Postumii, of which your fathers – who themselves heard it from their grandfathers – have learned many things, would be endowed with consular power. Certainly it was the Senate that added Africa to the Roman empire, the Senate that conquered Gaul, the Senate that subdued the Spains, the Senate that gave laws to the peoples of the east, and the Senate that made trial of the Parthians – and would have conquered them if the republic's fate had not appointed so covetous a *princeps*[18] to command the Roman army. It was definitely as a senator that Caesar subdued the Britains,[19] but he was not yet dictator. How much better would this Commodus have been if he had feared the Senate! In fact, up to Nero's time, the authority of the Senate was strong: it did not fear to condemn a base and unclean *princeps*, and at that time speeches were made against the man who was then holding the power of life and death, and the imperial position. Wherefore, fellow-soldiers, I for my part do not want the Caesarian name which Commodus has offered me. May the gods grant that no other man want it either! Let the Senate rule, let the Senate apportion provinces and make us consuls – and why do I say 'the Senate'? – I mean you yourselves and your fathers, for you yourselves shall be senators.

This speech was reported to Rome while Commodus was still alive. It enraged Commodus against Albinus and he at once

17. This statement at least is factual: Albinus *was* governor of Britain.
18. Presumably a reference to M. Crassus, ignominiously defeated by the Parthians at Carrhae in 53 B.C. The term *princeps* is here used in its old 'republican' sense, i.e. 'leading man'.
19. From Severus onwards there were two – ultimately four – provinces in Britain, which is thus referred to (anachronistically) in the plural.

sent out Junius Severus, one of his boon companions, as his successor. But the Senate was so pleased that it honoured Albinus in his absence with remarkable acclamations, both while Commodus was alive and then when he had been put to death, so that some even advised Pertinax to make him his ally and his authority had the most weight with Julianus in his plan to kill Pertinax. Moreover, so that it may be understood that this is true, I have included a letter of Commodus addressed to his prefects, in which he makes clear his intention of killing Albinus:

Aurelius Commodus to the prefects, greeting. I believe that you have heard, firstly, that the story has been invented that I have been killed by a plot of my household, and, secondly, that Clodius Albinus has delivered an address before my soldiers, commending himself at length to the Senate; and not in vain, as far as we can see. For whoever says there ought not to be one *princeps* in the republic, and whoever asserts that the republic should be completely ruled by the Senate, is seeking the imperial power for himself, through the Senate. So keep very careful watch: for now you know the person whom you and the troops and the people must avoid.

When Pertinax found this letter, he published it, in order to make Albinus hated. As a result, Albinus was the one who incited Julianus to kill Pertinax.[20]

20. The story that Albinus incited Didius Julianus to murder Pertinax (briefly mentioned in the first sentence of this *Life*) is also found in Victor, *de Caes.*, 20.9 and Eutropius, 8.18.4. It may have been invented by Severan propagandists.

ANTONINUS CARACALLUS*

BY AELIUS SPARTIANUS

O F the two sons which Septimius Severus left, one of
whom was named Antoninus by the army and the other
by his father,[1] Geta was declared a public enemy while Bassianus
obtained the imperial power. We regard it as pointless to
repeat the account of his ancestors, since everything has been
said quite adequately in the *Life* of Severus. In his boyhood,
then, he had winning ways, was talented, respectful to his
parents and pleasing to his parents' friends. With the people he
was popular and he was dear to the Senate, and his ability to win
affection was beneficial to himself. He did not seem backward at
his letters nor inactive in showing goodwill, neither niggardly
in largess nor slow to show mercy – but this was under his
parents. Indeed, if he ever saw condemned men thrown to the
wild beasts he wept or turned away his eyes; and this was more
than pleasing to the people. As a boy of seven, when he heard
that a playmate of his had been rather harshly beaten because of
his Jewish religion, for a long time he would not look at either
his own father or the boy's father, as being responsible for the
beating. By his intervention he restored their ancient rights to
the Antiochenes and Byzantines, with whom Severus was

---

* For a discussion of this *Life*, see Syme, *AHA*, pp. 34ff. Note his comment: 'Fatigue and impatience are also disclosed in the *Vita Caracallae*.
Everything from 213 to the Emperor's death in 217 gets reported in a
scrappy fashion, barely intelligible.' The nickname by which he was
subsequently known is usually given as Caracalla; the *Augustan History*
uses the form Caracallus.

1. See p. 18 above.

angered because they had aided Niger. He conceived a loathing for Plautianus because of his cruelty. Of his own accord he gave to his dependants or teachers the presents he had received from his parents for the Sigillaria. But these things he did when a boy.[2]

When he passed boyhood, either through his father's advice or through natural cunning, or because he thought he must make himself the equal of Alexander the Great, the Macedonian, he became more reserved, sterner, even somewhat ferocious in his expression, so much so that many who had known him as a boy did not believe that it was him. He had Alexander the Great and his deeds ever on his lips. Very often he praised Tiberius and Sulla in the assembly. He was haughtier than his father, his brother he despised for his great abjectness.

After his father's death, he went to the camp of the guard and complained before the soldiers that his brother was plotting against him, and so he caused his brother to be killed in the palace. He ordered that his body be cremated at once. Furthermore, he said in the camp that his brother had prepared poison for him, and that he had been disrespectful to their mother; and he publicly rendered thanks to those who killed him. Indeed, he gave them extra pay for being so loyal to him. Some of the soldiers at Alba[3] took the killing of Geta very hard, and they all said that it was to two sons of Severus that they had promised allegiance and that they ought tō maintain it to both. The gates were shut and for a long time the emperor was not admitted. The soldiers were only placated when their minds had been made easier, not only by the complaints and accusations that he uttered against Geta, but also by an enormous payment of money. Thereupon he returned to Rome. Then, wearing a breastplate under his senatorial clothes, he entered the Senate House with armed soldiers. He drew them up in the

---

2. Some of this is probably fiction.
3. The fortress of the legion II Parthica, at Alba, close to Rome.

middle, in a double line, among the seats, and in this manner
made a speech. He complained about his brother's plot in an
involved and confused fashion, accusing him and excusing
himself. This of course the Senate did not readily accept, since
he had said that he had granted everything to his brother and
had saved him from a plot, and that nevertheless his brother had
formed a most serious conspiracy against him and had not
requited his brotherly love.

After this he granted exiles and those that had been banished
the right to return to their homeland. Then he went to meet the
praetorians and remained in the camp. On the next day he
made for the Capitol and spoke cordially to those whom he was
preparing to kill, then went back to the palace leaning on the
arm of Papinian and Cilo. When he saw Geta's mother and
other women weeping for his brother's murder he tried to kill
the women, but was held back, to prevent him adding to the
cruelty of having killed his brother. He compelled Laetus[4] to
die, having sent him poison himself; for he, who had been
among the first to recommend the murder of Geta, was himself
among the first to die. Antoninus himself very frequently wept
at his death. Many who had been involved in Geta's murder he
put to death, and also a man who showed honour to Geta's
portrait. After this he ordered the killing of his father's brother's
son Afer,[5] to whom he had sent portions from a dinner the day
before. Afer jumped headlong in fear of the assassins and
crawled to his wife with his leg broken, but he was nonetheless
seized by the assassins with derision and killed. He also killed
Pompeianus,[6] grandson of Marcus, son of Marcus' daughter
and of the Pompeianus to whom Lucilla had been married

4. Conceivably identical with the 'Laenus' recorded by Dio (77.5.4)
as a man intended as a victim who survived through being ill at the time.

5. Perhaps the name should be Aper, in which case he may be the *cos.
ord.* 207, L. Septimius Aper: see stemma, p. 322.

6. Aurelius Pompeianus (*cos. ord.* 209): see stemma, p. 320.

after the death of the emperor Verus, and whom Marcus had made consul twice and placed in command of all his wars; and it was done in such a way that it seemed as if he had been put to death by brigands.[7] Then Papinian was struck down with an axe by soldiers, before his eyes, and killed. When this was done, Antoninus said to the assassin: 'You should have carried out my order with a sword.' Patruinus was also killed by his order, in front of the temple of the Deified Pius. Their corpses were dragged through the streets without any regard for human feelings. Papinian's son, too, who three days before as quaestor had put on a lavish spectacle,[8] was put to death. During these days countless numbers were killed who had supported his brother's party. The freedmen who had managed Geta's affairs were also killed. Thereafter there was slaughter everywhere. There was even murder done in the baths, and some were killed at dinner too, among them Sammonicus Serenus, many of whose books on learned subjects are still available.[9] Even Cilo, twice prefect and consul, came into extreme danger for the reason that he had advocated harmony between the brothers. In the case of Cilo, his senatorial robe had been taken off him and his feet were bare, and he had been seized by the urban soldiers before Antoninus checked the disturbance. He caused many additional murders in the city after this, not a few persons being seized by the soldiers, far and wide, as if he were punishing an insurrection. He put to death Helvius Pertinax, a suffect consul, for the sole reason that he was son of an emperor, and he never ceased, on different occasions, putting to death those who had been his brother's friends. Frequently he delivered arrogant invectives against the Senate and against the

7. See also *Commodus*, 5.12 (p. 166 above) for a similar story about the murder of another member of this family.

8. This would appear to date the death of Geta to late December A.D. 211 (rather than early 212): see T. D. Barnes, *Jn. Theol. Stud.* 1968, 523f.

9. A scholar whose writings were cited by Macrobius and other fifth-century authors.

people, issuing edicts or publishing speeches, even indicating that he would be a Sulla.

After these deeds he made for Gaul and as soon as he reached it he killed the proconsul of Narbonensis. Thereupon all who were holding posts in Gaul were thrown into a panic, and he earned the detestation felt for a tyrant, although sometimes he would pretend to be benevolent as well, whereas he was grim by nature. And after he had done many things against individuals and against the rights of communities, he fell ill and was in serious distress. Towards those who were looking after him he was most cruel. Then, while preparing an expedition to the east, he interrupted his journey and stopped in Dacia. In the vicinity of Raetia he put to death not a few barbarians, and as for his own soldiers he both exhorted them and gave them presents as though they were Sulla's soldiers. At least he did not allow them to call him by the names of the gods, as had been the practice with Commodus – for they used to call the latter Hercules because he had killed a lion and other wild beasts. After he had subdued the Germans, he called himself Germanicus,[10] either in jest or in earnest, for he was stupid and crazy and asserted that if he had conquered the Lucanians he would have had to be called Lucanicus.[11] At that time men were condemned for urinating in the place where there were statues or portraits of the *princeps*, as were those who removed garlands from his busts to replace them with others; and those who wore things round their necks as preventatives for quartan or tertian fevers were condemned too.[12]

10. The title was already in use at Rome by 6 October A.D.213: *ILS*, no. 451. During the campaign (against the Alamanni) Caracalla made important modifications to the Roman frontier system in the province of Raetia.

11. Presumably a joke by the author: Syme, *AHA*, pp. 34f. (the name means 'sausage'). *Germanus* means brother, hence there is an allusion here to Geta's murder.

12. This last item is spurious: the wearing of amulets was not a capital offence until the reign of Constantius II (Ammianus, 19.12.14).

He made a journey through Thrace with the prefect of the guard.[13] Then when he was crossing to Asia the sail-yard of the ship was broken and he ran into danger of shipwreck, so that he had to climb down into a rowing-boat with his bodyguards.[14] From this he was taken into a trireme by the prefect of the fleet and was rescued. He took wild boars on many occasions and even faced a lion, an achievement he boasted about in a letter sent to friends, in which he bragged that he had attained to the prowess of Hercules.

After this he turned to the Armenian and Parthian war, appointing as general for the war a man whose character accorded with his own.[15] Then he made for Alexandria, where he summoned the people to the gymnasium and rebuked them. He also ordered that the physically fit should be enrolled for military service. But those that he had enrolled he killed, after the example of Ptolemy Euergetes, the eighth to bear that name.[16] In addition, as he gave a signal to the soldiers to kill their hosts, he caused great slaughter at Alexandria.

After this, advancing through the lands of the Cadusii and the Babylonians,[17] he engaged in guerilla warfare with the satraps of the Parthians, even letting wild beasts loose at the enemy. On the dispatch of a letter to the Senate as if there had been a victory, he was named Parthicus, he had taken the name Germanicus while his father was alive.[18] Intending to make war on the Parthians a second time, he was

13. Presumably Macrinus.

14. The term *protectores* (which meant 'staff-officers' when it emerged in the later third century) is here used inaccurately and anachronistically.

15. The freedman Theocritus (Dio, 77.21.1–4).

16. Ptolemy VIII Physcon Euergetes (sole ruler of the Ptolemaic empire 145–116 B.C.) carried out a massacre at Alexandria in 125 B.C.

17. 'Both items are absurd . . . a vague reminiscence from geography or fable' (Syme, *AHA*, pp. 35f.).

18. An error: see p. 254 above.

wintering at Edessa. From there he had come to Carrhae to do
honour to the god Lunus, on his birthday, the eighth day before
the Ides of April [6 April A.D. 217],[19] during the Megalensian
festival. He went aside to perform natural functions, and was
put to death through a plot mounted by the prefect of the guard,
Macrinus, who laid hands on the imperial power in his stead.
Involved in the murder were Nemesianus and his brother
Apollinaris, and Triccianus who was serving as prefect of the
legion II Parthica and commanding the special cavalry, while
Marcius Agrippa, who was commanding the fleet, and most of
the headquarters staff – on the instigation of Martialis – were not
in ignorance about the matter. He was actually killed in the
middle of the journey between Carrhae and Edessa, when he
had dismounted from his horse for the purpose of relieving his
bladder and was doing so, between his bodyguards. When his
equerry was helping him on to his horse, he stabbed the
emperor in the side with a dagger, and everyone shouted out
that Martialis had done it.

Since we have made mention of the god Lunus, it should be
known that it is held by the most learned and has been committed to record – and is still generally believed, especially by
the people of Carrhae – that whoever thinks the moon ought
to be called by the feminine name and sex will be controlled by
women, and always subservient to them; but whoever thinks
that the deity is masculine shall dominate his wife and never put
up with any womanish wiles. Hence although the Greeks and
Egyptians, in the same way that they say a woman is 'man',
likewise call Luna a 'god', yet in mystic rites they use the name
Lunus.

I know that many have set down the story of Papinian's
death in such a way as to show that they did not know the
cause of his murder, each giving a different version. But I have

19. A typical, perhaps deliberate, error: Caracalla's birthday was 4
April and he was murdered on 8 April. The Megalensian festival lasted
from 4–10 April.

preferred to record a variety of opinions, rather than remain silent about the murder of so great a man. It is generally recorded that Papinian was a very close friend of the emperor Severus, indeed, according to some, he was related to him through his second wife; and it is said that it was to him in particular that both his sons were entrusted by Severus, and that this is why he urged harmony between the Antonine brothers.[20] Indeed he is even said to have wanted to prevent Geta being killed when Bassianus was already complaining about his plot; and hence that Papinian was killed by the soldiers, together with those who had been supporters of Geta, and Antoninus not only permitted but actually encouraged it. Many say that when his brother had been killed, Bassianus gave Papinian the task of explaining away the crime for him, both in the Senate and before the people, but that he replied that it was not so easy to defend fratricide as to commit it. There is also the story that he did not want to compose a speech in which he had to inveigh against the brother so that the murderer's case might be improved; and that, moreover, in his refusal he said that fratricide was one thing, but to accuse an innocent man who had been murdered was another. But this is not at all plausible, for a prefect of the guard would not compose a speech and it is well established that he was killed for being a supporter of Geta. It is in fact reported that when Papinian had been seized by the soldiers and was being dragged off to the palace to be killed, he predicted what would happen, saying that the man who was appointed to replace him would be a fool if he did not take revenge for the cruel assault on the prefecture. This is what came to pass: for Macrinus killed Antoninus, as we have related above. When Macrinus had been made emperor in the camp, together with his son who was called Diadumenus, he

20. See p. 221 above. It is not clear whether the relationship was through Severus' or Papinian's wife; the former is commonly assumed to be the link.

gave his son the name Antoninus, for the reason that Antoninus was greatly missed by the praetorians.

Bassianus lived forty-three years[21] and was emperor for six. He was given a public funeral. He left a son, who was afterwards also called Marcus Antoninus − Heliogabalus. (For the name of Antoninus had such a hold that it could not be plucked out of the minds of men, since it had taken possession of the hearts of all, just like the name Augustus.) His character was evil and he was more cruel than his relentless father. Greedy over food and an avid drinker of wine, he was loathed by his household and detested in all the camps except by the praetorian soldiers. In short, there was no similarity between the brothers.

The public works that he left at Rome include the splendid baths named after him,[22] and the sandal-shaped room (*cella solearis*) which, so architects say, cannot be imitated in its manner of construction. For beams of bronze or copper are said to have been set in position, on which the whole vaulting rests, and so great is the span that engineers say it was an impossible feat.[23] He also left a portico named after his father, which was to contain a record both of his triumph and of his wars. He himself got the name Caracallus from the garment reaching down to the heels that he had given to the people, which had not been worn before. Hence hooded cloaks (*caracallae*) of this kind are still called Antonine today, and are commonly worn, especially by the plebs at Rome. He also built a new street, alongside his baths (that is, the Antonine Baths), and a more beautiful one it would be hard to find among the streets of Rome. He brought the rites of Isis to Rome and built splendid temples to that goddess everywhere. He also celebrated the rites with greater reverence than they used to be celebrated

21. An error: he died at the age of 29.
22. The Baths of Caracalla.
23. The reference is apparently to the great entrance-hall of the Baths, the vaulting of which was supported by *iron* girders.

previously. In this matter, actually, it seems puzzling to me how the rites of Isis can be said to have come to Rome for the first time through him, since Antoninus Commodus celebrated them to such an extent that he even used to carry the Anubis figure and make the pauses – unless perhaps Bassianus increased the celebration of the rites, and was not the first to bring them in. His body was laid in the tomb of the Antonines, so that the spot which had given him his name might receive his remains.

It is of interest to know the way in which he is said to have taken his stepmother Julia as his wife. She was very beautiful and, as if through carelessness, had uncovered the greater part of her body; Antoninus said: 'I would want to, if it were permitted'. She is said to have replied: 'If you wish it, it is permitted. Don't you know that you are emperor and give out laws and do not suffer under them?' When he heard this his disordered madness was given strength to carry out the crime and he contracted the marriage which – if he really knew that he gave out the laws – he alone should have prohibited. For he took to wife his mother – she ought not to be called by any other name – and added incest to fratricide, considering that he joined to himself in marriage the woman whose son he had just killed.[24]

It is not out of place to subjoin a certain *plaisanterie* made against him. When he assumed the names Germanicus, Parthicus, Arabicus and Alamannicus (for he had conquered the people of the Alamanni), Helvius Pertinax, son of Pertinax, is said to have remarked, as a joke: 'Add Geticus Maximus, too, please' – because he had killed Geta and 'Getae' is a name for the Goths whom he had defeated in skirmishes while crossing to the east.[25]

There were many omens predicting Geta's murder, as we shall set forth in the biography of him. For although he was the

24. On this erroneous fable, see p. 221, n. 58, above.
25. 'Nonsense', in the view of Syme, *AHA*, p. 36.

first to die we have nonetheless followed the plan that the one that was born first and began to be emperor first should be written about first.

Of course, at the time when Antoninus was called Augustus by the army while his father was still alive – because the latter, crippled in the feet, appeared to be incapable of governing the empire – when the plot of the soldiers and tribunes had been crushed, Severus is said to have turned over in his mind the idea of killing him – but his prefects, men of weight, opposed this. Some, on the other hand, say that the prefects did want this to be done, but that Septimius was unwilling, lest the severity of such an act might be darkened by the name of cruelty; and whereas those responsible for the crime were soldiers, a young man might pay the penalty for his foolish temerity under the head of so heavy a punishment that he might seem to have been killed by his father.

Yet he, the most relentless of all men and, in a word, an incestuous fratricide, enemy of his father, mother and brother, was enrolled among the gods by Macrinus, through fear of the soldiers and especially of the praetorians. He has a temple, he has Salian priests,[26] he has the Antonine *Sodales* – he who took from Faustina her temple and her divine name, certainly the temple, which her husband had founded for her in the foothills of the Taurus, and in which afterwards his son Heliogabalus Antoninus built a temple either for himself or for the Syrian Jupiter or for the Sun – it is uncertain which.

26. There is no evidence for this remark.

ANTONINUS GETA*

BY AELIUS SPARTIANUS

I KNOW, Constantine Augustus, that many people as well as
Your Clemency may raise the question why I should treat of
Geta Antoninus also. Before I speak either of his life or of his
death I shall discuss the reason why he too was given the name
Antoninus by his father Severus. For there is not much that can
be told of the life of one who was removed from human affairs
before he could take control of the empire together with his
brother.[1]

Once when Septimius Severus asked about the future and
sought to have revealed to him who his successor might be
when he died, he saw in a dream that an Antoninus would
succeed him. Therefore he went at once to the soldiers and
named Bassianus, his elder son, Marcus Aurelius Antoninus.
When he had done this, after some fatherly reflection, or, as
some say, a warning by his wife Julia, who was skilled in dreams,
that by this act he had himself cut off his younger son from access
to the imperial power, he ordered that Geta his younger son
should also bear the name Antoninus. Hence Geta was always
given this name by Severus in family letters. He used to write,
if he happened to be away: 'Salute the Antonines, my sons and
successors.' But the precautions of a father availed nothing, for
the son who first received the name Antoninus was his sole
successor. So much for the name Antoninus.

---

* This *Life* is predominantly fiction, not least the title: Geta was never
called Antoninus (see p. 18 above).

1. This is inaccurate if it means that Geta was not a full emperor: he
was made Augustus in A.D.209.

He was called Geta, moreover, either after his uncle or after his paternal grandfather, concerning whose life and character Marius Maximus has reported in quite abundant detail in his *Life* of Severus, in the first section.[2] But another version why Geta was called Antoninus was that Severus had it in mind that all subsequent emperors should be called Antoninus as well as Augustus, because of his love for Marcus, whom he always used to call his father or brother, and whose philosophy and literary training he always imitated. Some say that it was not in honour of Marcus only that the name Antoninus was bestowed – since Marcus had it by adoption – but in honour of him who was surnamed Pius, namely Hadrian's successor. This was, actually, because Antoninus Pius had chosen Severus from practice in the law-courts to be an advocate of the fisc, since the happy augury of the first step or appointment given by Antoninus had opened the path to such great advancement for him.[3] At the same time, it was because no emperor seemed to him more auspicious for lending his name than that *princeps*, whose personal name had already been passed on to four *principes*.

As for this same Geta, Severus, knowing his horoscope, a subject in which, like most Africans, he was very skilled, is reported to have said about him: 'It seems remarkable to me, my dear Juvenalis, that our Geta is to be deified, since I see nothing imperial in his horoscope.' (Juvenalis was his prefect of the guard.) Nor was he mistaken. For Bassianus, when he had

2. The meaning of the term used, *septenarius*, is not clear: see Birley, *Severus*, pp. 322f.

3. The story that Severus had been *advocatus fisci* is also found in Victor, *de Caes.*, 20.30 and Eutropius, 8.18.2, and the latter adds the statement that Severus had been military tribune also. There are no grounds for believing either item, which contradicts the detail supplied in *Severus*, 2–3 (p. 202 above). See Birley, *Severus*, p. 302, n. 1, for the suggestion that Marius Maximus' *Life of Severus* may have contained the information that Severus' father had held the post; and that this was misunderstood by Victor, Eutropius and the *Augustan History*.

killed Geta, and feared that he would be branded as a tyrant for his fratricide, and heard that his crime could be mitigated if he declared his brother deified, is reported to have said: 'Let him be deified, so long as he does not live.'⁴ He did in fact enrol Geta among the deified emperors,⁵ and thus his reputation came back into favour one way and another, in spite of his being a fratricide.

Geta was born at Mediolanum [Milan], even though others have related otherwise, on the sixth day before the Kalends of June, when Severus and Vitellius were the consuls [27 May A.D. 189(?)].⁶ His mother was Julia, whom Severus had taken as his wife for the reason that he had found out that her horoscope foretold she should be the wife of a king. Severus was then a private citizen, but already of excellent standing in the republic. As soon as he was born, it was announced that a hen had laid a purple egg in the inner courtyard. When it was brought in, Bassianus his brother, behaving just as little boys do, took it and threw it to the ground, and broke it. Julia is reported to have said, as a joke: 'Accursed fratricide, you have killed your brother!' But this, said as a joke, Severus took more seriously than any of those present, although afterwards it was confirmed by those who had been standing round that it had been uttered as if by divine inspiration. There was another omen, too: a lamb was born with purple wool on its forehead, on the farm of a certain Antoninus, a commoner, on the same day and at the same hour as Geta was born. The man had heard from the soothsayer that 'Antoninus' would be emperor after Severus, and interpreted the omen as referring to himself – but feared the sign of such a destiny, however, and drove a knife into it. This

4. It is impossible to reproduce the play on the words *divus* and *vivus*.
5. False.
6. A piece of bogus scholarship: see Syme, *AHA*, p. 123; *EB*, pp. 64, 183. Geta was born at Rome (*Severus*, 4.3, p. 204 above) on 7 March A.D. 189 in the view of T. D. Barnes, *Jnl. of Theol. Studies*, 1968, pp. 522ff., which seems probable.

was another sign that Geta would be put to death by Antoninus, as subsequently became quite clear. There was, as well, a further important omen of this crime, as the remarkable outcome subsequently showed: when Severus was preparing to celebrate the infant Geta's birthday, a boy named Antoninus killed the sacrificial victim. This was not investigated or noted at the time, but afterwards it was understood.

As a youth Geta was handsome, a rough character but not disrespectful, greedy, interested in words, gluttonous, a lover of food and of wine variously flavoured. He made a famous remark when he was a boy and Severus, who was planning to kill men from the opposite factions, said to his family: 'I am ridding you of your enemies.' Bassianus was in favour of this, even to the extent of saying that if his advice were asked their children should be killed as well. But Geta is reported to have inquired how large a number were to be executed, and when his father had told him, he asked: 'Do they have parents, do they have kinsmen?' When the reply was that they had, he said: 'Then there will be more in the state that will grieve than will be glad at our victory.' His view would have prevailed, if Plautianus the prefect – or Juvenalis – had not urged against it, in the hope of having proscriptions, from which they became rich. They were supported by the excessive cruelty of Bassianus. When he was arguing and saying half in joke and half in earnest that everyone from the opposite factions should be killed, together with their children, Geta is said to have told him: 'You, who spare no one, are capable of killing even your brother.' That remark of his was thought nothing of at the time, but afterwards it was regarded as prophetic.

In his study of literature he stuck to the old writers. He was mindful of his father's opinions too, was always hated by his brother, and was more affectionate than his brother towards his mother. He had a resonant voice, with a slight stammer. He was very fond of elegant clothing, so much so that his father used to make fun of him. If he got anything from his parents he used it for his own external appearance, and never gave anything to anyone. After the Parthian war, when his father was at the height of his glory, and Bassianus had been named his colleague as emperor, Geta too received the name of Caesar, and that of Antoninus, according to some. He made a habit of propounding problems to grammarians, asking them to say what sounds different animals make, for example: lambs bleat, pigs grunt, doves coo, bears growl, lions roar, leopards snarl, elephants trumpet, frogs croak, horses neigh, bulls bellow – and he would confirm these from old writers. He was very intimately acquainted with the books of Serenus Sammonicus,[7] which were addressed to Antoninus. He also had the custom of ordering banquets, and especially dinners, according to single letters, with the help of knowledgeable slaves: for instance at one there was goose, gammon, gadwall, or again, pullet, partridge, peacock, pork, *poisson*, pig's trotters and other kinds of food beginning with this letter; or again, pheasant, farina, fig, and so on. For this reason he was regarded as a good companion even in his youth.

When he had been killed, some of the soldiers who had not been bribed took the fratricide very hard, and they all said that it was to two sons that they had promised allegiance and that they ought to maintain allegiance to two.[8] The gates were shut and the emperor was not admitted for a long time. In the end, if he had not uttered complaints against Geta and made their minds easier, and also given them enormous payments of money, Bassianus could not have returned to Rome. After this, in the end, both Papinian and many others who had either supported concord or had been in Geta's party were put to death, in such a way that men of both classes were cut down in the bath or while dining or in public. Papinian himself was struck down with an axe, and Bassianus found fault because the business had

7. See p. 253, n. 9 above.
8. This chapter, closely resembling *Caracallus*, 2ff. (p. 251f above), is apparently largely authentic.

not been done with a sword. Finally things reached the pitch of a mutiny of the urban soldiers. Of course Bassianus curbed them with no light authority. One of their tribunes was executed, as some say, or exiled, according to others. Bassianus himself, moreover, was so much afraid, that he entered even the Senate House wearing a breastplate under his broad stripe and, thus attired, rendered an account of his action and of the 'Getic murder'. It is said that at this time Helvius Pertinax, son of Pertinax, who was subsequently put to death by Bassianus, said to the praetor who was reading out auspicious news, and saying 'Sarmaticus Maximus and Parthicus Maximus', 'Add Geticus Maximus as well', meaning 'Gothicus', as it were. This remark sank deep into the heart of Bassianus, as was proved in the sequel by the murder of Pertinax, and not only of Pertinax, but others too, as was said above, on all sides and without just cause. Helvius, moreover, he suspected of aiming at an usurpation, because he was son of the emperor Pertinax, and that is something that is hardly very safe for any private citizen.

Geta's funeral is said to have been fairly elaborate for one who appeared to have been killed by his brother. He was laid in the tomb of his ancestors, that is, in Severus' tomb, which is on the *Via Appia* on the right as you go to the gate, built like the Septizodium, which Severus had adorned for himself in his lifetime.

Antoninus wanted to kill Geta's mother as well, his step-mother,[9] because she was mourning his brother, and with her the women that he found weeping after his return from the Senate House. Antoninus was, furthermore, such a monster that he used to be particularly charming to those he was intending to murder, so that his charm was feared more than his anger. It certainly seemed remarkable to everyone that even he used to weep for the death of Geta, whenever there was a mention of his name, and whenever he saw his portrait or statue. Of course,

9. See p. 221, n. 58 above.

there was so much capriciousness about Antoninus Bassianus, or rather so much bloodthirstiness, that he would kill at one moment Geta's supporters and at another his enemies, according as chance put them in his path. For this reason Geta was the more regretted.

OPILIUS MACRINUS*

BY JULIUS CAPITOLINUS

THE lives of those *principes*, or usurpers, or Caesars who were not emperors, for long lie hidden in obscurity, for there is nothing about their private life which is worth telling. They would not be known of at all if they had not aspired to empire, and about their position as emperor, which they did not hold for long, there is not much that can be said. Nonetheless, we shall bring out into the light of day what we have dug out from various historians, and these things at least shall be worthy of record. For there is no one who has not done something or other every day of his life; but it is the duty of a biographer to write down what is worth knowing. Junius Cordus[1] was of course devoted to publishing the lives of those emperors whom he regarded as the more obscure. But he did not achieve a great deal. For he found little, and that was not worthy of record, while he declared that he would pursue all the smallest details, as though, in the case of Trajan or Pius or Marcus, one had to know how often he went out, when he ate different kinds of food, when he changed his clothes, and whom he promoted and when. By writing such things he filled his books with 'mythical history', whereas either none of the trivial details should be recorded at all, or very few, – and only if character can be observed from them, for character is what really should

---

* Macrinus' *nomen* is spelled Opellius on coins and inscriptions, but the incorrect form Opilius is found in Victor and Eutropius as well as here. Most of this *Life* is fiction.

1. See p. 16 above.

be known about . . .,[2] but from one part, so that the rest may be inferred from it.

Now when Antoninus Bassianus had been killed, Opilius Macrinus, his prefect of the guard, who had previously been in charge of the Privy Purse,[3] seized the imperial power. Born to a lowly station and shameless both in his spirit and in his countenance, and although detested by all, both by the people in general and by the soldiers, he named himself first Severus and then Antoninus,[4] and at once set out for the Parthian war. Thus he gave the soldiers no chance to judge him and the rumours, by which he was being pursued, no chance to reach full strength. Nonetheless the Senate willingly accepted him as emperor, through hatred of Antoninus Bassianus, and there was at this time a single cry in the Senate: 'Anyone rather than the fratricide, anyone rather than the incestuous, anyone rather than the polluted, anyone rather than the murderer of the Senate and the people!'

It may possibly seem puzzling to everyone why Diadumenus[5] wanted to be called Antoninus, being the son of Macrinus, considering that the latter is said to have been responsible for the murder of an Antoninus. Concerning this matter I will set forth what has been related in the annals. The priestess of Caelestis at Carthage, who is accustomed to foretell the truth, inspired by the goddess, in the reign of Antoninus Pius predicted the future for a proconsul who was consulting her about affairs of state, as

2. The MSS. are defective here.

3. i.e. *procurator rei privatae*: Dio (78.11.1ff.), who gives a detailed account of Macrinus' previous career, does not mention this post, although he does say that Macrinus had received 'some brief appointments as procurator' from Caracalla before being made prefect of the guard. But the *Augustan History* is unaware of the important facts, given by Dio, that Macrinus was a Moor and a former protégé of Plautianus.

4. Incorrect: he used the name Severus, but not Antoninus.

5. Macrinus' son is called Diadumenus by Victor and Eutropius as well as here, but elsewhere he is called Diadumenianus.

was usual, and about his own prospect of becoming emperor.
When the subject of the *principes* was reached, in a clear voice
she commanded him to count how many times she said 'Antoninus'; and then, to universal astonishment, she uttered the
name Antoninus Augustus eight times. But whereas everyone
thought that Antoninus Pius would be emperor for eight years,
he went beyond that number of years, and it was agreed among
those who believed in her, both then and subsequently,
that something else was indicated by the priestess. In fact, when
all who have been called Antoninus are counted, the number of
Antonines is found to be exactly eight. For Pius was the first of
the Antonines, Marcus the second, Verus the third, Commodus
the fourth, fifth was Caracallus, sixth Geta, seventh Diadumenus and eighth Heliogabalus. Not to be included among
the Antonines are the two Gordians, either because they only
had the forename of Antoninus, or because they were actually
called Antonius, not Antoninus. Hence it is that Severus too
called himself Antoninus – and there have been a great many,
Pertinax too, and Julianus and this same Macrinus. But by the
Antonines proper, who were the true successors of Antoninus,
this name was kept in preference to their own personal names.
This is what some say. But others record that the reason why
Diadumenus was named Antoninus by his father Macrinus was
to remove the soldiers' suspicion that Antoninus had been put
to death by Macrinus. Others, again, say that there was such
great longing for this name that if the people and the soldiers did
not hear the name Antoninus, they would not regard a man as
imperial.

Of course, when it was announced that Varius Heliogabalus[6]
had been made emperor, and when the Senate had already

---

6. Elagabalus (as he is generally known now) was the son of Sex.
Varius Marcellus and Julia Soaemias, niece of Julia Domna: see stemma,
p. 322. His original names were Varius Avitus Bassianus.

named Alexander as Caesar,[7] things were said about Macrinus
in the Senate which made it apparent that he was ignoble, base
and common. In fact, these were the words of Aurelius Victor
surnamed Pinio: that, under Commodus, Macrinus had been
a freedman and a male prostitute, engaged in slave-duties in the
imperial household; that his honour was for sale and his life base;
that under Severus he had been dismissed even from the most
wretched of duties and banished to Africa, where, to conceal the
disgrace of his sentence, he had devoted himself to public reading, had pleaded minor cases, had been a declaimer, and
finally had had speaking parts in plays; but that he was granted
the gold rings[8] with the support of his fellow-freedman, Festus,
and that he became a treasury counsel under Verus Antoninus.[9]
However, these statements themselves are placed in doubt, and
other things are stated by other writers, and on these too we
shall not be silent. For many have said that he practised gladiatorial combat and went to Africa after receiving the staff of
discharge; that he had been a huntsman in the arena first, then a
notary too, and finally treasury counsel. Then, as prefect of the
guard, when his colleague had been banished, he caused the
death of Antoninus Caracallus, his own emperor. So many
were in the conspiracy that it was not obvious that Macrinus
was behind the murder. He bribed Antoninus' equerry and
offered the man great hopes, then brought it about that

7. Alexander was not in fact named Caesar until A.D.221 (*PIR²*, A
1610). As T. D. Barnes, *HAC* 1970, pp. 66f., suggests, the story that he
was made Caesar in 218, also found in *Heliogabalus*, 10.1 (p. 297 below),
the *Life* of Severus Alexander, 1.2, and in Victor, *de Caes.*, 23.3, 'may
derive ultimately from Marius Maximus and be a deliberate, contemporary invention from the reign of Severus Alexander'. Son of Julia
Mamaea, another niece of Julia Domna, and Gessius Marcianus, his
name was originally Gessius Alexianus Bassianus: see stemma, p. 322.

8. A symbolic way of wiping out the stigma of servile origin.

9. Macrinus (b. A.D.164: Dio, 79.40.3) was aged four at the time of L.
Verus' death. But the story is fiction anyway.

Antoninus' murder was attributed to a plot by the soldiers, because of Antoninus' unpopularity either for the fratricide or for the incest.

Macrinus seized the imperial power at once, then, and having taken his son Diadumenus as colleague, immediately ordered the soldiers to name him Antoninus, as said above. Then he sent the body of Antoninus back to Rome to be laid in the tomb of his forefathers. He charged his former colleague, the prefect of the guard,[10] to perform his proper duties and particularly to bury Antoninus with due honours, conducting a royal funeral, for he was aware that Antoninus had been greatly loved by the plebs on account of the clothes distributed to the people as gifts. There was the further point, also, that he was afraid there would be a disturbance among the soldiers, and if that happened it might jeopardize his position as emperor, which he had intended to seize but which he had accepted with a show of reluctance – as happens with men who say that they are compelled to take what they get for themselves even through crime. Furthermore, he feared his colleague too, in case he might wish to be emperor himself – everyone was expecting this and if there had been support from a single unit he would not have refused; and everyone would have done this with great eagerness through their hatred of Macrinus, either for his infamous life or because of his lack of nobility (seeing that all previous emperors had been nobles).[11] Besides this, he added to his own name that of Severus, although not connected to the latter by any kinship. Hence the joke: 'Macrinus is as much a Severus as Diadumenus is an Antoninus.' However, to put a stop to disturbances among the soldiers, he gave a donative both to legionaries and to praetorians at once, on a more ample scale than usual,

10. M. Oclatinius Adventus.

11. On Adventus' ambitions, see Dio, 78. 14.2–4. Herodian (4.14.1) claims that he was actually offered the position of emperor, but refused. Previous emperors had *not* all been 'nobles'; but they had all been senators, which Macrinus was not.

seeing that he was eager to mitigate the charge of having killed the emperor. As is usual, money assisted one whom innocence could not profit; for he was maintained as emperor for some time, although he was a person with all the vices.

Then he sent a letter to the Senate concerning the death of Antoninus, called him 'the Deified', clearing himself of guilt, and swearing that he did not know about his murder. Thus to his crime, in the manner of wicked men, he added perjury, an act which it was fitting for a shameless man to begin with, when writing to the Senate. It is of interest to know the nature of his address in which he cleared himself, so that his insolence may be appreciated and also the sacrilege with which this shameless man made his start as emperor. Passages from the speech of the emperors Macrinus and Diadumenus:

We might have wished, Conscript Fathers, to look upon Your Clemency with Antoninus safe and riding back in triumph. For then indeed would the republic be flourishing and we would all be happy and would be living under that *princeps* whom the gods had given us in place of the Antonines. But since that could not happen on account of the uprising of the soldiers, we announce, first, what the army has done concerning ourselves, and then we decree, for him to whom we swore our allegiance, divine honours – and this is our first duty. For the army has regarded no one as more fitted to avenge the murder of Bassianus than him whom he himself would have charged with punishing the conspiracy had he been able to detect it while he lived.

And further on:

They have bestowed the empire on me, and I, Conscript Fathers, having taken up the guardianship of it for the time being, will retain control if it please you also, as it has pleased the soldiers, to whom I have already given a payment of money and for whom I have commanded everything in the customary imperial fashion.

Again, further on:

To my son Diadumenus, who is known to you, the soldiers have given both the imperial power and the name – calling him Antoninus, that is to say – so that he might be graced first with the name and then too with the honour of kingly power. And this, Conscript Fathers, we seek that you approve with good and propitious omen, that you may not lack the name of the Antonines, which you most greatly revere.

Again, further on:

To Antoninus, moreover, the soldiers have decreed divine honours; we too decree them and, Conscript Fathers, although by right as emperor we could instruct you, yet we ask you, that you decree them also. And we dedicate to him two statues on horseback and two on foot, two in military uniform and two seated, in civilian dress, likewise two for the Deified Severus in triumphal costume. All of which, Conscript Fathers, you will command to be carried out, as we dutifully solicit on behalf of our predecessors.

So when the letter had been read in the Senate, contrary to the general expectation the Senate received the news of Antoninus' death with pleasure. Also, hoping that Opilius Macrinus would safeguard the freedom of the people, it first enrolled him among the patricians, although he was a new man and one who had but a little while before been in charge of the Privy Purse. This man, although he was a pontifex's clerk – today they call them minor pontiffs – it named Pontifex Maximus, decreeing for him the name Pius. For a long time, however, when the letter had been read, there was silence, since absolutely no one believed the story of Antoninus' death. But after it was established that he had been killed, the Senate reviled him as a tyrant. Then they at once conferred on Macrinus both the proconsular *imperium* and the tribunician power.

Of course, after he himself had received the name Felix, he named his son Antoninus, his previous name being Diadumenus, to avert the suspicion that Antoninus had been killed by himself. And in fact this name was also used subsequently by Varius Heliogabalus, who called himself 'son of Bassianus', a person of the basest kind and born of a prostitute. Indeed, there are verses by some poet in which it is shown that the name of Antoninus began with Pius and gradually passed down the Antonines until it reached the final sordid level, considering that Marcus alone appears to have enhanced that hallowed name by the character of his life, while Verus seems to have lowered, and Commodus actually to have profaned, the reverence of the sacred name. And then, what can be said of Caracallus Antoninus, or what of this Diadumenus? Finally, what can be said of Heliogabalus, the last of the Antonines, who is reported to have lived in the depths of foulness?

Having been named emperor, then, and having undertaken the war against the Parthians, Macrinus set out on expedition with a great array, eager to wipe out the baseness of his stock and the ill repute of his former life by the magnificence of a victory. However, after an engagement with the Parthians he was put to death in a revolt of the legions, which had deserted to Varius Heliogabalus. But he was emperor for more than a year.

To be sure, although worsted in the war which Antoninus had waged – for Artabanes exacted a heavy punishment for the killing of his citizens – Macrinus at first fought back. But subsequently, having dispatched envoys, he sought peace, which the Parthian granted in a willing spirit, considering that Antoninus had been put to death.[12] Then, after he had taken himself off to Antioch, and began to devote his attention to luxury, he provided justification to the army for killing him and following the supposed son of Bassianus, that is Heliogabalus Bassianus Varius, afterwards called both Bassianus and Antoninus.

There was a certain woman, Maesa or Varia,[13] from the city

12. From midway through this paragraph to midway through the paragraph after next, the account is derived, in places as a direct translation, from Herodian, 5.3.1–4.12.

13. Julia Maesa, sister of Julia Domna, was of course never called Varia: her elder daughter Soaemias was married to Sex. Varius Marcellus (see stemma, p. 322).

of Emesa, sister of Julia the wife of Severus Pertinax the African. After the death of Antoninus Bassianus she had been expelled from her home at court through the arrogance of Macrinus, although Macrinus did allow her to keep everything that she had collected together over a long period. She had two daughters, Symiamyra and Mamaea, the elder of whom had a son, Heliogabalus – for the Phoenicians call the sun Heliogabalus. Heliogabalus was outstanding for his beauty and stature, and for the priesthood, and was well known to all the people who used to come to the temple, especially to the soldiers. To them, Maesa, or Varia, said that Bassianus was the son of Antoninus, and this gradually became known to all the soldiers. Besides this, Maesa herself was very rich (for which reason Heliogabalus was most extravagant), and through her promises to the soldiers, the legions were seduced from their allegiance to Macrinus. For when she and her people had been taken into the town by night, her grandson was hailed as Antoninus and the insignia of the imperial power were bestowed upon him.[14]

When these events had been announced to Macrinus, who was based at Antioch, he, amazed at the audacity of the women and at the same time despising it, sent Julianus the prefect with the legions to besiege them. When Antoninus was shown to the troops, they all turned to him with remarkable affection, killed Julianus the prefect and all went over to him. Then, as part of the army had joined him, Antoninus proceeded against Macrinus, who was hurrying against him, and when battle was joined, Macrinus was defeated,[15] through the treachery of his soldiers and the affection for Antoninus. Macrinus in fact fled, together with a few men and his son, was killed with Diadumenus in a certain village of Bithynia, and his head was cut off and brought to Antoninus.

14. 16 May A.D.218.
15. 8 June A.D.218.

It ought to be known, in addition, that the boy Diadumenus, whom many have recorded to have been emperor jointly with his father, is said to have been Caesar not Augustus. The son also was killed, having gained nothing from the imperial power but his death at the hands of the soldiers. For there will not be anything in his life worth speaking of except this: that like an illegitimate child he was added on to the name of the Antonines.

In his life as emperor, however, Macrinus was a little more stiff and stern, hoping that he could cover all his previous acts with oblivion, whereas his very severity opened up the opportunity of criticizing and attacking him. He had wanted to be called both Severus and Pertinax, which seemed to him two names that connoted harshness, and when the Senate had named him Pius and Felix, he accepted the name Felix but did not want that of Pius. This it seems resulted in the not inelegant epigram against him which survives, by some Greek poet, which in Latin is expressed in the following terms:

> An actor now ageing, a base,
>   Severe, cruel, unjust man,
> To be both blest and impious,
>   Was his desire and plan.
> Although he would not be pious,
>   He wanted to be blest:
> But reason would not allow this,
>   Nature spurns the request.
> He could be called and seem to be,
>   Pious and blessèd both:
> If impious, now will he,
>   And ever, be unblest.

These verses some Latin-speaker or other placed in the Forum alongside the ones that had been put up in Greek. When he heard of them, Macrinus is reported to have replied with these lines:

Had fate produced a Greek poet,
Like that Latin gallows-bird,
The people would have learned nothing,
Nothing the Senate had heard,
From no huckster those offensive
Verses I should have incurred.

In these lines, far worse than the ones in Latin, Macrinus believed that he had made a reply, but he was ridiculed no less than the poet who had had to write in Latin translated from the Greek.

He was, then, arrogant and bloodthirsty, and wanted to be a military emperor, even criticizing the discipline of former times and praising Severus alone above all the others. He even crucified soldiers and always inflicted slaves' punishments on them. When he was faced with mutinies of the soldiers he very often decimated them – sometimes he only 'centimated' them, which was his own word. Then he used to say that he was merciful in 'centimating' those who deserved decimation or 'vicensimation'. It would be a lengthy business to expose all his acts of cruelty, but nonetheless I will describe one, not a great one, in his own opinion, but harsher than all his tyrannical enormities. Some soldiers had had intercourse with the maidservant of their host, although she had already had a low reputation for a long time. He learned of this through a commissary agent, ordered them to be brought before him and questioned them as to whether this was true.

When the facts had been established, he ordered two oxen of extraordinary size to be cut open suddenly, while still alive, and the soldiers to be thrust one into each, with their heads protruding so that they could talk to each other. Thus did he inflict a penalty on them, although punishments like this were not decreed even for adulteries by our ancestors or in his days. He did however fight against the Parthians and the Armenians and the Arabs, whom they called the 'blessed',[16] no less bravely than successfully.

A tribune who allowed the watch to be abandoned he dragged, bound under a wheeled carriage, alive and dead, throughout an entire march. He also brought back the punishment of Mezentius, who used to bind the living to the dead and forced them to die consumed by slow putrefaction. Hence, even in the circus, when public support for Diadumenus had been manifested, there was a shout:

> Outstanding in form is the youth –
> His father should not be Mezentius![17]

He also put men who were still alive into walls and built them up. Those guilty of adultery he always burned alive with their bodies bound together. Slaves who had fled from their masters and had been found he sentenced to the sword fight at the games. On informers, if they did not prove their case, he inflicted capital punishment. If they did prove it, he gave them a reward of money and sent them away in disgrace.

In the law he was not without shrewdness: thus he had even planned to cancel all the rescripts of former emperors, so that the law and not the rescripts should be acted upon, saying that it was a crime that the wishes of Commodus and Caracallus and men without skill should appear to be the laws, whereas Trajan never replied to petitions, in order that what might seem to have been done as a favour should not be applied to other cases. He was very generous in grants of grain, with gold he was very mean. In flogging the court staff he was so unjust, so unyielding and so harsh, that his own slaves called him not Macrinus but Macellinus,[18] because his house was stained with the blood of the household slaves like a slaughterhouse. He was very greedy

16. Or 'the Arabs of Arabia Felix'.
17. A conflation of Virgil, *Aeneid*, 12.275 and 7.654.
18. i.e. 'the butcher'.

over wine and food, sometimes even to the point of drunkenness – but in the evening hours. For if he had lunched, even in
private, very sparingly, he was very extravagant at dinner. He
invited to his banquets literary men, as though while talking
about liberal studies he would necessarily be abstemious.

But when people thought about his old-fashioned meanness
and saw the cruelty of his character, they could not endure the
rotten little man as emperor – especially the soldiers, who
remembered many acts of his that were very deadly and sometimes most base. Forming a plot they killed him, with the boy,
his son Diadumenus – surnamed Antoninus, to be sure, of
whom it was said that he had been Antoninus only in his
dreams. Hence too there survive the following verses:

> This too we saw in our dreams, unless I mistake,
> Citizens: that boy th' Antonine name did take,
> Born of a father corrupt, but a chaste mother;
> A hundred lovers she had, and chased another
> Hundred; the baldhead too was one, her spouse to be,
> A Pius, a Marcus – Verus never was he!

These lines were translated from Greek into Latin, for in Greek
they are very well composed, but they seem to have been
translated by some common poet. When Macrinus heard this,
he composed some iambics, which do not survive but which are
said to have been very pleasing. Of course they perished in the
same uprising in which he was killed, when everything of his
was looted by the soldiers.

The manner of his death, as we have said, was the following:
after the army had swung over to Antoninus Heliogabalus,
Macrinus fled and was defeated in the war, and was killed in a
Bithynian suburb, some of his own side having surrendered,
some being killed and some put to flight. Thus, Heliogabalus
was thought to have distinguished himself, because he appeared
to have avenged his father's death. Through this he attained the
imperial position, which he dishonoured by his monstrous

vices, his extravagance, baseness, wastefulness, arrogance and cruelty. But he too was fated to meet an end similar to his life. These things we have learned about Macrinus, although many give different versions of some of them, as is the case with all history. We have collected them together from a great many sources and presented them to Your Serenity, Diocletian Augustus, because we have seen that you are an enthusiast for the former emperors.

DIADUMENUS ANTONINUS*

BY AELIUS LAMPRIDIUS

THE life of the boy Antoninus Diadumenus, who was proclaimed emperor by the army with his father Opilius Macrinus, when Bassianus had been killed by Macrinus' conspiracy, contains nothing memorable, except that he was called Antoninus and that amazing omens were displayed to him, of imperial power that would not last long – as turned out to be the case. When it first became known among the legions that Bassianus had been killed, great sorrow filled the hearts of all because they did not have an Antoninus in the republic: for they thought that the Roman empire would perish with him. When that was announced to Macrinus, who was already emperor, he feared that the armies might turn to one of the Antonines, many of whom, relatives of Antoninus Pius, were among the generals. He at once ordered a speech to be prepared, and named his son, then a boy, Antoninus. This is the speech:

You see, fellow-soldiers, that I am already of an advanced age, and Diadumenus a boy, whom, if the gods are favourable, you will have for a long time as *princeps*. Furthermore, I appreciate that there remains among you an immense longing for the Antonine name. Wherefore, since it seems that not much life remains for me on account of the nature of human weakness, with your authority, I name this boy Antoninus, and for a long time to come he shall bring Antoninus back to life for you.

Acclamations:

* On the name, see p. 269, n. 5 above. There is now a detailed discussion of Diadumenianus by R. Syme, *Phoenix*, 1972, pp. 275ff. The *Life* is almost wholly fiction.

Emperor Macrinus, may the gods preserve you, Antoninus Diadumenus, may the gods preserve you! We all ask that Antoninus shall
live a long time, Jupiter Best and Greatest, grant long life to Macrinus
and Antoninus! You know, Jupiter, Macrinus cannot be defeated,
you know, Jupiter, Antoninus cannot be defeated. If we have an
Antoninus, we have everything! The gods have given us an Antoninus,
the boy Antoninus is worthy to be emperor!

The emperor Macrinus said:

Receive, therefore, fellow-soldiers, in return for the imperial power
three gold pieces each, for the name Antoninus five gold pieces each
and the customary promotions, but doubled.

After this, the little boy himself, the emperor Diadumenus
Antoninus, said:

I thank you, fellow-soldiers, for having given me both the imperial
power and the name, as you have considered myself and my father
worthy to be called Roman emperors, and to be entrusted with the
republic by you. My father for his part will take care that he does not
fail the empire, and I will endeavour not to fail the name of the
Antonines. For I know that I have taken upon myself the name of
Pius and Marcus and Verus, and it is very hard to live up to them. In
the meanwhile, however, in return for the imperial power, and in
return for the name, I promise all that my father has promised and as
much again, doubling the honours, even as my revered father Macrinus, who is present, has promised.

Herodian, the Greek writer, omitting this, says[1] that the boy
Diadumenus was called Caesar only by the soldiers, and that
he was killed together with his father.

After holding this assembly, coinage was at once struck at
Antioch in the name of Antoninus Diadumenus, but Macrinus'
coinage was deferred for the Senate's command. A letter was
sent to the Senate, also, in which the name Antoninus was
reported. Hence too the Senate is said to have accepted him as

1. Herodian, 5.4.12.

emperor gladly, although others think that it was done out of
hatred for Antoninus Caracallus. Now the emperor Macrinus
had planned to give cloaks to the people, red in colour, that
were called Antonine in honour of his son Antoninus, just as
the *caracallae* were called Bassian, claiming that his son had a
better right to be called Paenuleus or Paenularius than Bassianus
to be called Caracallus. He also promised an 'Antoninian'
largess by edict, as the text of the edict itself can show:

I would, fellow-citizens, that we were already with you in person:
your Antoninus would give you largess in his own name. In addition,
he would enrol boys as Antoniniani and girls as Antoninianae, which
would extend the glory of so favoured a name.

And so forth.

When these things had been carried out in this fashion, he
ordered the standards and the banners in the camp to be made
'Antonine' and had busts made of Bassianus in gold and
silver; and a thanksgiving was celebrated for seven days in
honour of the name Antoninus.

The boy was the best-looking of all, rather tall in stature, with
blond hair, black eyes, aquiline nose, his chin shaped with all
comeliness and a mouth ready for kisses. He was naturally
strong, although pampered by his upbringing. When he first
received the scarlet and purple garments and the other insignia
of imperial power used in the camp, he was star-like and
celestial in his radiance, so that he was loved by all because of
his charm.

Now let us come to the omens of empire which are amazing
enough in other cases but in this one especially so. On the day
that he was born, his father, who happened at that time to be
procurator of the greater treasury, inspected the purple robes,
and those which he approved for their brightness he ordered to
be taken into the very inner room in which Diadumenus was
born two hours later. Newly born infants are normally marked
out by nature with a caul, which midwives pull off and sell to

credulous advocates – because pleaders are said to be helped by this; but this boy, instead of a caul, had a kind of slender diadem, that was nonetheless so strong that it could not be broken, for the sinews were intertwined like the strings of a bow. Therefore, they say, the boy was named Diadematus, but when he grew older he was called Diadumenus after his maternal grandfather, although the name Diadumenus did not differ much from the previous appellation Diadematus. They say that twelve purple lambs were born on his father's estate, of which only one had spots. On the very day that he was born it is well known that an eagle gently brought him a tiny royal ring-dove, placed it in his cradle as he slept, and departed without harming him. Woodcocks built a nest in his father's house. About the time that he was born, astrologers, having been told his horoscope, cried out that he was both the son of an emperor and an emperor – as if his mother had committed adultery, as gossip maintained. Again, when he was walking in the country an eagle took away his cap. When the child's companions made an outcry, it is reported to have put it on a royal monument near the country-house where his father was then living, on the statue of a king, to fit its head. Many thought this an omen and one that portended death, but events were to show that it was something glorious. Besides this, he was born on the birthday of Antoninus and at the same hour and with the stars almost in the same positions, as Antoninus Pius. Hence astrologers used to say that he would be both the son of an emperor and an emperor, but not for long. On the day that he was born, a certain woman, a relative, is said to have exclaimed: 'Let him be called Antoninus!' But Macrinus is said to have been afraid, because no one in his family was registered under that name; and thus he avoided the imperial name, because at the same time a rumour had already spread about the meaning of his horoscope. Many have set it down in writing that there were these and other omens, but there is one in particular: when Diadumenus was in a cradle, a lion broke its chains, as some

say, rushed out savagely, came to the cradle, licked the boy –
and left him unharmed; whereas the nurse threw herself at the
lion, was taken in its jaws and perished; she happened to be the
only person found in the small open space where the child was
lying.

These are the things that seem to be worthy of record in the
case of Antoninus Diadumenus. I would have joined on his *Life*
to the deeds of his father, if the name of the Antonines had not
forced me to publish a separate account of the boy. Indeed, so
beloved was the name of the Antonines in those times that
those who did not have the support of that name seemed not to
have deserved imperial power. Hence too some think that
Severus, Pertinax and Julianus should be honoured with the
forename Antoninus, and that subsequently the two Gordians,
father and son, had the surname Antoninus. But it is one thing
when it is assumed as a forename and another when it is taken
as an actual family name. For Pius had Antoninus as his real
family name, and Pius as a surname. Marcus had Verissimus as
his real family name, but when this was set aside and cancelled
he received that of Antoninus, not as a forename but as a family
name. Moreover Verus had the family name Commodus, and
when this was cancelled he received that of Antoninus, not as a
forename but as a family name. Then Marcus gave Commodus
the name Antoninus and set this down in public records on the
day of his birth. As for Caracallus Bassianus, it is sufficiently
well known that it was actually because of a dream that Severus
had had, when he perceived that an Antoninus was his fore-
ordained successor, that he called him Antoninus. This was not
until his thirteenth year, at which time he is said to have conferred the imperial power on him too. As for Geta, whom
many deny to have been called Antoninus, it is quite well
known that he was called this for the same reason as Bassianus,
in order that he should succeed his father Severus, which actually came to pass. After this, it is sufficiently agreed that Diadumenus himself was called Antoninus so that he might be

commended to the army, Senate and people of Rome, since there was immense longing for Bassianus Caracallus.

A letter survives of Opilius Macrinus, father of Diadumenus, in which he boasts not so much that he had attained to the imperial power, after having been the second man in the empire, as that he had become the father of an Antoninus, a name more distinguished than any in those times, even than one belonging to the gods. Before I insert this letter, it is pleasant to quote some lines composed against Commodus, who had named himself Hercules. This is so that everyone may appreciate that the Antonine name was so distinguished that it seemed inappropriate to add to it even a god's name:

Lines composed against Commodus Antoninus

> Commodus wished the name of Hercules to bear,
> Thinking to be an Antoninus not so fair,
> Knowing no human law nor empire's majesty,
> Hoping that as a god he would get greater fame
> Than if he were a *princeps* of outstanding name –
> Neither god nor any sort of man shall he be.

These lines, composed by some unknown Greek, were translated into Latin by a poor poet, and I have seen fit to quote them for this reason, that all might know that the Antonines were greater than the gods, and this because of the love for three *principes*, enshrined by their wisdom, kindness and piety – piety in the case of Antoninus, kindness with Verus and wisdom with Marcus. I now return to the letter of Macrinus Opilius.

Opilius Macrinus to Nonia Celsa his wife.[2] The good fortune we have attained, my dear wife, is incalculable. Perhaps you may think that I am speaking of the imperial power; but that is no great thing, and one which fortune has bestowed even on the undeserving. I have become father of an Antoninus, you have become mother of an Antoninus. O happy are we, fortunate our house, famous the praise given the empire, prosperous at last! May the gods, and kindly Juno whom you worship, grant both that he shall make the name

2. The lady's name is not confirmed by any other evidence.

Antoninus one that he deserved, and that I, who am the father of an Antoninus, may seem worthy of it to all.

This letter shows what great glory he thought he had gained because his son was called Antoninus.

Even so, in his fourteenth month as emperor, the boy was put to death on account of his father's illiberal and harsh principate, together with his father, not through his own fault. However, I might discover in many accounts that he too was cruel beyond his years, as a letter he sent to his father shows. For certain men had incurred the suspicion of rebellion, and Macrinus had punished them most cruelly, during his son's absence. But Diadumenus heard that while the instigators of the rebellion had indeed been killed, yet their accomplices (one of whom was a general commanding in Armenia and another the legate of Asia and Arabia) had been released, on account of their long-standing friendship. He is said to have addressed this letter to his father (and an identical one to his mother as well), of which I have thought it right, for the sake of history, to give the text:

Augustus the son to Augustus the father. You do not seem, my dear father, to have kept up your old ways, in love for us, in that you have spared men implicated in attempted usurpation, either because you are hoping that they will be more friendly to you in the future if you spare them, or thinking that they should be released because of their long-standing friendship. This ought not to have been done and it will profit nothing, for, firstly, they cannot love you now, when they are festering with suspicion, and secondly, enemies who forget their old friendship and have joined your worst enemies are all the more cruel. Add to this the fact that they still have armies.

> 'If glory cannot move a mind so mean,
> Nor future praise, from flitting pleasure wean,
> Regard the fortunes of thy rising heir;
> The promis'd crown let young Ascanius wear.
> To whom th'Ausonian scepter, and the state
> Of Rome's imperial name, is ow'd by fate.'[3]

3. Virgil, *Aeneid*, 4.272–6 (Dryden's translation).

Those men must be struck down, if you wish to be secure. For through a vice of human nature, others will not be lacking if they be spared.

Some report that this letter was by him, others that it was by his teacher Caelianus, an African and former rhetorician. From this it is apparent how harsh the youth would have been if he had lived.

Another letter survives, addressed by him to his mother, as follows:

Our lord and Augustus loves neither you nor himself, in that he preserves his enemies. See to it then that Arabianus and Tuscus and Gellius are bound to the stake, lest if there be an opportunity they do not let it slip.

As Lollius Urbicus[4] says in his history of his own time, these letters, when made known by his secretary, are said to have done the boy great harm among the soldiers. For when they had killed his father, some of them wanted to spare him; but a chamberlain came forward who read these letters to the assembly of soldiers.

And so when both had been put to death and their heads carried round on spears, the army went over to Marcus Aurelius Antoninus, through affection for his name. He was said to be the son of Bassianus Caracallus, but, in fact, he was priest of the temple of Heliogabalus, the foulest of all mankind and one who by some act of fate disgraced the Roman empire. About him, since there is much to tell, I shall speak in the place reserved for him.

4. See p. 16 above – another bogus author.

ANTONINUS HELIOGABALUS*

BY AELIUS LAMPRIDIUS

THE life of Heliogabalus Antoninus, who was also called Varius, I should never have committed to writing – in order that no one might know that he had been *princeps* of the Romans – had not this same empire previously had a Caligula, a Nero and a Vitellius. But since the selfsame earth bears not only poisons but also grain and other wholesome things, and serpents as well as domestic animals, the discriminating reader may allow himself some compensation to set against these monstrous tyrants, when he reads of Augustus, Trajan, Vespasian, Hadrian, Pius, Titus and Marcus. At the same time he will appreciate the discernment of the Romans, in that the latter were emperors for a long time and died natural deaths, whereas the former were put to death, dragged along, even called usurpers, and no one is willing to mention their names.

When Macrinus had been killed, and his son Diadumenus, who with equal imperial power had received the name Antoninus as well, the position of emperor was conferred on Varius Heliogabalus,[1] for the reason that he was said to be the son of Bassianus. He was in fact priest of Heliogabalus, or of Jupiter or

---

* T. D. Barnes, *HAC*, 1970, pp. 53ff., has demonstrated that chapters 1–18 derive from a reliable source, which he identifies with Marius Maximus. The remainder is fiction. The name by which the emperor is usually referred to now is Elagabalus, but the form Heliogabalus was commonly used in ancient times.

1. For his correct names, see stemma, p. 322.

the Sun, and had taken the name Antoninus either to prove his
descent or because he had learned that that name was so dear to
mankind that even the fratricide Bassianus had been loved on
account of it. He was actually called Varius originally, then
Heliogabalus from his priesthood of the god Heliogabalus,
to whom he founded a temple at Rome, in the place where there
had previously been a shrine of Orcus, after he had brought him
from Syria with him. Finally, when he received the imperial
power, he was called Antoninus, and he was the last of the
Antonines to be Roman emperor.

He was so much under the control of his mother Symiamira[2]
that he would carry out none of the business of the republic
without her consent, although she lived like a whore and
practised baseness of all kinds at court – indeed she was notorious
for her fornication with Antoninus Caracallus, so much so that
this Varius or Heliogabalus was commonly thought to have
been conceived as a result of it. Some say that even the name
Varius was given him by his school-fellows because he appears
to have been conceived by the seed of 'various' men, as
happens with a whore. He is reported to have fled as to a
sanctuary to the temple of the god Heliogabalus when his
reputed father Antoninus had been killed by Macrinus' plot,
lest he be put to death by Macrinus, who wielded imperial
power with his extravagant and cruel son. But enough about
the name, although he polluted that hallowed name of the
Antonines, which you, Most Sacred Constantine, so revere that
you have made Marcus and Pius golden examples for yourself,
together with the Constantii and Claudius, as though they were
your own ancestors, adopting the virtues of the men of old

2. Her name was in fact Julia Soaemias Bassiana. The form Symiamira,
found only here (although Eutropius, 8.22, calls her Symiasera), may
possibly be explained as a simple transcription of a Semitic original
meaning 'Soaemias the princess', and doubtless represents contemporary usage.

which accord with your character and are pleasing and dear to you.

To return to Antoninus Varius, having obtained the imperial power, he sent messengers to Rome, and all ranks were stirred up. An immense longing for him was also created among the whole people through the name Antoninus, which seemed to have returned not as a title only, as it had been for Diadumenus, but actually in the blood, since he had written that he was the son of Antoninus Bassianus. Besides, he brought with him the reputation that is usually given to new *principes* who follow usurpers – although it does not last except with the highest virtues, and many mediocre *principes* have lost it. In short, when Heliogabalus' letter was read in the Senate, at once good wishes were spoken for Antoninus and curses against Macrinus and his son, and Antoninus was acclaimed *princeps*. All were in favour and eager to believe, as happens with the prayers of men who hasten to believe when they are longing for what they desire to be true. But when he first entered the city – to leave out what was done in the provinces – he enshrined Heliogabalus on the Palatine Hill next to the temple of the emperors, and built a temple for him, being eager to transfer to that temple both the emblem of the Mother Goddess and the fire of Vesta, the Palladium, the sacred shields[3] and all the objects sacred to the Romans, so that no god should be worshipped at Rome except Heliogabalus. He used to say, furthermore, that the religion of the Jews and Samaritans and the rites of the Christians ought to be transferred there, so that the priesthood of Heliogabalus might include the mysteries of every cult.

3. The cult of Vesta and her sacred fire (to which the Vestal Virgins ministered) was, with the worship of Jupiter Capitolinus, one of the 'two spiritual pillars' on which the Roman state had rested since earliest times. Vesta was frequently identified with the 'Great Mother' goddess, hence the reference to the 'emblem'. The Palladium was an image of the goddess Pallas, kept in the temple of Vesta (who was not represented in image-form herself), and the sacred shields (*ancilia*) were used by the Salian priests (p. 30 above).

Then, when the Senate held its first meeting, he ordered that his mother be invited to the Senate. When she had come, she was called to the consuls' benches and took part in the drafting, that is, she was a witness to the completion of a decree of the Senate. He was the only one of the emperors under whom a woman entered the Senate like a man, as if she were an 'honourable member'. He also set up a *senaculum*, that is a woman's senate, on the Quirinal Hill, where there had previously been an assembly of married women, but only on days of religious festival and occasions when some married woman was granted the insignia of a 'consular marriage', which the emperors of old bestowed on their kinswomen, especially those whose husbands had not been ennobled, so that they should not continue to lack nobility.[4] Under Symiamira ridiculous decrees of the Senate were enacted dealing with laws applying to married women: who should wear what clothing in public, who should yield precedence to whom, who should advance to kiss another, who might ride in a carriage, on a horse, on a pack-animal, on a donkey, in a mule-drawn or ox-drawn carriage, who might be carried in a litter, and whether the litter might be made of leather or bone, or covered with ivory or with silver, and who might wear gold or jewels on her shoes.[5]

After he had wintered at Nicomedia, then, and was living in a depraved manner, being debauched by men and being 'on heat', the soldiers at once regretted what they had done in conspiring against Macrinus to make this person *princeps*. They turned their minds to the cousin of this same Heliogabalus, namely Alexander, whom the Senate had called Caesar when Macrinus had been put to death.[6] For who could endure a *princeps* who was the recipient of lust in every orifice of his body, when no one would tolerate even a beast of this sort?

---

4. A ruling of Caracalla (*Digest*, 1.9.12). Both Soaemias and her sister had been married to non-senators.
5. These suspect items may be presumed to be the author's inventions.
6. See p. 271, n. 7 above.

In fact at Rome he did nothing else but keep agents to search out for him men with large organs, and to bring them to court, so that he could enjoy their *amours*. Furthermore, he used to perform the story of Paris in his house, taking the role of Venus himself, in such a way that his clothes would suddenly drop to his feet and he would kneel, naked, with one hand placed on his breast and the other on his private parts, with his buttocks projecting and thrust back on front of his debaucher. Moreover he used to make up his face to look like a painting of Venus, and was depilated all over his body – thinking that it was the principal enjoyment of life to appear worthy and suited for the lusts of the greatest number.

He sold both honours and ranks and powers, both in person and through his slaves and the agents of his lusts. He enrolled men in the Senate without regard to age, property-rating and family, in return for money. Even military special commands and tribunates and legateships and generalships were sold, procuratorships too and posts in the palace. As his associates, first in the chariot-race, and then as colleagues in the whole of his life and actions, he had the charioteers Protegenes and Gordius.[7] Many whose bodies had pleased him he took from the stage, circus and amphitheatre to the court. Hierocles, in fact, he loved to such an extent that he used to kiss him in the groin, which it is indecent even to mention, claiming that he was celebrating the festival of Flora. He violated the chastity of a Vestal Virgin[8] and profaned the sacred rites of the Roman people by removing the inner sanctuaries, and he wanted to extinguish the eternal flame. It was not only the Roman religious rites that he wished to wipe out, but those of the

7. On these men, see Barnes, *op. cit.*, pp. 58ff., who shows that the second name should be spelt Gordius rather than Cordius.

8. He married the Vestal Virgin Julia Aquilia Severa (*PIR*[2], J 648) late in A.D.220 or early in 221, as his second wife, subsequently divorced her and then married her again. But with a Vestal, even marriage was regarded as incest.

whole world, being eager for one thing, that the god Heliogabalus should be worshipped everywhere. He even broke into the sanctuary of Vesta, which is entered by the Virgins and
the pontiffs only,[9] being himself defiled by every moral stain,
together with those who had defiled themselves. He also tried
to carry away the sacred inner shrine, and seized an earthenware one[10] which the Chief Vestal Virgin had shown him as if
it were the real one, to deceive him. As he found nothing in it,
he threw it down and broke it. However, he did not deprive
the cult of anything, for several identical shrines are said to have
been made, to prevent anyone ever taking away the real one.
In spite of this, he nonetheless took away the image which he
believed to be the Palladium and having enriched it with gold
placed it in the temple of his god. He also received the rites of
the Mother of the Gods and underwent the *taurobolium*[11] in
order to take away the emblem and other sacred objects which
are kept hidden with it. Moreover he tossed his head among the
castrated devotees and tied up his genitals and did everything
that the eunuch-priests are accustomed to do. Having carried off
the sacred object he transferred it to the inner sanctum of his
own god. He also celebrated the rite of Salambo,[12] with all the
wailing and the frenzy of the Syrian cult, creating an omen of
his own imminent end. In fact, he used to say that all the gods
were the servants of his own god, calling some of them chamberlains, others slaves, others its attendants for various matters.
The stones which are said to be divine he wanted to take from
their own temple, including an image of Diana from its own
shrine at Laodicea, where Orestes had placed it.

9. An error: no male, even the Pontifex Maximus, was permitted to
enter the innermost sanctuary of Vesta (see Barnes, *op. cit.*, p. 68).

10. A confusion with the earthenware jars in which the sacred objects
were kept.

11. An initiation ceremony at which bull's blood was poured over
the neophyte.

12. A Phoenician fertility goddess.

Now they say, of course, that Orestes had not put one image of Diana in one place, but many of them in many places. After he purified himself at the Three Rivers in the region of Hebrus, in accordance with the oracle he founded the city of Oresta, as well, which was destined often to be stained with men's blood.[13] Hadrian actually ordered that the city of Oresta should be called by his own name, at the time when he began to suffer from madness, in accordance with an oracle, when it was told him that he should steal into the house or the name of some madman. Indeed, they record that thereby the insanity which had caused him to order many senators to be killed was alleviated. Antoninus gained the name Pius for saving them, because he brought to the Senate the men that they thought had all been put to death by order of the *princeps*.

Heliogabalus also sacrificed human victims, having chosen for this from all over Italy boys that were noble and good-looking and had fathers and mothers living. I suppose this was so that the sorrow should be the greater in the case of two parents. Finally, he used to have with him every kind of magician, and they used to perform daily while he urged them on and gave thanks to the gods whom he found showed friendship to them, while he inspected the children's innards and tortured the victims according to his own native ritual.

When he entered into his consulship he threw to the people not coins of silver or gold, or cakes or little animals, but fatted cattle and camels and asses and stags, to be fought over by the people. He used to say that that was an imperial thing to do.

He savagely attacked the reputation of Macrinus, but that of Diadumenus much more so, because he was named Antoninus, calling him Pseudo-Antoninus (like the Pseudo-Philip), and also because it was said that from being most profligate he had

13. The reference is clearly to the two great battles fought at Adrianople, in A.D. 324 (defeat of Licinius by Constantine) and 378 (defeat of Valens by the Goths): see p. 11f above.

become a most brave, good, serious and stern man. In fact he compelled a number of writers to recount unspeakable things – or rather, profanities – about Diadumenus' way of life and profligacy, as in a biography of him.

He made a public bath in the palace and at the same time made the baths of Plautianus available to the people, so that he might thereby collect paramours from among men with large organs. Careful attention was given to seeking out from the recesses of the whole city, and from among sailors, *onobeli*, which is what they used to call those who looked extra virile.

When he wanted to make war on the Marcomanni, something that Antoninus had carried out most gloriously, it was said by some that by means of Chaldaeans and magicians Antoninus Marcus had brought it about that the Marcomanni should be forever devoted to the Roman people and be their friends, and that this had been done by incantations and a rite of dedication. When he inquired what this was or where it was, it was kept secret. For it was well known that the reason why he was inquiring about the dedication was so that he might destroy it, and that his motive in particular was that he had heard that an oracle foretold that 'the Marcomannic war must be ended by Antoninus' – although he was called Varius and Heliogabalus and a public laughing-stock, and was in fact defiling the name of Antoninus that he had usurped. The story was revealed, of course, in particular by the opponents of those with large organs and greater resources for practising lust. Hence plotting to murder him began. So much for affairs at home.

But the soldiers could not endure that pestilential person being clad in the imperial name and they began discussions, at first among themselves and then in groups, all turning to Alexander, who had already been declared Caesar by the Senate at the time that Macrinus was put to death. He was cousin of this Antoninus, for Varia, from whom Heliogabalus had the name Varius, was grandmother of both of them.

Under Heliogabalus, Zoticus had such influence that he was

treated by all the heads of department like their master's
husband. Furthermore, this same Zoticus was one to abuse a
relationship of this kind and used to sell 'for smoke' everything
that Heliogabalus said and did, piling up enormous riches to the
greatest possible extent, threatening some, making promises to
others and deceiving all of them. He used to come out from the
emperor's presence and approach each one and say: 'I said this
about you, I heard this about you, this will happen in your
case.' As is the way with men of this sort, if admitted to over-
close intimacy with *principes*, they sell reports not only about
bad *principes* but good ones too, and through the stupidity or
innocence of emperors who do not realize this they feed on
shameless rumour-mongering. Heliogabalus married Zoticus
and had intercourse with him, to the extent of even having a
matron of honour and shouting: 'Lay on, Magirus!'[14] – and
this at a time when Zoticus was ill. Then he used to ask philosophers and men of great seriousness whether they themselves had
experienced as young men what he was experiencing. This was
said with complete lack of shame, for he never refrained from
filthy words, while he even used to make indecent signs with
his fingers. He had no sense of shame at public meetings, even
when the people could hear.

He appointed freedmen as governors, legates, consuls and
generals, and defiled every office with low-born profligates.
When he had summoned nobles from his entourage of the
vintage-festival and had taken his seat by the grape-baskets, he
began to interrogate all the most serious-minded as to whether
they were capable of sex, and when the old men began blushing,
he would cry out: 'He is blushing, things are all right!' –
regarding silence as a confession. Furthermore he added
information about what he used to do himself, without any
cloak of modesty. When he saw that the old men were blushing
and silent, because either their age or their rank was restraining

14. Dio (79.16.1) explains that Zoticus was nicknamed 'Magirus'
(cook) after his father's trade.

them in such matters, he turned to the young men and began to inquire of them about everything. When he heard from them things that accorded with their age, he began to joke, saying that it was truly a bacchanalian vintage-festival that he was celebrating in this manner. Many record that it was he who first thought up the practice of jokes – which he himself had composed, mainly in Greek – being made against masters at vintage-festivals. Marius Maximus quotes a number of them in his *Life* of Heliogabalus. There were in his entourage men who were depraved, some of them old and looking like philosophers, who used to wear hair-nets on their head, and say that they were having depraved experiences and boast that they had husbands. Some say that they pretended this so as to gain increased favour with him by imitating his vices.

To the prefecture of the guard he appointed a dancer who had performed as an actor at Rome.[15] He made Gordius, a charioteer, prefect of the watch, and Claudius, a barber, prefect of the grain-supply. To the other offices he appointed men whose enormous private parts recommended them to him. He ordered a muleteer to take charge of the five per cent tax on inheritances, likewise a courier, a cook and a locksmith. Whenever he entered either the camp or the Senate House, he took with him his grandmother, Varia by name, of whom there was mention above, so that he might be accorded more respect through her authority – since he could get none on his own account. Until his reign, as we have said already, no woman had ever entered the Senate actually to be asked to draft a decree and express an opinion. At banquets he mainly used to put perverts next to himself and take especial pleasure in fondling or touching them, and no one else would give him his cup when he drank.

In the midst of these evil deeds of his disgusting life, he ordered that Alexander, whom he had adopted,[16] should be

15. P. Valerius Comazon (*cos. ord.* 220).
16. The adoption was formalized on 26 June A.D. 221.

removed from his presence, saying that he regretted the adoption; and he instructed the Senate to deprive him of the name of Caesar. When this had been revealed there was profound silence in the Senate, seeing that Alexander was an excellent youth, as was shown in the sequel by his conduct as emperor, whereas he displeased his 'father' simply because he was not shameless. He was in fact his cousin, as some say, was loved by the soldiers as well, and was popular with the Senate and the equestrian order. Yet Heliogabalus' insanity went to the length of a most evil design – for he dispatched assassins against him. It was in fact done as follows: he withdrew to the Gardens of Spes Vetus, as if forming designs against some new youth, having left his mother in the palace, and his grandmother and cousin. Then he ordered the slaughter of an excellent young man and one whom the republic needed; and he sent a letter to the soldiers in which he commanded that Alexander should be deprived of the name of Caesar. He sent men to smear mud on the inscriptions on his statues in the camp, as is normally done in the case of tyrants. He also sent to those who looked after him, ordering them, if they hoped for rewards and distinctions, to kill him by whatever means they wished, either in the baths or by poison or by the sword. But evil men accomplish nothing against the innocent. For no power could induce anyone to commit so great a crime, while the weapons which he was making ready against others were turned against himself, and he was put to death by the forces with which he was attacking others.

When the inscriptions were first smeared with mud, all the soldiers were incensed, and they set off, some for the palace, others for the Gardens where Varius was, to rescue Alexander, and, at last, to cast out that foul person and intending murderer from the republic. When they reached the palace, they guarded Alexander, together with his mother and grandmother, and then with the greatest care led them to the camp. Symiamira, the mother of Heliogabalus, followed them on foot, being anxious for her son. Then they went to the Gardens, where Varius was found, making preparations for a chariot-race, but waiting very intently for the moment when it should be announced to him that his cousin had been killed. Terrified by the sudden clattering of soldiers he hid in a corner and covered himself with the curtain which was in the bedroom entrance, having sent off the prefects, one to the camp to quieten the soldiers, and one to calm those that had come to the Gardens. Antiochianus, then, one of the prefects, by reminding them of the oath of allegiance, persuaded the soldiers who had come to the Gardens not to kill him, for not many had come and most of them stayed with the banner, which the tribune Aristomachus had kept back. So much for what happened in the Gardens.

But in the camp the soldiers told the prefect, who was making an appeal to them, that they would spare Heliogabalus if he would dismiss from his presence the foul persons and charioteers and actors and return to a decent way of life, removing in particular those who to the general sorrow had the most influence with him and were selling everything of his, either in actual fact or 'for smoke'. He did in fact dismiss Hierocles, Gordius and Myrismus and two other disgusting favourites who were making him more of a fool than he was. Furthermore, the prefects were instructed by the soldiers not to allow him to live like that any longer, and to guard Alexander so that no violence should be done to him; and at the same time to ensure that the Caesar should not see any of the friends of the Augustus, so that there should be no imitation of their baseness. But Heliogabalus not only, with earnest entreaty, kept asking to have back Hierocles – a most disgusting person – but was also daily increasing his plotting against the Caesar. At last, on the Kalends of January, when they had been designated consuls jointly, he refused to appear in public with his cousin. Finally, when his grandmother and mother told him that the soldiers were threatening to destroy him unless they saw that there was concord between the cousins, he put on the bordered toga and at the sixth hour went to the Senate, having summoned his grandmother to the Senate and taking her to a seat. Then he refused to go to the Capitol to assume the vows and carry out the ceremonies, and everything was done by the urban praetor, as though the consuls were not there.

Nor did he give up the murder of his cousin, but, fearing that the Senate might turn to someone else if he killed him, he ordered the Senate to leave the city at once. All of them, including those who lacked either carriages or slaves, were ordered to set off at once; some were carried by porters and others by any beasts of burden they could find, or hired for money. Sabinus, a man of consular rank, to whom Ulpian wrote books,[17] he ordered to be killed because he had remained in the city, summoning a centurion in a low voice. But the centurion, being rather deaf, thought he was being ordered to eject him from the city, and did so. Thus a centurion's infirmity saved Sabinus. He also got rid of both Ulpian the jurist, because he was a good man, and Silvinus the rhetorician, whom he had appointed as the Caesar's teacher. Silvinus was in fact killed, but Ulpian was saved. But the soldiers, especially the praetorians, either knowing that Heliogabalus was planning evil things against Alexander, or because they saw that they would gain displeasure because of their love for Alexander, joined together and formed a conspiracy to liberate the republic. First his associates in lewdness were killed, in various ways – some they slaughtered by tearing out their vitals, and others they pierced up the anus, so that their death fitted their lives; – and after this an attack was made on him, and he was killed in a latrine where he had taken refuge.[18] Then he was dragged along in public and the corpse was further insulted when the soldiers threw it in a sewer. But the sewer happened not to be large

17. An extraordinary slip: Ulpian wrote *ad Sabinum*, which meant not 'to Sabinus' but '*on* Sabinus', i.e. a commentary on the writings of the first-century jurist Masurius Sabinus.

18. 12 March A.D.222.

enough for it, so it was hurled into the Tiber from the Aemilian Bridge, with a weight attached to prevent it floating, so that it might never be buried. His body was also dragged around the track of the circus before it was hurled into the Tiber. His name, that is Antoninus, was erased by order of the Senate (that of Varius Heliogabalus remained), since he had held it by usurpation, wishing to appear to be the son of Antoninus.

After his death he was called Tiberinus and Tractatitius and Impurus and many other things, which were to indicate what seemed to have been done under him. He alone of all *principes* was both dragged along and thrown into a sewer and hurled into the Tiber. This befell him as a result of the general hatred of all, which emperors must particularly guard against, seeing that those who do not earn the love of Senate, people and soldiers do not even earn a tomb.

Of his public works, none survive apart from the temple of the god Heliogabalus, which some call the Sun, and others Jupiter, and the amphitheatre[19] as restored after destruction by fire, and the Baths in the Vicus Sulpicius which Antoninus son of Severus had begun.[20] The Baths, of course, Antoninus Caracallus had dedicated, both by bathing in them and by admitting the people to them, but the portico was lacking; this was subsequently built by the spurious Antoninus, and completed by Alexander.

He was the last of the Antonines (although many think that the Gordians subsequently had the surname Antoninus; but they were called Antonius, not Antoninus), so detestable in his life, his character and his depravity that the Senate erased even his name. I too would not have called him Antoninus, except for the sake of identification, which makes it necessary to pronounce even names which have been abolished. With him was also killed his mother Symiamira, a most depraved woman and one worthy of her son. Before anything else, after Antoninus

19. The Flavian amphitheatre, better known as the Colosseum.
20. i.e. the Baths of Caracalla (cf. p. 258 above).

Heliogabalus, it was laid down that no woman should ever enter the Senate, and that the life of him that should cause this to happen should be forfeit to the kingdom of the dead and accursed.

Concerning his life many obscene items have been put in writing, but since they are not worthy of record I have decided that I should relate the things that are relevant to his extravagance, some of which he is reported to have done as a private citizen and some when already emperor. For he himself as a private citizen used to say that he was imitating Apicius,[21] but as emperor, Nero, Otho and Vitellius.[22]

He was the first of all private citizens to cover his couches with golden coverlets, because it was then lawful to do this, by authority of Antoninus Marcus, who had held a public sale of all the imperial furnishings. Then he gave summer banquets in various colours, one day a green one, glass-coloured on another day, on another a blue one and so on, always a different one on all the days of summer. Again, he was the first to have cooking-pots of silver, and cooking-dishes too, and again, engraved silver vessels weighing a hundred pounds, some of them defiled with very lewd designs. Wine flavoured with both mastic and pennyroyal, and all these things which extravagant people still use now, were first invented by him. For he made rose-wine, which he had got from others, more fragrant by adding ground up pine-cones. In fact, these types of wine-cup are not found in books before Heliogabalus. Indeed, for him, life was nothing but a search for pleasures. He was the first to make forcemeat out of fish, mussels and oysters, and shellfish of this type, and from lobsters, crabs and prawns. He also strewed his dining-rooms with roses and every kind of flower – lilies, violets, hyacinths and narcissi. He never swam except in swimming-pools in which a superior perfume or saffron had been mixed. He did not readily recline on cushions unless they

21. See p. 93, n. 14 above.
22. What follows may be regarded as pure fiction.

were of rabbit-fur or feathers from under the wings of partridges, and he changed the pillows frequently.

He often showed such contempt for the Senate that he used to call them slaves in togas, regarding the Roman people as the tiller of a single farm and the equestrian order as having no position at all. Often he used to invite the urban prefect to drink after dinner, having summoned the prefects of the guard too, in such a way that, if they refused, the heads of the secretariat would compel them. He also wanted to create a separate prefect of the city for each of the city-regions, so that there would be fourteen in the city. If he had lived, he would have done this, being about to promote all the basest people and those of the lowest of callings.

He had couches both for dining and sleeping made of solid silver. In imitation of Apicius he very often ate camels' heels, and cocks' combs taken from living birds, and the tongues of peacocks and nightingales, because those who ate them were said to be immune from the plague. Again, to the palace staff he served huge dishes filled with mullets' innards, flamingoes' brains, partridge eggs, thrushes' brains and the heads of parrots, pheasants and peacocks. Indeed, he used to order mullets' beards to be brought on, so large that he served them like cress, parsley, kidney-beans and fenugreek, filling dishes and bowls. This was exceptionally remarkable.

He fed dogs on goose liver. Among his pets he kept lions and leopards which had been rendered harmless, and as they had been trained by tamers, he used to order them suddenly during the second and third course to get up on the couches to stir up panic, no one being aware that they were harmless. He sent grapes from Apamea to the stables for his horses and fed the lions and other animals with parrots and pheasants. He served wild sows' udders for ten successive days, thirty a day, with their wombs, also serving peas with gold pieces, lentils with onyx, beans with amber, and rice with pearls. Besides this he sprinkled pearls instead of pepper on fish and mushrooms. He

loaded his parasites with violets and other flowers in a banqueting room with a reversible ceiling, in such a way that some
of them expired when they could not crawl out to the surface.
He invited the common people to drink and he himself drank
such an amount that it was thought, on seeing what he alone had
drunk, that he had been drinking from a swimming-pool. As
banquet-presents he gave eunuchs, or four-horse chariots,
saddle horses, mules, sedan-chairs and four-wheelers. He also
gave a thousand gold pieces and a hundred pounds of silver a
head. Indeed, at his banquets he had lucky chances written on
spoons, such as one that went 'ten camels', another 'ten flies',
another 'ten pounds of gold', another 'ten pounds of lead',
another 'ten ostriches', another 'ten hens' eggs', so that they
were really lucky chances and fortune was tested. He also
presented these at his games, when he had as chances ten bears,
ten dormice, ten lettuces or ten pounds of gold. He was the
first to begin this custom of chances, which we still see at the
present time. But he really did invite the performers to take a
chance, making the chances dead dogs, or a pound of beef, or
again, a hundred gold pieces, a thousand silver pieces, a hundred
copper coins, and so on. The people responded to this with
pleasure and afterwards rejoiced that he was emperor.

He is said to have given naval displays on the circus-canals
which had been filled with wine and to have sprinkled cloaks
with wild-grape perfume; also to have driven a chariot drawn
by four elephants on the Vatican, destroying the tombs which
were in the way,[23] and to have harnessed four camels to a chariot
as well, at a private show in the circus. He is said to have collected snakes with the help of priests of the Marsian people, and
to have let them loose suddenly, before dawn, when the
people usually assemble for games that are attended by large
numbers; and many are said to have been hurt, by bites and in
the rush to escape. He wore an all-gold tunic, and a purple one

23. Perhaps a sly anti-Christian joke by the author (cf. *Verus* 6.4,
p. 143 and n. 7 above).

and a Persian one, with jewels, on which occasions he used to say that he was weighed down by the burden of luxury. He had jewels on his shoes too, and engraved ones at that. This provoked the derision of all – as if engraving by famous crafts-men could be seen on jewels that were attached to his feet! He wanted to wear a jewelled diadem, too, to make himself more beautiful, and to make his face more like a woman's; and he did wear it in his house. He is even said to have promised his guests a phoenix, or, in place of this, a thousand pounds of gold, so that he might give them an imperial send-off. He provided swimming-pools with sea-water, especially in places inland, and handed them over to individual friends who swam in them. On another occasion he filled them with fish. He made a mountain of snow in the pleasure garden of his house in the summer, having had snow carried there. At the seaside he never ate fish, but in the places furthest away from the sea he always served sea-food. He fed the country people in the inland regions with murenas' and pikes' milk.

The fish he ate were always cooked in a blue sauce, as if in sea-water, to retain their proper colour. He supplied swimming-pools scented with rose-wine and with roses, and bathed with all his household, supplying nard-oil for the hot rooms. He likewise supplied oil of balsam for the lamps. He never had intercourse with the same woman twice except for his wife, and he provided brothels at his house for his friends, clients and slaves. He never dined for less than a hundred thousand sesterces, that is thirty pounds of silver. In fact, sometimes he dined at a cost of three million sesterces, when everything he spent was reckoned up. Indeed, he surpassed even the banquets of Vitellius and Apicius. He used oxen to haul out fish from his ponds, but while passing through the market-place he lamented the public poverty. He used to tie his parasites to a water-wheel and by turning it plunge them under water and bring them up to the surface again – calling them river-Ixions. He also paved the courtyards in the palace which he named 'Antoninian' with Laconian marble[24] and porphyry. This paving survived to within our memory, but was recently dug up and cut in pieces. He had also intended to set up a single huge column which could be ascended on the inside, and to place the god Heliogabalus on top of it. But he did not find such a large quantity of stone, although he was thinking of bringing it from Egyptian Thebes.

He would often shut his friends up when they were drunk and suddenly, in the night, let in lions and leopards and bears – rendered harmless – so that when they woke up they would find at dawn, or what is worse, at night, lions, bears and panthers in the same bedroom as themselves. Several of them died as a result of this. Many of his humbler friends he used to seat on air-pillows instead of cushions and would let out the air while they were dining, so that often the diners were suddenly found under the tables. Finally, he was the first to think of setting out a semi-circle on the ground, not on couches, so that the air-cushions might be loosened by slave-boys at their feet, to let out the air.

In stage performances of adultery he ordered that what was usually simulated should actually be done. He often purchased harlots from all the procurers and set them free. Once when a discussion arose during private conversation how many men with hernias there could be in the city of Rome, he ordered all of them to be marked out and put on show at his baths. Then he bathed with them, some of them being respectable men, too. Often he put on gladiatorial fights and boxing-matches before a banquet, and spread a couch for himself in the upper gallery. While he dined, he exhibited criminals and wild-beast hunts. He often served his parasites, at the second course, food made of wax, or wood, or ivory, sometimes of pottery, and on occasion even marble or stone, so that everything that he was

24. Laconian marble was a green stone quarried in southern Laconia, and this, together with the red Egyptian porphyry, was imported in large quantities to Rome.

eating himself was served them, but made of different materials, only to be looked at, and in the meanwhile they would just drink with each course and wash their hands as if they had eaten.

It is said that he was the first of the Romans to have worn entirely silk clothing, whereas partly silk garments were already in use. He never touched washed linen, saying that only beggars wore linen clothes that had been washed. Often he was seen in public after dinner wearing a Dalmatian tunic, calling himself Gurges Fabius or Scipio,[25] because he had on the same clothes in which Fabius and Cornelius were brought out in public in their youth by their parents, to improve their manners. He gathered together into a public building all the prostitutes from the circus, the theatre, the stadium and all public places, including the baths, and delivered a sort of military speech to them, calling them 'fellow-soldiers', and lectured them on types of posture and pleasures. Afterwards he invited to a similar gathering pimps, catamites, collected from all sides, and the most profligate little boys and youths. Whereas he had appeared in front of the prostitutes in women's dress, with protruding breast, he met the catamites in the costume of boys that are prostituted. After his speech, he announced a donative, as if they were soldiers, three gold pieces for each, and asked them to pray the gods that he might have others to commend to them. Of course he used to play jokes on his slaves, even asking them to bring him a thousand pounds of spiders' webs, having offered a prize, and he is said to have collected ten thousand pounds of spiders' webs, from which, he said, it could be appreciated how large Rome was. He used to send his parasites as annual salary, for provisions, vessels containing frogs, scorpions, snakes and other reptiles of this kind; and he used to

25. Gurges is presumably Q. Fabius Maximus Gurges, consul three times in the first half of the second century B.C. It is not clear which Scipio is meant, and in any case no further details are known of this story.

shut up a vast number of flies in vessels like this, calling them tamed bees.

He always produced four-horse chariots from the circus in his banqueting-rooms and porticoes, while lunching or dining, compelling his aged guests to drive, some of them men who had held office. When already emperor, he used to order ten thousand mice to be brought to him, or a thousand weasels, or a thousand shrew-mice. He had such good confectioners and dairymen that whatever different kinds of food his cooks had served, either meat-cooks or fruit-cooks, they would serve them up now made of sweetmeats, now of dairy-products. He served his parasites with dinners made of glass, and sometimes used to send to table embroidered napkins depicting the food which had been set out, the same quantity as the courses that he was going to have, so that they were served only with what was made by the needle, or tapestry-work. Sometimes, however, paintings too were served up to them, so that they were served with everything, as it were, and yet were tortured with hunger. He mixed jewels with apples and flowers, and he threw out of the window the same amount of food that he served to his friends. He had commanded, also, that a supply of grain equal to a year's tribute to the Roman people should be given to prostitutes, pimps and catamites within the walls, having promised another supply to those outside, since there was at that time, thanks to the foresight of Severus and Bassianus, a grain-supply at Roman equal to seven years' tribute.

He harnessed four huge dogs to his chariot and drove about within the royal residence, and did the same thing on his estates when a private citizen. He even appeared in public with four huge stags yoked together. He harnessed lions too, calling himself the Mother of the Gods, and tigers, calling himself Liber [Bacchus]. And he appeared in the same dress as the gods that he was imitating were depicted. He kept at Rome little snakes from Egypt (which they call 'good *genii*'), and also hippopotami, a crocodile, a rhinoceros, and everything Egyptian that was of such a kind that it could be supplied. Sometimes he served ostriches at banquets, saying that the Jews had been commanded to eat them.

One thing he is said to have done certainly seems strange. He strewed a semi-circular couch with saffron when he had invited leading men to dinner, saying that he was serving them hay of a kind that fitted their rank. He performed the business of the day at night and that of the night in the day, reckoning it one of the signs of luxury to rise from sleep and begin to hold his levée late, but to start sleeping in the morning. He used to give largess to his friends every day and rarely let anyone go without a present, except those whom he had discovered to be thrifty, regarded by him as past recovery.

He had jewelled and gilded carriages, scorning those that were of silver, ivory or bronze. He also harnessed very beautiful women, in fours, twos or threes, or more, to a little one-wheeler, and would drive about like this, usually naked, and they were naked as they pulled him. He also had the custom of inviting eight bald men to dinner, or again, eight one-eyed men or eight men with gout, eight deaf men, eight dark men, eight tall men or eight fat men – in the latter case, because they could not all be accommodated on one semi-circular couch, it was to provoke laughter at all of them. He also presented to the guests all the silver that he had in the banqueting room and the whole supply of goblets; and he did this often. He was the first Roman leader to serve watered fish-sauce at a public gathering, whereas previously it had been a soldier's dish, a practice that subsequently Alexander at once restored. Besides this, he used to propose to those guests by way of a topic, that they should invent new sauces for flavouring dishes and to the one whose invention should please him he used to give a very large prize, even presenting a silk garment, which was regarded as being a rarity and an honour. But anyone whose invention did not please him, he used to order to continue to eat it until he invented something better. Of course he always sat among expensive flowers or perfumes. He used to love hearing the prices of the food served at his table exaggerated, declaring that this was an appetizer for the banquet.

He made himself up as a confectioner, a cook, a shopkeeper or a pimp, and he even practised all those occupations at home all the time. At one dinner he served the heads of six hundred ostriches, at many tables, for the brains to be eaten. Sometimes, too, he gave such a great banquet that he had twenty-two courses of enormous dishes, but between each one both he himself and his friends would bathe and have intercourse with women, taking an oath that they were deriving pleasure from it. Again, he once gave a banquet where one course was served at the house of each friend, and although one lived on the Capitol, one on the Palatine, one beyond the Rampart, one on the Caelian and one across the Tiber, yet the individual courses were eaten in order in their houses where each lived, and they went to the homes of all of them. Thus a single banquet was scarcely finished in a whole day, since they also bathed between each course and had intercourse with women. He always served a course of Sybariticum, made of oil and fish-sauce, which the Sybarites invented in the year in which they perished. He is also said to have built baths in many places and to have bathed in them once and immediately demolished them, so that he might not gain any practical use from the baths. It is said that he did the same thing with houses, military headquarters and summer houses. However, both these matters and some others which pass belief were, I think, invented by people who wanted to depreciate Heliogabalus to win favour with Alexander.

It is also reported that he purchased a very famous and beautiful harlot for a hundred thousand sesterces and kept her untouched like a virgin. When someone said to him, when he was still a private citizen: 'Are you not afraid of becoming poor?' he is said to have replied: 'What could be better than that I should be my own heir, and my wife's?' He

had, besides, resources bequeathed to him by many out of
regard for his father. He also used to say that he did not want
sons, in case one of them happened to be thrifty. He would
order Indian perfumes to be burned without coals, to fill his
summer houses with the fumes. When a private citizen he
never made a journey with less than sixty carriages, and his
grandmother Varia used to say that he would waste all his
possessions: but as emperor he would take as many as six
hundred carriages, declaring that the king of the Persians
travelled with ten thousand camels and that Nero had set off
on a journey with five hundred four-wheelers. The reason for
the carriages was the vast number of pimps, bawds, prostitutes,
catamites and perverts with large organs too. At the baths he
was always with the women, to the extent of even treating
them with a depilatory ointment. He himself applied the
ointment to his beard as well, and, a shameful thing to say, in
the same place where the women were being treated and at the
same hour. He also shaved the groins of his minions, using the
razor with his own hand, and afterwards shaved his beard with
it. He strewed a portico with gold and silver dust, lamenting
that he could not strew amber dust too, and he did this often
when he made his way on foot to his horse or carriage, as is
done today with golden sand.

He never put on the same shoe twice, and he is even said not
to have worn the same ring a second time. He often tore up
expensive clothes. He took a whale and weighed it, and sent his
friends what its weight was reckoned at, in fish. He sank laden
ships in the harbour, saying that this denoted greatness of soul.
He emptied his bowels in a golden vessel and urinated in vessels
of murra or onyx. 'If I have an heir', he is reported to have said,
'I will give him a guardian who will force him to do what I
myself have done and am going to do.' He also had the practice
of serving himself with dinners of a particular type: one day
he would eat nothing but pheasant, and put out pheasant-meat
for every course; likewise another day only chicken, on another

one kind of fish and then another kind; on another day pork and on another ostrich, or greens, or apples or sweetmeats or dairy products. Often he shut up his friends with little old Ethiopian women in overnight rest-houses, and kept them there until it was light, telling them that very beautiful women were kept there. He did the same thing with boys too, for then, as it was before Philip, it was lawful. Moreover sometimes he laughed so much that he alone could be heard in public at the theatre. He himself sang, danced, performed on the pipes, played the horn and the pandura[26] and performed on the organ. He is also reported to have gone in one day to all the prostitutes of the circus, the theatre, the amphitheatre and all the public places of the city, covered up with a muleteer's hood so that he would not be recognized. But, without satisfying his lusts, he gave all the prostitutes gold pieces, adding the words, 'Don't tell anyone, but Antoninus is giving you this.'[27] He invented certain kinds of lust, surpassing the spintrians of the emperors of old, and he knew well all the arrangements of Tiberius and Caligula and Nero.[28]

It was once predicted to him by Syrian priests that he would die a violent death. He had therefore got ready ropes woven with purple and scarlet silk, so that if it should be necessary he might end his life by the noose. He had prepared golden swords, too, with which to stab himself if any violence should beset him, and poisons concealed in onyxes and sapphires and emeralds with which he might make away with himself if anything serious should threaten. He had also made a very high tower with gilded and jewelled boards spread underneath in front of him, so that he could cast himself down from it, saying that even his death ought to be costly and of an extravagant pattern, so that it might be said that no one else had ever perished in this

26. An instrument that resembled the mandolin.

27. The story is repeated from Suetonius, *Caligula*, 11, *Nero*, 26; cf. *Verus*, 4.6 (p. 141 above).

28. cf. Suetonius, *Tiberius* 43.1, *Caligula* 24–26, *Nero* 28–29.

fashion. But these things availed him nothing, for, as we have
said, he was killed by guards and dragged through the streets,
thrust into the sewers in the most sordid fashion and dropped
into the Tiber. This was the end of the Antonine name in the
republic, everyone being aware that this Antoninus was as false
in his life as in his name.

Perhaps it may seem strange to some, revered Constantine,
that this scourge that I have described occupied the position of
princeps – and indeed for nearly three years. But at the time
there was such a lack of anyone in the republic to remove him
from the government of Rome's majesty, whereas there was
never any lack of a tyrannicide in the case of Nero, Vitellius,
Caligula and the others of this kind. But first of all I ask pardon
for having set down in writing these things that I have found in
various authors – although I have kept silent on many items
that are disgusting and cannot even be mentioned without the
greatest shame. Indeed, such matters as I have spoken of I have
covered up, as much as I could, by using veiled language. Then
I have felt that what Your Clemency is accustomed to say must
always be remembered: 'Being emperor depends on fortune.'
For there have been kings that are not so good and ones that are
very bad. But care must be taken, as Your Piety is wont to say,
that those whom some force of fate has brought to the destiny
of ruling are worthy of imperial power. Since he was the last of
the Antonines and this name was never subsequently repeated
in the republic in the position of *princeps*, this too must be added,
so that no error may arise when I begin to tell the story of the
two Gordians,[29] father and son, who wanted to be called after
the family of the Antonines: firstly, they did not have it as a
family name but as a forename; secondly, as I find in many
books, they were called Antonius, not Antoninus.

So much concerning Heliogabalus, whose biography you

29. The author here makes the same error as Victor and Eutropius,
that there were only two Gordians. Later, his study of Herodian made
him realize that there were three.

wished me (unwilling and reluctant though I was) to compile from Greek and Latin sources, set down in writing, and present it to you, since I have previously brought you the lives of others. Now I shall begin to write of those who followed after. Of these Alexander was the best and should receive serious treatment, as he was *princeps* for thirteen years. The others lasted for six months or barely one or two years, while Aurelian[30] is outstanding, and the glory of them all is Claudius, the founder of your family.[31] About this man I fear to tell the truth when writing to Your Clemency, lest I seem to the spiteful to be a flatterer; but I shall be delivered from the envy of evil men when they have seen that he was illustrious even in the eyes of others. To these must be joined Diocletian, father of the golden age, and Maximian, father of the iron, as is commonly said, and the others as far as Your Piety. But as for you, revered Augustus, those men to whom a more kindly nature has granted this gift shall describe you in many and more eloquent pages. To these emperors shall be added Licinius, Severus, Alexander and Maxentius,[32] all of them men whose power passed under your control, but I shall write of them in such a way as not to detract at all from their virtues. For I shall not follow the common practice of many writers and belittle the merits of those who have been defeated: I realize that it enhances your glory if I declare all the good qualities that they possessed, with truthfulness.

30. Aurelian (*PIR*[2], D 135), reigned A.D. 270–75.
31. Claudius II Gothicus (*PIR*[2], A 1626), reigned A.D. 268–70; he was to be claimed as an ancestor by Constantine.
32. Four of Constantine's rivals: Licinius, Augustus from A.D. 308–24, killed in A.D. 325; Valerius Severus, made Caesar in 305, Augustus 306–7 and killed by Maxentius in the latter year; L. Domitius Alexander, proclaimed Augustus in Africa in 308 and overthrown by Maxentius' generals in 309 or 310; Maxentius, son of Maximian, proclaimed emperor in 306 and defeated by Constantine at the battle of the Milvian Bridge in 312.

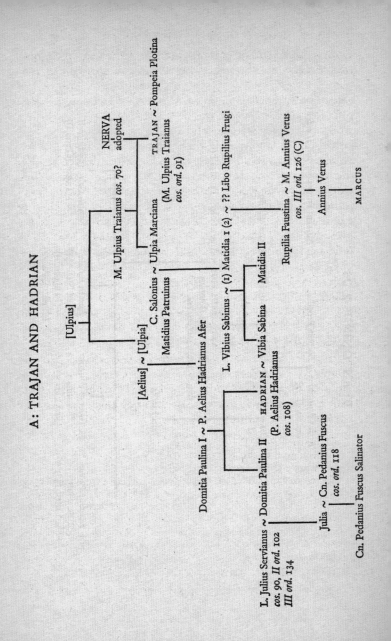

A: TRAJAN AND HADRIAN

B: ANTONINUS PIUS

Arrius Antoninus ~ Boionia Procilla   T. Aurelius Fulvus *cos.* 70?, II *ord.* 85
cos. 69, II 97?

P. Julius Lupus ~ (2) Arria Fadilla (1) ~ T. Aurelius Fulvus *cos. ord.* 89

ANTONINUS PIUS ~ Annia Galeria Faustina I (C)
(T. Aurelius Fulvus Boionius
Arrius Antoninus *cos. ord.* 120)

Julia Fadilla

M. Aurelius Fulvus   M. Galerius Aurelius   Aurelia Fadilla   Annia Galeria Faustina II
Antoninus   Antoninus   (died latest 138)   ~ MARCUS (C and D)
(died latest 138)   (died latest 138)   ~ [? Fundanius]
                                                         Plautius [? Aelius]
                                                         Lamia Silvanus

C: MARCUS

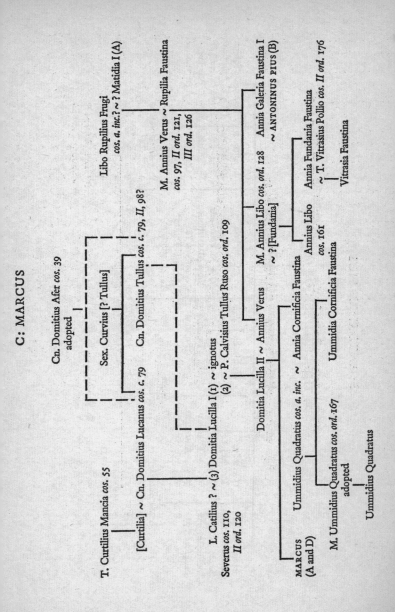

D: THE CHILDREN OF MARCUS

MARCUS ~ Faustina II (B and C)

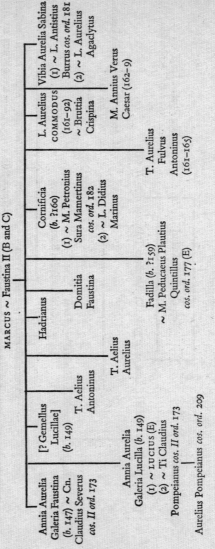

Annia Aurelia
Galeria Faustina
(b. 147) ~ Cn.
Claudius Severus
cos. II ord. 173

[? Gemellus
Lucillae]
(b. 149)

T. Aelius Antoninus

T. Aelius
Aurelius

Hadrianus

Domitia
Faustina

Cornificia
(b. ?160)
(1) ~ M. Petronius
Sura Mamertinus
cos. ord. 182
(2) ~ L. Didius
Marinus

L. Aurelius
COMMODUS
(161–92)
~ Bruttia
Crispina

Vibia Aurelia Sabina
(1) ~ L. Antistius
Burrus cos. ord. 181
(2) ~ L. Aurelius
Agaclytus

M. Annius Verus
Caesar (162–9)

Annia Aurelia
Galeria Lucilla (b. 149)
(1) ~ LUCIUS (E)
(2) ~ Ti Claudius
Pompeianus cos. II ord. 173

Fadilla (b. ?159)
~ M. Peducaeus Plautius
Quintillus
cos. ord. 177 (E)

T. Aurelius
Fulvius
Antoninus
(161–165)

Aurelius Pompeianus cos. ord. 209

E: LUCIUS VERUS

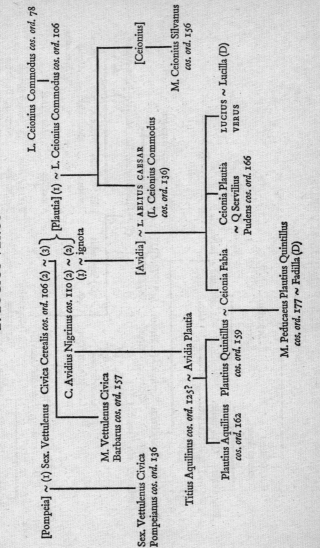

[Pompeia] ~ (1) Sex. Vettulenus Civica Cerealis *cos. ord.* 106 (2) ~ (3) [Plautia] (1) ~ L. Ceionius Commodus *cos. ord.* 106

L. Ceionius Commodus *cos. ord.* 78

C. Avidius Nigrinus *cos. 110* (2) ~ (2)
(1) ~ ignota

M. Vettulenus Civica
Barbarus *cos. ord.* 157

Sex. Vettulenus Civica
Pompeianus *cos. ord.* 136

Titus Aquilinus *cos. ord.* 125? ~ Avidia Plautia

[Avidia] ~ L. AELIUS CAESAR
(L. Ceionius Commodus
cos. ord. 136)

[Ceionius]

M. Ceionius Silvanus
cos. ord. 156

Ceionia Plautia
~ Q Servilius
Pudens *cos. ord.* 166

LUCIUS ~ Lucilla (D)
VERUS

Ceionia Fabia

Plautius Aquilinus
cos. ord. 162

Plautius Quintillus ~ Ceionia Plautia
cos. ord. 159

M. Peducaeus Plautius Quintillus
cos. ord. 177 ~ Fadilla (D)

F: SEPTIMIUS SEVERUS

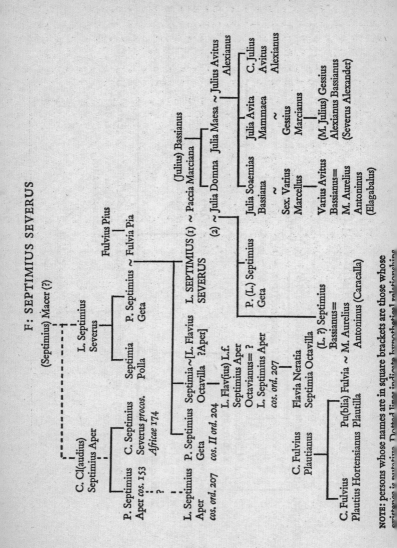

NOTE: persons whose names are in square brackets are those whose existence is putative. Dotted lines indicate hypothetical relationships.

c.A.D. 142
c.A.D. 122
York
BRITANNIA
London
R. Rhine
Cologne
CHATTI
GERMANIA INFERIOR
GERMANIA SUPERIOR
R. Elbe
R. Vis
BELGICA
MARCOMANNI
QUADI
LUGDUNENSIS
Carnun
RAETIA
NORICUM
PANNONIA
SUPERIOR
Lyons
Aquileia
Milan
INFERIOR
Sirmiu
AQUITANIA
Nîmes
NARBONENSIS
ITALIA
DALMATI
Narbo
Ancona
Salonae
TARRACONENSIS
CORSICA
ROMA
LUSITANIA
Tarraco
SARDINIA
Naples
Italica
BAETICA
Uccubi
Tarentum
Gades
SICILIA
Tinges
Carthage
Syracus
Iol Caesarea
MAURETANIA
Cirta
Sicca Veneria
TINGITANA
CAESARIENSIS
Hadrumetum
NUMIDIA
AFRICA
Leptis Magn

0   500 miles

- - - - -   *Provincial boundaries*
─────   *Frontiers*

-H.A.S-

INDEX

Exigencies of space have made it necessary to restrict this almost exclusively to proper names, and some of these have had to be omitted: Rome (and most topographical features within the city), Italy, consuls given as dates, most of the sources in the notes to pp. 29–53, and some of the names on pp. 317–322. Most Romans will be found under the *nomen*, e.g. Aelius Lampridius under Aelius, but consistency has proved impossible. In many cases the name is given more fully here than in the text, to supplement the notes.